MARXISM AND SOCIOLOGY

Studies in Critical Social Sciences Book Series

Haymarket Books is proud to be working with Brill Academic Publishers (www.brill.nl) to republish the *Studies in Critical Social Sciences* book series in paperback editions. This peer-reviewed book series offers insights into our current reality by exploring the content and consequences of power relationships under capitalism, and by considering the spaces of opposition and resistance to these changes that have been defining our new age. Our full catalog of *SCSS* volumes can be viewed at https://www.haymarketbooks .org/series_collections/4-studies-in-critical-social-sciences.

MARXISM AND SOCIOLOGY

A Selection of Writings by
Kazimierz Kelles-Krauz

EDITED BY
HELENA CHMIELEWSKA-SZLAJFER

ESSAYS TRANSLATED BY
JONATHAN WEBER

Haymarket Books
Chicago, IL

First published in 2017 by Brill Academic Publishers, The Netherlands.
© 2017 Koninklijke Brill NV, Leiden, The Netherlands

Published in paperback in 2019 by
Haymarket Books
P.O. Box 180165
Chicago, IL 60618
773-583-7884
www.haymarketbooks.org

ISBN: 978-1-64259-008-1

Distributed to the trade in the US through Consortium Book Sales and
Distribution (www.cbsd.com) and internationally through Ingram Publisher
Services International (www.ingramcontent.com).

This book was published with the generous support of Lannan Foundation and
Wallace Action Fund.

Special discounts are available for bulk purchases by organizations and
institutions. Please call 773-583-7884 or email info@haymarketbooks.org for more
information.

Cover design by Jamie Kerry and Ragina Johnson.

Printed in United States.

10 9 8 7 6 5 4 3 2 1

Library of Congress Cataloging-in-Publication Data is available.

Contents

Acknowledgements

I would like to thank Professor Marcin Król, Professor Timothy Snyder, and Doctor Bartłomiej Błesznowski for making the publication of this book possible.

The English translation of this volume was funded by The National Programme for the Development of Humanities, grant no. 0054/NPRH4/H3a/83/2016.

A Revised Introduction to the English Edition: Kazimierz Kelles-Krauz's Theory, Practice, and Purposeless Change

Helena Chmielewska-Szlajfer

Introduction

Kazimierz Kelles-Krauz was quite an extraordinary figure on the Polish political scene at the turn of the 20th century. A Marxist and patriot, academic and politician, a strong supporter of Poland's independence and of the idea of socialism, he was also the author of a sociological theory according to which the needs of the nation could be reconciled with international socialism. His works, though Marxist at heart, linked concepts stemming from the concepts of German idealists, French positivists, as well as contemporary sociologists, or 'social psychologists', who offered a bridge between research on individuals and the workings of social systems. What seems most unique in Kelles-Krauz's theory is that while labelling himself a Marxist, in his analysis of society he repeatedly transcended Marxist tenets, drawing interpretations from other schools of thought. In his writings, one can easily find imaginative reflections on the links between economic materialism and the ideas of Giambattista Vico, Auguste Comte and Jean-Jacques Rousseau next to Immanuel Kant and Georg Wilhelm Friedrich Hegel. Kelles-Krauz's major work is that on laws, which determine the role of the past in shaping new social theories. However, his scholarly intuition led him down other avenues as well, and he wrote on issues – still topical today – such as constructing national imaginary to serve partisan goals, or manufacturing (or, as Benedict Anderson wrote almost a century later: inventing[1]) traditions for contemporary needs; he also questioned the idea of norm and deviation within a social order.

After the Second World War, the great Polish Marxist and philosopher Leszek Kołakowski wrote of Kelles-Krauz as "the chief theoretician and ideologist of the main stream of the Polish socialist movement",[2] and a unique advocate

---

1   See: Anderson, Benedict, 1983, *Imagined Communities: Reflections on the Origin and Spread of Nationalism*. London, UK: Verso.

2   Kołakowski, Leszek, 1978, *Main Currents of Marxism: The Founders, the Golden Age, the Breakdown*, New York: W.W. Norton & Company, p. 208.

of philosophical Marxism. Nonetheless, after the end of the First World War, barely a decade after Kelles-Krauz's death, he became largely and surprisingly forgotten in Poland. This disappearance from public debates did not deter Timothy Snyder from describing Kelles-Krauz more recently as a "great figure in the intellectual and political histories of Central Europe" in his extensive biography.[3] According to Snyder, the Polish thinker played a key role in defining the issues that were discussed on the Polish political scene during his lifetime. By providing space for practical discussions on nationhood, he influenced the way Poland, still stateless at the time, marked her presence in the larger European political debates.

Kelles-Krauz's most developed interpretation of historical materialism, and at the same time his greatest achievement, was the law of revolutionary retrospection, according to which all revolutions draw on past ideals. His other essays, for example on the role of art and on psychiatry, published in journals ranging from the French *Annales de l'Institut International de Sociologie*, to the Polish *Prawda* and *Poradnik dla samouków*,[4] revealed the pertinent intuition of the socialist-sociologist. The issues raised by Kelles-Krauz could be found in the writings of his contemporaries including Émile Durkheim and Georg Simmel, but the key ideas resonated in later works of major Polish sociologists of the first half of the 20th century, Stefan Czarnowski and Stanisław Brzozowski, as well as in the writings of major post-war social thinkers such as Thomas Kuhn and Michel Foucault, as well as historians including Eric Hobsbawm, Ernest Gellner, and Benedict Anderson. Still, Kelles-Krauz's works are an interesting read not just because of their historical value. His observations based on the reality of the turn of the century still have bearing, since many of the topics concerning nationhood, memory, and social norms have again become intensely visible today. On a broader scale, Kelles-Krauz's analyses open up questions on the significance of social changes that took place in the preceding tumultuous century, as once more we are forced to face many of the issues he hoped to solve in his own lifetime.

3   Snyder, Timothy, 1997, *Nationalism, Marxism, and Modern Central Europe: A Biography of Kazimierz Kelles-Krauz, 1872–1905*. Cambridge, MA: Harvard University Press, p. ix.

4   'Prawda' means 'truth' in Polish; 'Poradnik dla samouków' could be translated as 'Teach Yourself'. The essay 'A Few Main Principles in the Development of Art' was originally published in *Poradnik dla samouków* (Warsaw 1905, 2, pp. 887–1013); the essay 'Psychiatry and the Science of Ideas' was first published in French, titled 'La psychiatrie et la science des idées' in *Annales de l'Institut International de Sociologie* (1895, 1, pp. 253–303). See also: K. Radosławski (pseud.). 1901. 'Literatura francuska. Idealizm Zoli', *Prawda* 35, pp. 427–429; 1902. 'Muzyka i ekonomia', *Prawda* 1–2, pp. 20–22; 1903. *Konrad czy Hamlet* 11–13, pp. 127–128.

Life and Politics

Kazimierz Kelles-Krauz was born in 1872 in Szczebrzeszyn, in Congress Poland. His family belonged to the landed gentry and shared a long story of participation in national uprisings, after Poland had been partitioned between Russia, Prussia, and the Austro-Hungarian Empire at the end of the 18th century. Kelles-Krauz's father fought in the anti-Russian January Uprising of 1863. Later, the Russian authorities punished the family by confiscating their estate. In the aftermath of the Poles' failed anti-Russian revolts – the January Uprising in 1863 and the earlier 1830 November Uprising – nonetheless served the purpose of upholding Poles' national spirit. However, as a result Kazimierz's education came at a time of severe post-1863 Russification. Denied the chance to read books deemed at odds with the ideology of the Russian invaders, Kelles-Krauz formed a secret educational group known as 'Aryele', the name inspired by the character in Shakespeare's *The Tempest*.[5] During its clandestine meetings the young men read the works of major Polish 19th century writers and poets – Adam Mickiewicz, Juliusz Słowacki and Ursyn Niemcewicz – next to the scholarly writings of Charles Darwin, Herbert Spencer, Auguste Comte and Lewis Morgan. The latter, a 19th century anthropologist, became known for his theory of stages of human progress in societies throughout history.[6] Morgan's ideas were to prove a significant influence on Kelles-Krauz's law of revolutionary retrospection. Edward Bellamy, the author of *Looking Backward: 2000–1887*,[7] a science-fiction novel on future socialist utopia, was another writer who captured the imagination of the young Kelles-Krauz. According to Snyder, Kazimierz Kelles-Krauz's generation – which did not remember the 1863 January Uprising or the repercussions that came later – was fascinated by patriotic romanticism. They shared "a cult of science beside the cult of Mickiewicz",[8] and trusted it would fix all social problems. Thus, socialism became the new science as remedy. In contrast, positivism, which had inspired the previous generation of the Polish *intelligentsia* traumatised after the failed January Uprising, was seen by their children as passive resignation.

Kelles-Krauz's knowledge and his enthusiasm for books was also the source of his troubles, and that at an important time during his education.

---

5 See: Gawin, Magdalena, 2011, 'Płeć i socjalizm. Przypadek Kazimierza Kelles-Krauza', *Kronos* 17 (2), pp. 220–229.

6 Morgan, Lewis H, 1877, *Ancient Society or Researches in the Lines of Human Progress from Savagery through Barbarism to Civilization*. London, UK: MacMillan & Company.

7 Bellamy, Edward, 1888, *Looking Backward: 2000–1887*. Boston, MA: Ticknor & Co.

8 Snyder, Timothy, 1997, *Nationalism, Marxism, and Modern Central Europe*, p. 14.

In 1890, the year of his secondary school final exams, he was expelled from school for his involvement in a conspiracy: to help other students, he wrote answers to the famously difficult exam questions that had been stolen earlier on. After much effort, Kelles-Krauz was allowed to retake the exam a year later in Kielce, following which for several months he studied law at the Imperial University of Warsaw. However, since during that time education at the university essentially meant further Russification, and since Kelles-Krauz had in the meantime transformed into an enthusiastic socialist, he decided – like many other Poles – to continue his studies in Paris.

He achieved this a year later. From the beginning of his emigration, Kelles-Krauz supported himself by writing articles for Polish newspapers, including the conservative *Kurier Warszawski*, *Głos*, *Prawda* and *Krytyka*. In his own words, he engaged in 'literary prostitution'. During the period of his creative work, which lasted until his untimely death in 1905, Kelles-Krauz maintained two identities: one was Casimir de Kellès-Krauz, the other Michał Luśnia. He used the *nom de plume* to write political pieces for the Polish Socialist Party (PPS) and the congresses of the Second International. These safety measures were not without reason; after his arrival in Paris, Kelles-Krauz was closely watched by the Tsarist Okhrana.

In the last decade of the 19th century, when Kelles-Krauz moved to the French capital, Paris was home for around six thousand Poles. The older generation of wealthy aristocratic emigrants from 1863 had settled on the right bank of the Seine, and the left bank attracted the younger generation of socialists and students. Interestingly, at the end of the century nearly one third of all students from Congress Poland, controlled by Russia, were studying abroad.

In Paris, Kelles-Krauz began his studies in the natural sciences at the Sorbonne; he had plans to pursue sociology and history of law later. In the meantime, he soon became the leader of Polish socialist students. Suspected of undercover activity, Kelles-Krauz was arrested on Polish territory in 1893, and was forced to spend a year there awaiting vindication. He returned to Paris in 1894 together with his newlywed wife, Maria Goldsteynówna; they had met while still at school in Radom. Their daughter, Janina, was born four years later. The forced stay in Poland prevented Kelles-Krauz from taking part in founding the Polish Socialist Party or in its partition into PPS and Social Democracy of the Kingdom of Poland. The latter organisation was headed by Rosa Luxemburg, who soon became his key political opponent.[9] Nonetheless, after settling down in Paris, Kelles-Krauz caught up quickly. By the end of the year he had co-founded the Paris section of the Association of Polish Socialists Abroad

---

9   See also: Snyder, Timothy, 2011, 'Love and Death', *New Republic*, June 9.

(ZZSP), the foreign branch of PPS. In the following year he became editor-in-chief of the PPS Foreign Bulletin, *Bulletin Officiel du Parti Socialiste Polonais*. Finally, during the ZZSP meeting in 1897 Kelles-Krauz was elected a member of the executive committee named Centralizacja. The next two years, until ZZSP was incorporated into PPS, were the period of his most intense activity during which the socialist-scholar strongly influenced the line of ZZSP and the organisation's newspaper, *Przedświt*.[10]

From the beginning of his stay in France, Kelles-Krauz kept in touch with powerful Polish emigre socialist thinkers and activists, such as Bolesław Limanowski and Edward Abramowski. What's more, as a member of ZZSP Kelles-Krauz met many of the key socialist leaders, including Karl Kautsky, Jean Jaurès, Gieorgi Plekhanov, Jules Guesde and Victor Adler. Strictly political activity was, however, only one of Kelles-Krauz's preoccupations. As a member of the Polish students' association in Paris, he took part in a campaign to move the remains of the great Polish 19th century poet Juliusz Słowacki to Poland. At the same time, Kelles-Krauz's flat in the Latin Quarter soon became a place of heated debate and a support centre for young Polish socialists. In addition, from 1897 Kelles-Krauz served as secretary for the Polish Red Cross, which gave money to bail out arrested students and socialists. That same year he started holding lectures on Marxist sociology at Collége Libre, next to the already famous French social thinker, Garbiel Tarde. In fact, the young scholar pursued his own studies under the direction of Tarde and also Georges Sorel at the private École Libre des Sciences Politiques, while his doctoral dissertation, in which he developed the law of revolutionary retrospection, was supervised by Lucien Lévy-Bruhl at the Université Nouvelle in Brussels. In addition to this work, in 1901 Kelles-Krauz began holding lectures on social dialectics at that university. At the same time, in 1901 he moved to Vienna where he took up law studies; and in addition to studying and holding lectures, the Polish scholar published scholarly papers. At the turn of the 20th century his articles were already to be found in journals such as the French *Annales de l'Institut International de Sociologie*, the German *Neue Zeit*, and also the Polish *Prawda* and *Przegląd Filozoficzny*, a prestigious philosophical journal. In 1904, a year before his death, he participated in the launch of Advanced Vacation Courses in Zakopane, a major Polish mountain resort close to Krakow, which was particularly popular among artists and scholars at the time. The summer school itself was

---

10   The name of the paper means 'daybreak' in English. See also: Żarnowska, Anna. 1962. *Kazimierz Kelles-Krauz (1872–1905)*, in: *Kelles-Krauz, Kazimierz. Pisma wybrane*, Warsaw, Poland: Książka i Wiedza; Bieńkowski, Wiesław, 1973, *Kazimierz Kelles-Krauz: życie i działalność*, Warsaw, Poland: Państwowe Wydawnictwo Naukowe.

inspired by the Collége Libre in Paris and Université Nouvelle in Brussels, and it offered studies on a wide range of topics. Kelles-Krauz held lectures on modern social movements as the new Renaissance, next to the prolific and scandalising Polish artist and writer, Stanisław Ignacy Witkiewicz.

At the same time, Kazimierz Kelles-Krauz was one of the most active members of the Paris section of the Association of Polish Socialists Abroad (ZZSP), and in his interpretation of Marxism he soon developed a visibly patriotic streak. Since he strongly supported the Polish Socialist Party's (PPS) efforts to establish an independent Polish state, Kelles-Krauz was seen as one of the party's key intellectuals, despite his declared Marxism. The interpretation of Marxism that Kelles-Krauz offered bridged nationalist narratives with the needs of the working class. "[N]ational consciousness is an intrinsic part of the political consciousness of every worker", while socialists "lacking an international policy of their own, would respond at crucial moments with patriotic formulas" , Snyder wrote on Kelles-Krauz's position.[11] The socialist-sociologist made his own stance clear in the form of a resolution of the Polish Socialist Party (PPS) at the Congress of the Second International in 1896. In consequence, his ideas sparked a major conflict between him and Rosa Luxemburg, which continued until his death in 1905. According to Luxemburg, a vocal supporter of supra-national Marxism, nationalist aspirations were pointless in light of the true goal of the working class's revolution. In contrast, Kelles-Krauz, an advocate of small steps and Poland's independence, claimed just the opposite and called for the establishment of a democratic national state. Unlike Luxemburg's, his opinion was that class consciousness could be raised only with gradual change. What's more, according to his law of revolutionary retrospection sudden revolutions were sure to devour their own children, but not necessarily to introduce the change desired.

Despite his fundamental disagreement with Rosa Luxemburg, what brought the patriotic Marxist from PPS together with the apostle of international revolution from the Social Democracy of the Kingdom of Poland was a very specific fear. Namely, they were afraid that in the midst of national struggles for independence, the petite bourgeoisie, stuck between the proletariat and the capitalists, would distort the ideals of the working class. But while Luxemburg found patriotic ambitions an obstacle standing in the way of socialism, Kelles-Krauz considered them an essential stage in what was possible in a class-based reality – a 'class possibilism'.[12] In general, the arguments offered by the speakers at

---

11   Snyder, Timothy, 1997, *Nationalism, Marxism, and Modern Central Europe*, p. 143f.

12   The source of the term is the Possibilistes, a group formed within the late-19th century French socialist movement. The Possibilistes claimed that, unlike a major revolution desired by the workers, reforms were realistic goals worth fighting for.

the Second International justified national interests by using internationalist rhetoric. For Kelles-Krauz this rhetoric was additional evidence that national issues shaped basic outlooks even among the most devoted socialist internationalists.[13] He pointed out this paradox later when discussing Comte and the failure of the French Revolution. In essence, the Polish thinker accused the French bourgeoisie of exploiting revolutionary ideals for their own class needs.

Despite the disputes with Luxemburg and other internationalist Marxists, Kelles-Krauz was a well-respected figure within the Polish Socialist Party, including among its more revolutionary-oriented young members. He was known for his strong personal moral authority, and was appreciated for both his efforts to bridge Marxism and patriotism and his ability to avoid petty conflicts – the latter, according to the Polish historian Wiesław Bieńkowski, a unique quality among the Polish émigré community. The late-19th century emigrants, unlike their fathers, did not share the trauma of failed uprisings and felt much more enthusiastic about cooperating with Russians in establishing socialist ideals. Nevertheless, though Kelles-Krauz tried to reconcile the feuding groups within PPS, which had vastly different generational experiences, soon after his death in 1905 the party split into the Polish Socialist Party-Left (PPS-Lewica) and Polish Socialist Party-Revolutionary Fraction (PPS-Frakcja Rewolucyjna). In an obituary for Kelles-Krauz, the Polish writer and poet Władysław Bukowiński[14] described bitterly how the socialist-sociologist, overworked, poor, and lacking the support he had expected from a Warsaw organisation that provided aid for scholars, died of pneumonia at a sanatorium on the outskirts of Vienna. Kazimierz Kelles-Krauz was barely thirty-three years old.

Marxism as a Scientific Method

Kazimierz Kelles-Krauz considered himself a Marxist, hence his political affiliations. Still, contrary to the dominant trends in Marxism at the time, rather than relying on determinism the Polish thinker offered a standpoint of historical development. At the same time he argued that economic materialism should not be considered as dogma but as a scientific method. What's more, instead of analysing Marxism as Engelsian 'dialectics of nature', Kelles-Krauz saw it rather as a distinct method for studying society, which is the natural habitat

---

13   According to Snyder, Kelles-Krauz pointed at a national version of 'class apperception', yet he did not notice it when discussing the national interests of Marxists. The author of Kelles-Krauz's biography called this 'national apperception'. See: Snyder, Timothy, 1997, *Nationalism, Marxism, and Modern Central Europe*, p. 122.

14   Bukowiński, Władysław, 1905, 'Kazimierz Krauz', *Prawda* 25 (1278), p. 293.

of humans (see: *Economic Materialism*). Furthermore, given the uniqueness
of Marxism as a method it should not be treated as a simple translation of the
natural sciences, such as Morgan's and Spencer's evolutionism or Comte's or-
ganicism. To emphasise this fundamental difference, in *Economic Materialism*
Kelles-Krauz invoked Engels's arguments that it is not the goal of Marxism to
find an economic basis in each and every phenomenon. According to the Polish scholar, Engels showed that as a scientific method Marxism was not dogmatic but, on the contrary, self-critical. According to this interpretation, the
method offered a study of "human society in which all relations are naturally
psychological, and among these relations there is one key, leading category:
economic".[15] In his critical attitude toward literal interpretations of Engels's
ideas, Kelles-Krauz rejected the idea of treating the economic base, which he
called 'substance', as a simple explanation of all facets of the superstructure,
which he called 'form' in his own theory. The Polish scholar stressed the role of
social influence on the economic foundation; moreover, he viewed substance
and form as dialectically linked in a way that makes the tie valid even after
the socialist goal is achieved. Going further in his analysis of Engels's thought,
Kelles-Krauz located the source of all social change in the individual minds
which constitute society, since this is where the economic groundwork is intertwined with social form. This was also the reason why he considered sociology
as, in fact, social psychology.

This psychological intuition, and, perhaps, traces of Durkheim's sociology,
are visible in Kelles-Krauz's general descriptions of society. He sees it as a 'social fact', irreducible to the sum of its parts. One can also notice similar insight
in the Polish scholar's analysis of form, or rather of societal influence on social
substance: it is an institutionalisation of norms and habits – the inspiration
coming from Lévy-Bruhl, who believed that habits impose themselves on individuals differently than intellectual facts.[16] According to Kelles-Krauz, forms
free themselves from economic substance, thus gaining their own power.
This power, however, can be undermined solely by changes that occur within
the technology of production of goods, while the goods in turn influence the
change of social forms. In essence, Kelles-Krauz asserts that every single economic activity is fundamentally social. The base is always tied to the superstructure, and so is substance to form. This inseparability is key, and it makes
Marxism a more perfect science than positivism or Hegelianism. Not only that,
Kelles-Krauz accused both these currents of separating idea from reality, and
of subjecting the latter to the mind, as if human intellect were independent

---

15   [Translation: Helena Chmielewska-Szlajfer] see: Kelles-Krauz, Kazimierz, 1903, 'Darwin-
       izm w socyologii', *Prawda* 23, pp. 512–513.
16   See: Lévy-Bruhl, Lucien, 1926, *How Natives Think*. New York: Alfred A. Knopf.

from the surrounding world. In addition, unlike positivism and Hegelianism, economic materialism applies dialectic also to itself. It is open to criticism because it includes the continuous process of change of economic substance and social form, as well as its own contextual setting in a particular space and time. In spite of this, sociology, while answering the needs of its time as much as any other element of social life at a given time, serves a unique function: that of a distanced science and of a litmus test, which monitors the development of socialism.[17] According to Snyder, this immersion of science in everyday life is so deep that for Kelles-Krauz sociology-as-science and socialism-as-goal merge into one.[18]

The lack of a predetermined goal in the historical process of dialectical change is striking, given the Polish scholar's Marxist beliefs. Contrary to the universalist positivist vision of a world ruled by objective progress, Marxism as a scientific method was a product of its own time, which answered the needs of a particular reality. Thus, one could assume that as a consequence of another social transformation a different science would emerge that would better fit new social needs. Kelles-Krauz's description of economic and social transformations, which are based on cycles of dominance of either substance or form, rather than orthodox Marxism, bring to mind Dilthey's hermeneutics and Husserl's phenomenology: the location of humans in a particular time and space limits their horizon of economic and social needs. Likewise, in science scholars can only attempt to discover their own historical conditions, without claims to forming absolute, objective laws.[19]

From the lack of a historical goal stems the "necessity of individuals' active role" in social life, their active influence on substance and forms, which Kelles-Krauz describes in *A Glance at the Development of Sociology in the 19th Century* in this volume. Interestingly, from the point of view of social process, this stance presages Florian Znaniecki's 'humanistic coefficient':[20] if there is no ultimate utopia that should be brought to life by humankind, and what we are left with are ever-changing visions of social accord, which depend on particular substance and form, individuals play an active part in shaping temporary

---

17   According to the Polish sociologist Ludwik Krzywicki, the task of sociology is "to check which system will be the most successful in making us poor, suffering mortals happy"; see: Krzywicki, Ludwik, 1883, 'Jeszcze o program', *Przegląd Tygodniowy* 18, pp. 177–179 [translation: Helena Chmielewska-Szlajfer].

18   See: Snyder, Timothy, 1997, *Nationalism, Marxism, and Modern Central Europe*, p. 205.

19   And indeed, over half a century later Thomas Kuhn uncovered the social context of science-making. See: Kuhn, Thomas, 1962, *The Structure of Scientific Revolutions*. Chicago, IL: Chicago University Press.

20   Znaniecki, Florian, 1927, 'The Object-Matter of Sociology', *American Journal of Sociology* 32 (4), pp. 529–584.

models of social order. According to Kelles-Krauz, these very circumstances shape social change. What's more, on the level of Marx's base, or the Polish scholar's substance, these types of shift take place all the time – in accordance with the rule of perfecting tools, namely to produce the largest number of goods at the lowest cost. Subtle shifts in technology emerge on the level of substance, which then in turn influence social forms. Briefly put, minute innovations in the economic base trigger subsequent transformations of institutions, from ethics and law to philosophy and art. The process of two-way influencing of economic substance and social form, their unique mutual 'vibrations', as Kelles-Krauz describes it in *Psychiatry and the Science of Ideas*, shapes the human horizons of both existence and thought within a 'philosophy of action'. According to the scholar, it is a fundamental pursuit of harmony in the process of constant economic and social change, while reality which undergoes endless transformations determines its transient ideals. This is why instead of a more-or-less linear quest for a predetermined, final goal, Kelles-Krauz offers a vision according to which even the ideal of harmony is subject to transformation. It is a purpose hammered out through the actions of individuals in a concrete social reality. In this manner, the Polish Marxist-sociologist overcomes the contradiction between idealism and materialism.

In the essay *What is Economic Materialism?* Kelles-Krauz presents human life as a relationship between an individual's biological conditions, the natural environment, and broader society. The basic pursuit of individuals is the growth of their productivity, and they approach this goal by adapting the natural environment to their own needs. They do so with the help of tools, which are inventions made possible thanks to the co-operation of individuals. In effect, technology determines the mode of production, while the mode of production determines social life. Thus, if the human desire to maximise production lies at the foundation of society, society's basic substance is the 'economy of social phenomena', i.e. the possibility of fulfilling the needs of productivity within society. In this way Kelles-Krauz translates Marx's category of labour. As the scholar writes in *The Crisis of Marxism*, it is both an 'expenditure of life force' and a measure of value shared by all. Although the physical aspect of labour falls well into evolutionary thought, in agreement with Comte's organicist theory, where tools are an extension of human organs, the fact that Kelles-Krauz lends 'value' to labour makes it a deeply social feature. In fact, Kelles-Krauz goes even further by treating society as human 'artificial nature', even if created thanks to human invention, nonetheless equally inevitable as natural phenomena.[21]

---

21   Interestingly in the context of 'nature' in Marxist social thought, György Lukács used the term 'second nature' two decades later to describe society ruled by relations between

The influence of positivists on Kelles-Krauz is particularly noticeable in his vision of society as a type of building. Each subsequent floor in the structure is the form for the substance of the floor below. However, while for Comte, who also used this comparison, the starting point for analysing this social 'edifice' was the human brain, for the Polish thinker it was economic materialism.[22] Moreover, the autonomous status of socially constructed institutions described by Kelles-Krauz not only brings to mind Émile Durkheim's qualitative distinctiveness of social facts but William Isaac Thomas's theorem, according to which defining occurrences as real makes them real in their consequences.[23] For Kelles-Krauz the autonomous development of social forms lasts until the detachment from substance becomes so unbearable that it sparks a palpable need for change.

In his analysis of the relationship between substance and form, and especially in the descriptions of the social influence of these relations, the Polish scholar imaginatively expounded Gabriel Tarde's law of imitation.[24] However, unlike the French sociologist, Kelles-Krauz argued that not ideas but the economic base constitutes substance. In contrast, form lags behind substance because it is subject to inertia, and it 'solidifies' in its own dogmas. Initially the aims of these dogmas coincide with the economic basis, which begot them in the first place. However, as Kelles-Krauz writes in *Psychiatry and the science of ideas*, material substance reveals itself only through social form. Thus, one can draw the conclusion that the need for social change depends on the level of agreement or discord between them. As for the Polish scholar, he located the source of desire to change existing forms in the growing number of new unsatisfied needs, which these forms constrained. Thus, in this case Hegel's rule – quantity turns into quality – worked both ways: firstly, when new substance created new forms that were compatible with it, which then emancipated themselves to dominate it; and, secondly, when as a result of this emancipation of forms, more and more unsatisfied needs on the level of substance led to the qualitative transformation of forms.

---

goods. See: Lukács, György, 1967, *History and Class Consciousness. Studies in Marxist Dialectics*. Cambridge, MA: MIT Press, p. 86.

22   The subsequent floors in Kelles-Krauz's theory are: I. The economy of social phenomena (economy); II. Law, politics, science, and art (law and ethics); III. Philosophy (knowledge, art, religion, and philosophy). See: *What is Economic Materialism?* in this volume.

23   See: Durkheim, Émile, 1982, *The Rules of Sociological Method*. New York: The Free Press; Thomas, William I., 1928, *The Child in America: Behavior Problems and Programs*. New York: Alfred A. Knopf.

24   See: Tarde, Gabriel, 1989, *L'opinion et la foule*, Paris, France: Les Presses universitaires de France.

The Law of Revolutionary Retrospection and the Golden Age

"The ideals with which any reformative movement desires to replace the existing social norms are always similar to the norms from a distant or not so
distant past", Kelles-Krauz wrote in *The Sociological Law of Retrospection*. The
law of revolutionary retrospection, inspired primarily by the works of Lévy-
Bruhl and Tarde, is considered the Polish thinker's most developed sociological theory. It explains the mechanism of social change, which is driven by a
vision of a future society, yet is based on an idealised past, the 'golden age'.
While Kelles-Krauz borrowed this idea from Giambattista Vico, a similar notion could also be found later in Rousseau's 'state of nature'.[25] In the *Social
dialectic in the philosophy of Vico*, Kelles-Krauz describes the rule of cycles and
returns (*ricorsi*), which according to the Enlightenment philosopher governs
social history. Vico's mythical 'golden age' existed in the 'pre-social state', a period of freedom for individuals who were self-sufficient and bound solely by
divine judgment.[26] At the same time, this mythical era was characterised by
'democratic anarchy'. This is how Providence punished people for having left
the path toward civic monarchy, which according to Vico was the perfect state.
The 'golden age' implied a time of a radical freedom of individuals, yet the lack
of basic laws meant it was impossible to create society. The Italian philosopher
argued that only civic monarchy, a society bound by rules warranted by the
king, could secure social unity; Rousseau's social contract echoed this idea.

Aside from the fundamental goal of a perfect social organisation, in Vico's
writings Kelles-Krauz found what later became the basis of his own theory,
namely the importance of human habits. In fact, he quotes the Enlightenment
philosopher in his essay, *The Social Dialectic in Vico's Philosophy*: "when men
change they retain for some time the impression of their previous customs".[27]
In a Marxist context, Kelles-Krauz argued that social institutions change more
slowly than the economic base which is their source. Unlike Vico, however, he
did not think of history as a chain of events determined by a transcendental divine goal, where the individual can merely delay the moment of the definitive

---

25   See: Vico, Giambattista, 1948, *The New Science of Giambattista Vico*, Ithaca, NY: Cornell
      University Press; Rousseau, Jean-Jacques, 2005, *On the Origin of Inequality*, New York: Co-
      simo Classics.

26   In many respects, this vision resembles the state of total freedom and war described by
      Thomas Hobbes in *Leviathan*. See: Hobbes, Thomas, 1996, *Leviathan*. Oxford, UK: Oxford
      University Press.

27   *The Social Dialectic in Vico's Philosophy* in this volume. See also: Vico, Giambattista, 1948,
      The New Science of Giambattista Vico, p. 338.

arrival of the perfect society. What for Vico was a diversion from God's plan, which later the positivists replaced with the progress of the mind, Kelles-Krauz viewed simply as change guided solely by its own, intrinsically material rules. Moreover, sentiment toward the past was merely the result of disappointment with the present, while previous, mythologised history served as an aesthetic basis, the 'fabric of dreams' for new developments.

If in Vico's writings Kelles-Krauz found his point of departure to analyse the role of habits in a changing society, in Jean-Jacques Rousseau's works he found shifting historical ideas of a perfect past. The Middle Ages were supposed to be the gate to paradise lost, but after the advent of the Renaissance and the advance of science that came with it, the status of the mythical, perfect form of organisation was bestowed upon the state of nature. Thus, in stark contrast to Vico, Rousseau found the human instinct for self-preservation and co-operation at the very beginnings of human activity. To make the juxtaposition between Vico and Rousseau even stronger, according to the latter this instinct also characterised the beginning of human nobility, which in Vico's theory had to be developed in time. For the French philosopher, the dawn of humankind already bore high moral value. Thus, the term 'golden age' signified a stage that followed the state of nature, and which was a period of creating technologies of production as well as war, and the first social contract. While Rousseau agreed with Vico in regard to monarchy – it was the best possible form of social organisation because people need wise monarchs – Rousseau considered kings merely as 'crutches' for 'old men'[28] in a world where the individual had irreversibly gained consciousness. The mind, thanks to which people could shape their tools for survival, for Rousseau was but a meagre imitation of the state of nature. Nevertheless, the author of the *Social Contract* postulated the establishment of small municipal democracies.[29] This was his own *ricorso* to the ancient *polis*, in the context of a growing 18th century bourgeoisie – the future capitalists.

Kelles-Krauz viewed the turn toward the past, which he understood as the basis for thinking and doing in the future, as Hegelian dialectic in material action: "consequence, which becomes the cause of its own cause".[30] Yet this process did not carry an intrinsic moral value as was the case with *ricorsi* or the state of nature. According to the Polish scholar, in Vico's philosophy the reproduction of the past was a sin against the ultimate plan of Providence, a

---

28   See: *The Golden Age, State of Nature, and Development in Contradictions* in this volume.

29   See: Rousseau, Jean-Jacques, 1920, *The Social Contract & Discourses*. London, UK: J.M. Dent & Sons.

30   See: *The Golden Age, State of Nature, and Development in Contradictions* in this volume.

regression which delayed the achievement of the set goal. In comparison, for Rousseau inspiration which came from the past could lead to good, since it was defined by a social contract of a higher order. But while for Vico the 'golden age' was a goal attainable in the divine plan, for Rousseau it was paradise lost forever. Kelles-Krauz had a different idea yet: he saw it as a changing aesthetic category, which fuels contemporary needs. Nonetheless, influenced by Rousseau, Kelles-Krauz did find constructive values in the initial social stage of 'primitive communism'. Although he maintained the concept of paradise lost – albeit a Marxist one – for him the past, in its idealised form, usually provided a pretext justifying the need for change, not a return to the past itself. What is particularly noteworthy is that unlike his predecessors, Kelles-Krauz saw both the past and the future as features of a dialectic process, the result of which is determined by contemporary needs of this concrete world.

Categories: Stages and Minds

Based on his interpretation of the works of Vico and Rousseau, Kelles-Krauz viewed history as a series of subsequent stages of humankind. He also showed a hermeneuticist's intuition when stressing that historical context, which defined the oeuvre of the authors, at the same time limited their perspective. In effect, the choice of ideal social states depended on the dominant substance and form of their day. In the article *A Glance at the Development of Sociology in the 19th Century*, Kelles-Krauz attributed retrospective trends to particular time periods. According to him, rationalism was based on a vision of classic Antiquity, while 19th century sociology, especially that of Henri Saint-Simon, turned toward the Middle Ages. The French thinker interpreted the period as an age of freedom and democracy, suspended between primeval self-sufficiency and modern, capitalist organisation of production and the social institutions that come with it. Yet according to Snyder,

> [Kelles-Krauz] makes a historical claim that the first retrospection was the Greek idea of the golden age, which reflected dim but existing historical memories of the primeval communalism which preceded Greek civilization. In the argument which seems to justify a passage to socialism by way of democracy, Kelles-Krauz now claims that consistent bourgeois democrats who long wholeheartedly for Greek antiquity also began to long for what the Greeks themselves longed for: primeaval communalism.[31]

---

31   See: Snyder, Timothy, 1997, *Nationalism, Marxism, and Modern Central Europe*, p. 210.

In terms of the future, the 20th century belonged to historic materialism, which, for the Polish scholar was itself a retrospective turn towards primitive societies. Within the law of revolutionary retrospection, the history of change – not progress – was to come full circle and, despite Kelles-Krauz's repeated assertions that no ultimate goal exists, return to its mythologised sources. In order to show how revolutionary retrospection worked in other contexts, he pointed at these dialectical returns in the works of other scholars. For example, Vico analysed the history of mankind through the lens of the evolution of monarchy, which he viewed as the best of possible social orders. The first, archaic version was the patriarchal familial monarchy. It later evolved into monarchy based on the dominance of a minority over a majority; this concept of monarchy was also an inspiration for Kelles-Krauz's idea of class apperception. Finally, monarchy transformed into a social order in which citizens were equal to their ruler. Unlike Vico, Comte found the driving force of history in basic human curiosity and the struggle to avoid suffering. These two desires guided humanity from the theological phase, through the metaphysical one, to finally reach the positive stage. Kelles-Krauz described the latter as 'historic realism', a period based on faith in the progress of the mind. On the one hand, according to Comte's interpretation it was science that served people's existential needs but – like Kelles-Krauz's form – it had to separate itself from these needs in order to develop to its ideal form. On the other hand, for Rousseau the ideal, the state of nature, was a time irrevocably lost. Based on these two rather contradictory approaches, Kelles-Krauz posed the question: should the state of nature be of a historical or merely logical status? After all, while no human creation, i.e. civilisation, is perfect when compared to nature, the social contract is still the highest achievement of the mind. People protected by regulations and subject only to laws,[32] autonomous institutions and not susceptible individuals, can retain their freedom from each other. In the end, for Kelles-Krauz these authors showed the history of thought in relation to a transcendental ideal. Still, the peak was reached by Hegel; the philosopher analysed the gradual birth of a consciousness of the absolute spirit, which was a certainty of reality bearing the magnitude of truth. Kelles-Krauz's goal, however, was to fulfil the Marxist ideal of placing dialectic back on its feet: to set both the mind and the certainty of truth on a material foundation.

In the law of revolutionary retrospection, in place of historical teleology the Polish sociologist presented stages of recurring (or spiral) transformations. The subsequent periods differ from each other in historical contexts, as the goal of social harmony is determined by the relations between substance and form. In the period of 'primitive communism', which many thinkers brought

---

32   See: Rousseau, Jean-Jacques, 2004, *Discourse on the Origin of Inequality*.

up by Kelles-Krauz idealised, people produced goods, governed by nature and the pre-economic 'social will'. Only in the age of 'proper' history did people's lives become subject to the production of goods, and the economic foundation transformed into the source of social norms such as law, ethics, art and philosophy. Under these new conditions the social form solidified in institutions, outlasted the economic substance, and – not without difficulty – adapted to new needs borne out of the changes in the technology of production. What is particularly significant in Kelles-Krauz's theory is that this process takes place because it is a practical consequence of material transformation, and not an autonomous, parallel evolution of thought. Moreover, in his interpretation the differences in interests that are based on people's class can become visible, since the workers are much closer to the economic substance than the owners of capital. Still, perhaps surprisingly, the Polish thinker did not discuss the implications of this dichotomous class setup. Instead, Kelles-Krauz focused on the mechanisms of negotiating the economic foundation with social institutions. This is why on the level of social interests – a reconciliation of substance and form – he called upon Gabriel Tarde's law of imitation, which too makes "the sap of tradition circulates in the new graft of progress".[33] Inspired by the French social thinker's concept, Kelles-Krauz portrayed social change as a two-step process: new, individual interests accumulate in the 'dictionary' period. Next, in the 'harmonisation' (or 'grammar') period, the multitude of these different individual needs is transformed to benefit the 'average individual', to use Tarde's own words.[34] For him, the human being is the fundamental source of all things social.

Kelles-Krauz on the one hand described the long-gone past as a mythologised, even theoretical ideal, which served as an inspiration for the future. On the other, he considered the less distant past a 'nightmare', which does not want to fade and persists thanks to the inertia of institutions. In this, one could notice clear inspiration from Marx's *The Eighteenth Brumaire* of *Louis Bonaparte*: "The tradition of all dead generations weighs like a nightmare on the brains of the living".[35] A longing for imaginary ideals from bygone times set the tone for new forms, these in turn were supposed to emerge for the new, changed substance. This is why Leszek Kołakowski argued that for Kelles-Krauz the past gained substantial autonomy over the material foundation and

---

33   *The Sociological Law of Retrospection* in this volume. See also: Tarde, Gabriel, 1903, *The Laws of Imitation*, New York: Henry Holt and Company, p. 173f.

34   See: Tarde, Gabriel, 1903, *The Laws of Imitation*, p. 294.

35   Marx, Karl, 2008, *The Eighteenth Brumaire of Louis Bonaparte*. New York: International Publishers, p. 15.

shaped the horizon of goals for future institutions. The process of maximising production was governed by its own logic, while social development was ruled by a sentiment toward an idealised freedom envisioned in the 'state of nature', but defined according to contemporary needs. The paradox, or even dialectical contradiction, was the result of the difficulty in linking increasingly advanced technologies of production with a growing yearning for the idealised vision of the primeval community. For Kelles-Krauz this paradox would be overcome by Communism. The new social order would resolve the conflict between the existing history of development of reflective thinking and technology on the one hand, and the need to shape a society of free individuals, independent from the command of economic calculation, on the other.

Tarde's charge against Marxists was that they reduced people to rationally acting individuals, and their actions to logically planned metaphysical constructions within the scheme of the gradual development of consciousness that would finally lead to Communism. Ironically, it was an accusation that could also be made against the Polish scholar. At first glance, in Kelles-Krauz's theory the goal set out by Marxism could only be defended as a temporary pursuit, which answered contemporary needs. Although the economic foundation was supposed to be the sole source of change, the author of *The Sociological Law of Retrospection* found all phenomena that take place in society, i.e. social facts, as psychological, thus occurring in people's minds. For example, in the law of revolutionary retrospection he presented a classification of personalities in relation to social changes.[36] In his typology of minds – reluctant to change, opportunistic, and hungry for novelty – he was most interested in the latter category. According to him, such personalities can draw radical conclusions from existing rules or transgress existing forms and create new ones. Minds that desire change, search for inspiration in the past. For Kelles-Krauz, who based his idea on history as well as on the works of thinkers including Tarde and Hegel, visions of the future were shaped by the discrepancies between contemporary technology of production and existing social norms, as well as previous ideals. For Tarde novelty could only be the result of an intersection of current

---

36 A similar categorisation was also offered by the Polish sociologist Wacław Nałkowski in his essay *Forpoczty ewolucyi psychicznej i troglodyci* (the title may be translated as *The vanguard of mental revolution and troglodytes*). The author distinguishes between progressive 'brainers' and three subcategories made up of the crowd, which he labels 'troglodytes': human-bulls, human-timber, and human-swine; see: Nałkowski, Wacław, 1904, *Jednostka i ogół: szkice i krytyki psycho-społeczne*, Krakow, Poland: Czatowicz, pp. 36–9. Furthermore, Durkheim famously described different types of social deviance in *Suicide*; see: Durkheim, Émile, 1951, *Suicide. A Study in Sociology*. New York: The Free Press.

imitation trends, but Kelles-Krauz extended this idea to embrace, as the Polish thinker described it, Hegel's 'solution of contradictions'. It was the necessity, as Kelles-Krauz put it, to abandon the "boundless accumulation of novelties, in order to replace one with the other, to harmonise and reconcile them".[37]

Since all these endeavours found their outlet not in society but in individual minds, the greater was the role of the workers, since they were supposed to feel most acutely the disparity between substance and form. Yet surprisingly Kelles-Krauz mentioned this issue only in passing. At the same time, this contrast could easily be noticed by anyone who rose above the one-sided perspective of their own class, that is their own 'social apperception'. According to the social thinker this part was to be played by minds desiring novelty and change. Based on his work, however, it is difficult to determine who in fact was capable of such desires, or whether they could be shared by members of the working class.

Although Kelles-Krauz searched for the germs of revolution in material needs, claiming that "social tasks stand before the human consciousness, when – at least in a hidden state – the means for their resolving and fulfilling have already been given",[38] he granted them a strongly autonomous status. One may wonder if the revolution was thus to be the adjustment of form for the changing substance, or whether it merely used material needs as a pretext to alter forms resulting from the development of the mind. Kelles-Krauz blamed the bourgeoisie, the children of the French Revolution for this, and accused them of resting on their class and capitalist laurels.

Class and Apperception

Social apperception, which Kelles-Krauz at times named 'class apperception', was a key element in his theory, and the main feature responsible for the growing disparity between substance and form. This social 'blindness' of sorts stemmed from class divisions, in which only the few had access to managing

---

37   *The Sociological Law of Retrospection* in this volume. Taking the argument even further into the future of social thought, one could find an echo of Kelles-Krauz's idea on the intrinsic logic of shifts in technology – which eventually leads to revolution in form – in Thomas Kuhn's descriptions of paradigm changes. The American philosopher viewed them as the result of subtle changes within existing methodologies and logic of discovery. See: Kuhn, Thomas, 1962, *The Structure of Scientific Revolutions*.

38   *What is Economic Materialism?* in this volume.

the production process. The class of owners of the means of production wielded power, which allowed them to shape as a whole. For this reason, the class struggle over the means of production was essentially a fight over control of social forms. This particular type of power made it possible to create laws, ethics, philosophy, as well as art according to the goals of the dominant class, which then imposed it on others. The scholar defined social apperception as "imposing upon the whole of social life forms brought to light by one category of needs, and that non-noticing of slow changes until they become serious changes".[39] Although social forms had value only when they met particular needs, they nonetheless formed the basis of the entire social order, Kelles-Krauz argued. Furthermore, the function of social order – even if it boiled down to oppression – was often also emphasized by Vico and Rousseau: it ensured security. Given the Polish thinker's favourable theoretical stance towards the concept of change, his all but pragmatic vision of social harmony, indispensable even at the cost of freedoms of a part of society, strikes as an interesting paradox.

For Kelles-Krauz the bourgeoisie was a missed opportunity to balance substance and form. The 'bourgeois class' won the battle with feudal order, but its own degeneration caused by the class's apperception made it possible for the working class – the child of feudalism and the bourgeoisie – to start a revolution. Only the proletariat could finally bring back equilibrium between the production of goods and social organisation. According to the scholar, the bourgeoisie followed three principles that corresponded with its own aims. These were, firstly, determinism and historical materialism in place of supernatural power and graces, which had been the domain of feudal rulers and priests; secondly, the renouncement of past certainties in favour of individual rationalism and fundamental faith in one's own agency; and, thirdly, a positivist, universal belief in fast and limitless progress. These principles, enacted on the level of form, emerged on the level of substance as the organization of the industrial system. It is interesting to note Snyder's comment on the role given by Kelles-Krauz to the mechanisms of social apperception, or – simply put – the social forms which aim to maintain the *status quo*:[40]

---

39   *The Sociological Law of Retrospection* in this volume.

40   It is worth noting that Snyder appreciated Kelles-Krauz's shrewdness in descriptions of national identity as a construction shaped in relation to social needs. In the 20th century, this concept was developed by leading social thinkers and historians including Eric Hobsbawm, Ernest Gellner, and Benedict Anderson. See: Snyder, Timothy, 1997, *Nationalism, Marxism, and Modern Central Europe.*

Capitalism transforms static feudal economic order into numerous, mobile, and overlapping classes. The individual, uprooted from his traditional economic and social position, finds a single constant in the new capitalist economy: his native language. (...) Capitalism demands an educated population, and thus traditional myths "in the very interest of capitalism" will reach the nation as a whole, rather than its elites only. Here intellectuals catalyze "retrospection". (...) Mass culture also allows for the transmission of the liberating ideas of "equality and democracy" to the oppressed.[41]

Positive philosophy was supposed to complete the hierarchy of forms of the bourgeois class. Still, Kelles-Krauz considered bourgeois capitalism, industrial society, and the nation itself solely as necessary elements in the process of achieving socialism. (This does not mean he did not fall into the same traps; Snyder accused the Polish scholar of ignoring his own 'national apperception' in the pursuit of Poland's independence.) Furthermore, Kelles-Krauz followed Saint-Simon when he argued that within the classification of the past into organic and critical periods, the industrial period was irrefutably an example of the former.[42] One may wonder if, according to this line of reasoning, the next critical stage to follow that of positivism would be a period of the development of totalitarian regimes, and their outcome, world war.

Bourgeois faith in the agency of the individual and the cognitive power of science was clearly visible in law and morality, which were made to be as perfect as possible, since they were based on rational and material premises. For Kelles-Krauz, they constituted the foundation for approaching Marxism. Yet another feature necessary for Marxism to fully emerge sprung from the opposite current: anti-rationalist, historical, based on the relative, shifting nature of truths and institutions in the historical process. The bourgeoisie, who rejected 'miracles' and 'metaphysics' in favour of objectivity of rational cognition, could be labelled the most perfect creation of positivist philosophy and the industrial system. But for Kelles-Krauz the bourgeoisie was only an indispensable element in the historical process, which led directly to classless Communism. It was because of the degeneration of positivist philosophy that the ideals of

---

41   Snyder, Timothy, 1997, *Nationalism, Marxism, and Modern Central Europe*, p. 198.

42   These classifications bring to mind Tarde's dictionary and grammar periods, as well as Comte's periods of critique, which emerge between subsequent stages of the development of the mind. See: Tarde, Gabriel, 1903, *The Laws of Imitation*; Comte, Auguste, 1903, *A Discourse on the Positive Spirit*. London, UK: W. Reeves.

rationalism and individualism (in other words, forms) could finally meet their material base (or substance) created by the workers.

Art, Health, and Morality

Aside from focusing on analysing social history within the theory of economic materialism, Kelles-Krauz was also interested in the ways society affected basic human needs. In *A Few Main Principles in the Development of Art*, he described the development of artistic creativity as an endeavour that transforms from a biological activity, direct and 'vital', into an occupation deeply rooted in social forms. According to his interpretation, the primeval task of art was to give pleasure and to appeal to people's emotions. Yet on the level of substance, the developments in the organisation of labour, subject to economic calculation and social forms, produced a growing distance between artistic activity and 'pure' life activities: "art, created socially, is also socially constrained",[43] Kelles-Krauz explained. The greater the autonomy of social forms, the more they turned into an end in themselves, and the more art drifted away from actual 'life', independent and unmediated by laws, morality, or economic system.

According to the Polish scholar, when art ceases to be an integral part of issues that concern life-production it becomes a luxury, leaving the everyday context behind. Being an 'ethics of instincts', art is placed by society at the very top of social hierarchy. Art is thus saturated with social creation but, being an activity intended to move and to give pleasure, it can transcend set social norms and return to 'life before' the shackles of forms of social order. In its pursuit of substance, art is akin to science, although it favours direct emotion over intellectual analysis. What's more, in this particular context Kelles-Krauz's idea of the psyche reveals itself in its ambivalence. Although the thinker usually treated it on par with the mind, in *A Few Main Principles in the Development of Art* he described the psyche in a different manner, namely from the point of view of emotions. His sociological intuition again proved valid, the question of emotions directed toward art in capitalism and the industrial society became a particularly fruitful topic soon after, and was discussed by such classic social thinkers as Georg Simmel and Walter Benjamin.[44]

---

43 See: *A Few Main Principles in the Development of Art* in this volume.

44 Simmel, Georg, 2005, *Rembrandt. An Essay in the Philosophy of Art*. New York: Routledge, see also: Simmel, Georg, 1950, *The Sociology of Georg Simmel*. New York: The Free Press; Benjamin, Walter. 1968. The Work of Art in the Age of Mechanical Reproduction. In: Benjamin, Walter, *Illuminations*. New York: Schocken Books, pp. 217–252.

Unlike later interpretations of art, which emphasised the importance of 'art for art's sake', for the Polish scholar art was fundamentally useful. Art enjoys this status because it is not only interlinked with 'life' itself but is also democratic. After all, "in every person lies dormant an artist to some degree or other".[45] This is also why art transcends set norms. What's more, because art strives for freedom and novelty, it remains in conflict with social institutions reluctant to change. Interestingly, the paradoxical position of art indicates the different modes of understanding 'usefulness', and these modes, too, transform influenced by social forms. In the initial version – and the final one, after the goal of Communism was achieved – art relates to the creative and somewhat egoistic activity of the individual, who wants to "discharge thoughts or urges".[46] However, in the face of society art becomes its servant. Kelles-Krauz argues that in a class society utility is intertwined with morality, duty, obedience, and, finally, fear. And since art transcends binding norms by default, it becomes either limited to the function of pleasure and luxury for the dominant classes or, deemed unnecessary, it is banished from the sphere of social norms. Furthermore, given his occupation, the artist is more critically aware of social forms to be broken than the worker. In the desire for change, the artist represents Kelles-Krauz's third type of mentality, even though he is not guided by the retrospective idea of change but by the desire for emotion. Therefore, the artist's retrospection is both Marxist, as it relates to the ideal of art imagined in the primeval society, and ahistorical, since it relates to humans' 'biological' needs.

This problematic status of art in society is based on the resistance of artists toward class order and the morality that comes with it. The artist is thus paradoxically either at the top of class order, meeting the aesthetic needs and offering emotions to the class of capital-owners, or he becomes a pariah with a sense of superiority toward society that rejected him. It is worth noting that the suspicious attitude toward artists, as useless members of society who undermine social order, was already to be found in Plato's idea of state.[47]

In the first case, the artist is made part of the social system, and turns into a professional creator of aesthetic products, which are intended to confirm the validity of the order imposed by the dominant class. Such creations do not touch upon the substance – important existential issues – that could undermine the legitimacy of the enforced system. Kelles-Krauz thus refers to Marx when he writes that "the bourgeois gladiators found the ideals and the

45   See: *A Few Main Principles in the Development of Art* in this volume.
46   See: Ibidem.
47   Plato, 1931, *The Republic*. London, UK: Oxford University Press.

art forms, the self-deceptions, that they needed to conceal from themselves the bourgeois-limited content of their struggles".[48] In the second case, the artist may create tendentious art, which serves the need for change in general ideas. The difference between these two version of the artist is that in the latter he shares the idea of social change, which art should aid. Nonetheless, it still makes for utilitarian art.

However, Kelles-Krauz offers a third option, by which the artist rejects society as such and in solitude creates art for art's sake. In doing so, he opposes utilitarian art but, as the scholar notes, 'art for art's sake' is not the same thing as 'idea-less art'. The first type of artistic creativity opposes contemporary morality; thus, it is itself 'immoral'. However, the second type, 'idea-less art', does not refer to social forms at all, which makes it potentially 'amoral', 'a-class', and allows it to return to the unmediated, free substance. Nevertheless, art is inevitably immersed in concrete historical conditions, and its fundamental pursuit is the ceaseless labour to break away from constraints visible in social reality. In the end, it is a Sisyphean task. In this particular argument, Kelles-Krauz employs a similar mechanism to that used in his analysis of historical processes: ultimate goals are merely inventions of their own time. Instead of confronting the human being with perfect ideas, it makes more sense and is more practical to offer different contexts and aspirations. Going further, the ideas the Polish scholar criticises are turned by him into ideal types.[49] In *A Few Main Principles in the Development of Art*, Kelles-Krauz offers the following:

> [...] there exists in everybody a natural aspiration to combine everyday life and everyday work with some kind of emotion, and if only this miraculous transformation of the everyday obligation really does come to be, transformation of the ordinary utilitarian action and its connected dictates and beliefs into selfless pleasure and emotion, this sweet and radiant transformation of life into art, that that is precisely when, that is only when one can be sure that life such as it is and as it must be in the particular system, life thus defined and confined as the given ruling system wants to have it, has set its deepest roots in the people's souls and become the most resistant to all attempts at change and revolution.[50]

---

48 See: *Psychiatry and the Science of Ideas* in this volume; see also: Marx, Karl, 2008. *The Eighteenth Brumaire of Louis Bonaparte*, p. 16.

49 See: Weber, Max, 2011. Objectivity in Social Science and Social Policy. In: Weber, Max, *Methodology of Social Sciences*. Brunswick, NJ: Transaction Publishers, pp. 49–112.

50 See: *A Few Main Principles in the Development of Art* in this volume.

In the end, life is supposed to be art, and art should transform itself into life; this is one of Kelles-Krauz's few claims, which he finds objective, beyond time.

Nevertheless, this does not change the fact that for the class society, which he observed, such quests for altruism stood in stark contrast with the idea of obedience to social order. In consequence, if artists cannot be socialised, they should be banished from society. What's more, in Psychiatry and the Science of Ideas Kelles-Krauz described an analogous method of control, this time concerning the right to be a rightful member of society. In his writings, he anticipated a phenomenon later analysed by Michel Foucault: biopower.[51] In the essay, the Polish scholar offered a scathing critique of Max Nordau's theory of health and mental illness, deeming them a simplistic affirmation of commonly shared social norms. Nordau, a physician and philosopher who was Kelles-Krauz's contemporary, considered all human endeavours that were inconsistent with class order as mental disorders requiring treatment. Hence, according to his theory both artists and revolutionaries – or, in general, any minds striving for change – were not only maladapted to social life but objectively ill. Kelles-Krauz strongly opposed such a determinist and static view of society, in which any freedom of thought was akin to losing one's mind. For him Nordau's theory was a clear example of social apperception; furthermore, the physician equated the typical with the moral. The Polish sociologist condemned Nordau's approach that dominant values are essentially good values. The difficult history of mass societies in the 20th century showed that Kelles-Krauz was right to have such reservations.

While not attempting to formulate a definition of health (or illness), the scholar offered his own theory of ethics of socialism. According to his argument, it stemmed from previous ideals, since "we can only seek salvation in what is known to us".[52] By adding ethics to his concept of Marxism, Kelles-Krauz expanded the Marxist programme, which is based on the economy, with features found in the superstructure; in doing so he highlighted the value of the superstructure within Marx's dialectic of history.

Retrospective ideas related to social forms had a key role in reaching successive stages, which were ultimately to lead to communism. Snyder summed up this approach, "Marxism consists in the constant dialogue between means and ends, with the ethical ideal of socialism serving to light the path from one step to the next".[53] Late 19th century German Marxists attempted to interpret Kant in order to create an objective ethics of socialism. Critical theory of the

---

51   See: Foucault, Michel,1990, *The History of Sexuality*. New York: Vintage Books.

52   See: *Psychiatry and the Science of Ideas* in this volume.

53   Snyder, Timothy, 1997, *Nationalism, Marxism, and Modern Central Europe*, p. 249.

individual together with the superior plan of nature became its foundation. Unlike them, however, Kelles-Krauz stressed that moral values, too, undergo change and they are dependent on specific historical conditions. After all, social contexts of health and art showed particularly well how deeply unstable 'objective' norms are.

Conclusion. Marxism?

Leszek Kołakowski was critical of Kelles-Krauz's interpretation of the relations between base and superstructure; the philosopher found them inconsistent. Although Kelles-Krauz claimed to have found the source of all social forms in the technology of production, his argument on the growing independence of these forms went so far that instead of writing about the economic base, he described the mutual influence of substance and form in history. Kołakowski wrote:

> Kelles-Krauz did not ask how far it made sense to speak of a 'monistic' interpretation of history while at the same time accepting the common-sense view that changes in art, science, philosophy, or religion depend on other factors besides changes in the relations of production – especially the logic of their own internal development and the operation of 'auton-omized' needs in respect of each. (...) [H]e ignored the question how the relative independence of the spiritual life and of the institutions of the superstructure, could be Rican style with a belief in the 'ultimate cause' of human history, and what limits it imposed on the general formulas of historical materialism.[54]

Nevertheless, the Polish historian Andrzej Mencwel pointed out that such harsh treatment of Kelles-Krauz is unfair, since it does not include his political activity within the Marxist canon;[55] a similar sentiment was shared by the sociologist Grzegorz Ekiert.[56] Still, despite the criticism, Kołakowski admitted

---

54   Kołakowski, Leszek, 1978, *Main Currents of Marxism: The Founders, the Golden Age, the Breakdown*, p. 525f.

55   Mencwel, Andrzej, 2010, 'Kazimierz Kelles-Krauz – przyszłość przeszłości', *Kulturologia polska XX wieku*, http://andrzejmencwel.pl/2010/06/22/przeszlosc-dla-przyszlosci/, accessed 30 July 2017.

56   Ekiert, Grzegorz, 1984, 'Kazimierz Kelles-Krauz: From Marxism to Sociology', in: Sztompka, Piotr (ed). *Masters of Polish Sociology*, Wrocław, Kraków, Poland: Zakład Narodowy im. Ossolińskich.

that at the end of the 19th century Kelles-Krauz was probably the only Polish thinker who understood Marxism as philosophical – and not merely historical or dialectical – materialism, and bridged it with the role of chance in history. Such a combination would be unthinkable for the positivists or the enthusiasts of historical determinism. Furthermore, while Mencwel's argument does little to counter the claims made against Kelles-Krauz's ideas, his activity was nonetheless unique in 'translating' Marxist thought at the turn of the century to push the case for the independence of Poland. Indeed, his endeavours as an activist and thinker had a visible and positive effect on the image of the stateless country on the European socialist scene.

Furthermore, Kelles-Krauz's interpretation of Marxism was distinctive because, unlike many, the Polish scholar did not view the doctrine as a system, which provided a total and finite description of the world. This view remained in stark contrast with those shared by the representatives of the dominant trends of the Second International, including Karl Kautsky and Georgij Plekhanow. In contrast, for Kelles-Krauz Marxism was a scientific method, in which its features such as foundation, superstructure, class, and nation should be treated as 'ideal types' or, as the Polish philosopher Andrzej Walicki put it, "social a priori".[57] According to Kelles-Krauz, sociology was a science that managed to overcome internal contradictions and that could isolate basic laws of society the way hard or natural sciences do. In addition, taking from positivism, the scholar emphasised the crucial role of individuals and their interpretations of reality as the foundations of the scientific method. In place of objective, abstract ideals, he offered a phenomenological approach, which took into account the particular horizons of experience. Kołakowski on the other hand found this interpretation problematic, given the premise of ultimate goals. Nonetheless, it opened new avenues in analysing the position of the individual in society, which goes through both rapid and unceasing revolutionary changes, as well as minute shifts.

Although Kelles-Krauz viewed the needs that emerge from the development of the modes of production as the drivers of change, his arguments formulated in the law of revolutionary retrospection suggest that these needs (i.e. economic substance) become visible in the human psyche as social forms, which are the ideals of the past. Half a century later, the Polish philosopher Bronisław Baczko argued that the law of revolutionary retrospection was an

---

57   Walicki, Andrzej, 1983, 'Kazimierz Kelles-Krauz'. In: Borzym, Stanisław, Floryńska, Halina, Skarga, Barbara and Walicki, Andrzej (eds), *Zarys dziejów filozofii polskiej 1815–1918*, Warsaw, Poland: PWN, p. 425.

attempt at "revising Marxism from an idealistic standpoint",[58] which, however, ignored the role of Marx's class conflict. While according to Baczko, by doing so Kelles-Krauz in fact broke with Marxism, Walicki noted this interpretation of idealism was later developed by Karl Mannheim in his own theory of 'utopia'.[59] Still, Ekiert points out that Kelles-Krauz was widely criticised by scholars in the Stalinist period, including Baczko, for his anti-dogmatic approach. And while the late 19th century Polish thinker was not always consistent in his justifications of the shifts in social forms thanks to the technologies of production, he saw the material tools, and not abstract ideas, as triggers of change. Although it may appear a stretch, it is hard not to notice a similar trend today, with tools of communication becoming the impulse and technology for social change.[60]

Ekiert, in another interpretation of Kelles-Krauz's major work, argued that the law of revolutionary retrospection should not be limited to the sphere of social consciousness. This claim echoed Kołakowski's stance on the problematic status of relations between form and substance in Kelles-Krauz's theory. What's more, one can also wonder if the longing for the past was in itself the effect of the changes in the mode of production. Still, Kelles-Krauz offered more sociological observations concerning the level of form than substance, which may have been the result of the undisputed assumption that the working class would bring social change. On the level of superstructure, Walicki interpreted the role of social habits through Georg Simmel's 'philosophy of life',[61] but it is worth asking whether the faith of Marxists in the upcoming revolution was not an illustration of these very habits. Still, one cannot deny Kelles-Krauz's insight in terms of social alienation, which he studied using the example of the isolation of art, as well as in the context of substance and form in the psyches of individuals. This is why Mencwel rightly argued that Kelles-Krauz's interpretation of society had a strong cultural streak, which was most clearly visible in his essay A Few Main Principles in the Development of Art. The theory used by the scholar to link artistic activity with everyday life still continues to offer an interesting view on the role of the artist and art today. In addition, the co-existence of the two realities of art – professional versus amateur, purposeful versus purposeless – ceaselessly imposes questions on the paradoxical role of artists in a changing society.

58   [Translation: Helena Chmielewska-Szlajfer] Baczko, Bronisław, 1949, 'Prawo retrospekcji przewrotowej Kelles-Krauza', *Myśl Współczesna* 1949, 8–9, p. 58.

59   See: Mannheim, Karl, 1997, *Ideology and Utopia*. New York: Routledge.

60   For example, see: Castells, Manuel, 2012, *Networks of Outrage and Hope*, Malden, MA: Polity Press.

61   See: Simmel, Georg, 2016, *The View of Life*, Chicago, IL: University of Chicago Press.

Interestingly, Kelles-Krauz also had high hopes for art in the future. In a series of short essays, titled The Underground Future of Humanity, published in the Polish newspaper Życie,[62] which were inspired by the futurist writings of Tarde and Bellamy, the Polish thinker envisioned the world to come in the 25th century. Perhaps ironically, he foresaw an environmental disaster – although caused by abnormal occurrences on the Sun and not by human activity – which forced people to go underground, while the surface of the Earth became a freezer full of food. What is particularly noteworthy is that contrary to his Marxist beliefs, Kelles-Krauz thought the social order of the future would be not Communism but global monarchy. In a fully man-made underground civilisation people would become artists and scholars, while all the labour would be done by machines. His vision, while undeniably amusing, was also chauvinist – for example, 'the love of women' was the prize for men's achievements in art and science – and, moreover, static. The underground future would have to be a boring, socially unchanging place, as people would lack the main driver of human activity Kelles-Krauz found in history: economic materialism. And, indeed, the scholar predicted outbursts of revolts as a result of people's frustration and their desire to see the Earth's surface. Thus, for Kelles-Krauz even in a perfect future the law of revolutionary retrospection would remain in place.

In conclusion, Kelles-Krauz was both a typical and talented representative of the Polish intelligentsia in partitioned Poland under Russian rule. He was a descendant of declassed nobility; he had to leave the country in order to study and engage in political activity; he believed in Poland's significant role in Europe, in merging Marxism with the fight for independence. As a scholar, he often transgressed the imposed Marxian frame of economic materialism. Instead, he put forward interpretations, which were developed into separate sociological approaches by other social thinkers after his death. However, what made Kelles-Krauz so distinct was the bridging of political activity with far-reaching anti-dogmatism in his scholarly work. Alongside Edward Abramowski, Ludwik Krzywicki, and Stanisław Brzozowski, he was the creator of one of the most original sociological interpretations of Marxism in Poland at the turn of the century.

---

62   See: Kelles-Krauz, Kazimierz, 'Podziemna przyszłość ludzkości' in Życie, issues no. 9–14/ 1897 and 1–2/1898.

The Sociological Law of Retrospection: The Law of Revolutionary Retrospection as a Consequence of Economic Materialism[1,2]

The year 1888 saw the publication in Leipzig of a work by a young Romanian researcher, Paul Weisengrün, entitled *Die Entwickelungsgesetze der Menschheit* [*The Laws of Development of Mankind*]. It is a rather non-systematic work, in many a place unclear, and here and there containing generalisations that are too quick and too risky. Nevertheless, one cannot but be surprised that it is so poorly known beyond specialist circles, and circles of only German specialists at that, since this is perhaps the sole attempt at presenting the economic materialism of Marx, Engels and Morgan in the form of a developed system.[3] In this presentation, the author, aspiring to construct a whole, filled many gaps with ideas of his own, the greater part of which cannot be accepted without discussion. As I do not wish to enter such discourse on this occasion, I shall cite only a few of the laws he formulated that deviate least from the thoughts of the said system's first creators and that accurately summarise it.

These laws are as follows:

---

1 Source: Socjologiczne prawo retrospekcji Prawo retrospekcji przewrotowej jako wynik materializmu ekonomicznego, "Ateneum" 1897, vol. 3, pp. 264–277, 465–481.

2 This work comprises two talks that I had on 4 October 1894 and 2 October 1895 [the dates given are incorrect: the talks were on 4 November 1894 and 2 November 1895; editor's note] at the sittings of the 1st and 2nd congresses of the International Institute of Sociology; they constitute a logical whole. I present the Polish reader with the second almost unmodified; significant alterations have been made to the first. The title of the talk was *Psychiatry and The Science of Ideas* [published in this volume; editor's note], and it was above all a critique of Max Nordau's *Degeneration*. The critique was printed in its original form in 'Głos' (1894, issues 14 and 15). By fighting the overuse of psychiatric terminology in regard to reminiscences of a distant, idealised past so common among poets and artists, I have confronted them with the law of retrospection. I have now developed this in greater breadth and detail, while I have totally removed those sections that did not refer directly to this law, but were specially directed against *lombrosism* [from Cesare Lombroso (1835–1909), an Italian psychiatrist and supporter of social Darwinism; editor's note] in artistic critique [Kelles-Krauz's footnote].

3 When these words were written, the splendid book by the Russian sociologist N. Beltov [pseudonym of Georgi Valentinovich Plekhanov; translator's note], *The Development of the Monistic View of History*, Petersburg 1895, had not yet been published [Kelles-Krauz's footnote].

1 and 2: One may distinguish three periods in the history of mankind according to the relevant factors defining the entire development of society. In the first period, reproductive urges and forms of reproduction are such a factor; this embraces primitive communism.[4] Its disintegration leads to centre stage being taken by the factor of wealth creation, an economic factor that has control over real history right up to our times, over the entire age of individual production; as for the impact of reproductive urges, in this age it only applies through economic forms. Finally, we are living on the eve of the third period, which will dominate when production is guided by social will; family and economic activities will depend on forms of consciousness, and will break apart, so to say, before their execution in those forms that, having become independent, will become a factor defining growth and will give man the greatest sense of free will. What we really have here are two laws, which may be called the law of defining factors, and the law of the consequences of these factors.

3: The ways in which wealth is created are therefore decisive in the period of real history; they constitute the foundations for the superstructure of ethical, legal, political, philosophical, religious and scientific, and literary and aesthetic forms; the economic conditions, the conditions for production, constitute content, that is to say the social content to which this entire social form is applied. This is a fundamental law of economic materialism: the law of the economic base.

Finally, 4: The social form experiences the social content.

The third law may be worded differently. Namely, an appropriate shaping of the social classes together with the domination of one of them corresponds to each of the methods of production that have succeeded one another right up until our times. When change that has occurred in the method of production transfers political power from the hands of one class to another, the new ruler naturally strives to strengthen – or one should even say to immortalise – their power. To achieve this goal it is essential to bring about an equilibrium in the needs existing in society, an equilibrium both mutual and in regard to such methods and means of satisfying these needs that correspond to the specific form of production, the structure of the classes, and the needs of the ruling class. The resultant relations, between all aspects of the psyche on the one hand and the relevant class foundation on the other, constitute the subject matter of a separate section of sociology – a section now in the stage of its

---

4   In any case, this liberation of the familial factor, defining economic matters at any time, is a
    matter of great contention [Kelles-Krauz's footnote].

THE SOCIOLOGICAL LAW OF RETROSPECTION 31

emergence – and namely class psychology, which may also be called historical sociology, as it only begins where the class-less prehistoric age ends. Following what we have said, we may formulate the following fundamental truth of class psychology: wherever a view of man's tasks and duties becomes a factor, then – digging deeper – one will always find some kind of class base or another.

This dependence of systems and moral dictates on the class foundation is almost obvious for the impartial and sober mind; it is harder to discern and demonstrate in regard to phenomena further removed from the economic base, in regard to the higher storeys of the social construction that scientific and aesthetic theories constitute. One should bear in mind here that a direct casting (*moulage*), so to say, is not the sole way in which the economic base influences social form. Admittedly what I understand by the word casting, namely the direct mental reaction to every fact of satisfying a need, constitutes a fundamental process: by protracting, a certain manner of satisfying needs degenerates into habit, an expression of which becomes a certain ethical or legal dictate, a certain political institution. This fundamental process takes place unceasingly; it creates social totalities, then disassembles them before modelling new integrals from the atoms torn asunder. Yet the time arrives when society begins trailing behind a traditional baggage of sundry systems that influence the formation of new ones; then we are dealing with a second way in which the class conditions have an influence. Though more superficial, this way is mighty; we would call it the sifting (*triage*). This involves each class receiving a certain relevant blindness that veils from its spiritual gaze all components of tradition absolutely incapable of entering a harmony and equilibrium with its economic base. The rest undergoes transformation *ad usum Delphini*; and it is no longer the *tabula rasa* of the pre-societal human animal but the type of social apperception thus generated that serves as the skeleton for the proper casting of social forms.

The victorious class shapes the whole of society in its fashion and in all fields establishes a certain generally binding norm, the infringing of which is considered an offence, since it threatens the existence of this society in its given form, equated with the existence of society as such. This norm is codified by law and public opinion, while religion and philosophy rush to sanction it; its idealisation suffuses art; and for these activities of the human mind an entire host of special sciences accumulates materials. Philosophy emerges from all sciences, from astronomy to psychology; and through it they too are all connected by bonds, some tighter some looser, to social human existence. The crowning of every philosophy is ethics; and from ethics it is infected with blindness, or class colour-blindness, and with this in turn it infects all the sciences that it comprises. This is because ethics is the very first need of any social form; it is determined in practice before it is embraced in theory. In the emergence of practical morality, the process of casting prevails over the sifting process. When ethics is connected later on, by a religious or philosophical path, to the general understanding of the world of which it seems but a result, the sifting begins to assume its role: an appropriately steered mind discerns from the cosmic or historical relations only those that may serve as premises for ethical results. Objectively – the conclusion defines the premises; the mirror of the subject presents this relationship to us in reverse. The postulates of philosophy in turn influence in the same manner the premises that are to emerge in the individual sciences. The further removed science is in this sequence from ethics, the less it succumbs to the process of casting and the weaker is the sifting taking place within its womb.

This paragraph would require the support of numerous examples. I believe that to break down the resistance of the reader, accustomed to belief in the Olympian independence of knowledge, and for the clarification of my thought, that perhaps sufficient will be an important incident in the recent history of knowledge tied rather closely to philosophy, yet to all appearances bearing no connection to ethics; I speak here of the emergence of the theory of panspermia and microbiology, and of its battle with the theory of spontaneous generation. As we know, Pasteur undertook a number of experiments that led him to panspermatism, with the aim of disproving the hypothesis of spontaneous generation, offending his religious beliefs, Christian beliefs, so tightly bound to the ethics of punishment and reward. Spontaneous generation in turn was the natural result of the great materialistic movement in philosophy, carrying with it the ethics of determinism and non-responsibility. As for materialism and idealism, determinism and the non-causality of will – these constitute a weapon in the battle between the waning and waxing classes, constantly recurring in history. As it turns out in the ultimate generalisation, what we see here is feudalism coming out in the person of Pasteur against the bourgeoisie. And that representative of the revolutionary bourgeoisie, Pouchet, in creating his hypothesis of spontaneous generation, was so focused on the entirety of materialism and determinism, for which it was supposed to be a new premise, that microscopic powders bringing into the vessel the seeds of microorganisms remained unnoticed to him on the sieve of the ideological sifting.[5]

---

5 Let us not forget that it was the Parisian Academy of Sciences, permeated like all academies with such a dose of conservatism as may only be reconciled with the irrefutable accomplishments of knowledge at any particular moment, that first proclaimed a crusade against Pouchet's theories, and in the year 1866 promised a reward of 2000 fr. to he who would incontrovertibly refute them. This prize went to L. Pasteur, for whom the said Academy facilitated

This entire process of shaping society in the fashion of the ruling class takes place in human minds, which possess diverse speeds of adaptation. As the process moves forward, one can differentiate three distinct categories. Minds endowed with the lowest speed of adaptation are long unable to part with the form of superseded social content, with views and feelings conveyed by the past; they desire a revival of the past, and stubbornly defend legal institutions that the new spirit has not managed to uproot; in a word, they constitute the regressive camp. The second category – of medium speed of adaptation – may be termed opportunistic, as it adapts with ease to the conditions whatever they are, and while possessing neither distant memories nor far-reaching hopes, it lives for the now. Finally, we have the third category – of the briskest of minds, those most thirsty for what is new – that runs through social forms like a train through stations, barely slowing to stop. No sooner does one see the establishing of courts of some kind that develop opinion-forming systems, then an onslaught of other images dismantles them, making room for the new; the impressions received and notions formed barely manage to satiate them and already they crave again. And this third category is not yet homogeneous. One of its divisions, having shown deeper concern in the prevailing system – and that frequently due to purely external conditions – cannot step beyond its own boundaries, and it satisfies its hunger for thought and impressions by drawing as far-reaching consequences as possible from this system's principles. These consequences upset the system's equilibrium, they undermine the existing norm, leading it logically to an abnormal absurd. The minds of this division, that embraces all creators of paradoxes, all Proudhons and Drumonts, are in a sense the *enfants terribles* of the existing form. Hence by no means strange is the indignation of the contemporary bourgeois opportunist, such as for example Nordau, at the idea of the mechanical woman (the 'Future Eve' of Villiers de L'Isle-Adam[6]), or Nietzsche's *Übermensch* – although these are but extreme reinforcements of the bourgeois principles: of artificiality of life and class inequality. Alongside these unwitting destroyers of the existing form, in the second division of the third category we have minds breaking down the borders of contemporariness: they sense the future and live with visionary images of an approaching social form. Depending on strength of will and the conditions of one's milieu, all these moods are manifested in actions or remain in the realm of contemplation.

---

all experimentation. Pouchet and Joly also began performing experiments before the Academy, but stepped aside protesting against the difficulties placed before them [Kelles-Krauz's footnote].

6 Auguste Villiers de L'Isle-Adam, *L'Ève future*, 1886.

Of course this experimental classification of minds possesses some kind of deeper foundation resting within their very nature. The speed of adaptation appropriate to a certain mind must depend on its psychophysiological attributes, such as speed and clarity of perception, healthy will, the degree of concentration of attention, and the strength of emotions, etc. We leave a closer inspection of these conditions to the psychophysiologists, such that sociology could duly employ them. Nordau, for example, made a significant step on this path in his two introductory chapters to each of the two volumes of *Degeneration*, in which he investigates the psychophysiological causes of mysticism and egotism; except that Nordau, encroaching upon the field of the sociological science of ideas, made ill use of his psychological research, since he based the demarcation between moral health and illness on totally arbitrary grounds, and instead of a classification constructed a biased hierarchy of minds. The anthropological race must also exert an influence on the speed of minds' adaptation; and this factor, manifested *en masse*, generates differences in pace of development between a few societies experiencing identical periods of development. Ludwik Krzywicki ascribes just such a significance, by no means contradicting economic materialism, to race in sociology.

We have seen that both divisions in the third psychophysiological category of minds constitute, each in a different way, a historical spur, an *esprit mouvant* of every class: the first – through negation, through paradox, through recognised things turning strange; the second – through the indication of new forms in place of those, which, "frayed, lay devoid of strength in the dust". Yet there is an interesting phenomenon occurring here, one seemingly contradicting the preeminent character of these last minds: the past plays a significant role in their sympathies, due to which these sympathies are partially similar to the freshly-fought ideals of the most conservative of minds.

Who, for example, has not been struck in the present day by the all too frequent and contralateral coalitions of the social left and right against the middle ground? For example, the entire so-called 'bankruptcy of modern philosophy' that the Brunetières of all countries expound upon is the result of a misunderstanding, deriving from the fact that the latest philosophical idealism directed a few arguments against classic materialism, arguments seemingly the same as those used earlier by religion. Such coalitions are particularly frequent today in politics. How many times for example have political chroniclers racked their brains over cases of the overthrowing of opportunists in the French parliament (who are a particular example there of the broader concept of social opportunism of which we spoke above) by the combined votes of extreme radicals and socialists on the one hand, and clericals and royalists on the other? These manoeuvres of parliamentary strategy, ultimately of secondary significance, have a deeper social cause: for example, a proponent of pre-revolutionary guilds and a proponent of labour syndicates really do share a common foe in such a person as, let's say, Yves Guyot, the extreme spokesman of Manchesterian economics, and together they must set their principle of the affiliation of people against his drive for the absolute separation of individuals in the fight for a livelihood.

Despite this, it is obvious that a guild association and a syndicate association answer completely different conditions and goals, and constitute profoundly different forms of life. Yves Guyot, and with him the entire class represented by him, are happy to forget this difference: whatever recollects the past is, for them, reactionary. Ibsen, shattering today's form of the family, is for Nordau an obscurant of the latter kind because in Asyria girls, before getting married, obtained a dowry as the price of their body! Altogether this conformity between reformative movements and certain traditions of the past is frequently and deftly exploited as an argument by defenders of the social form predominant at any time. In the meantime, it constitutes a normal, fixed and essential result of human development, which has rightly been compared to a spiral line: a line that constantly returns to the same points in the circle, but on each occasion is ever higher above them.

This phenomenon may be formulated without metaphor as the following sociological law, which we shall call the law of revolutionary retrospection:

> The ideals with which any reformative movement desires to replace the existing social norms are always similar to the norms from a distant or not so distant past.[7]

Let us see how this works.

What does the phenomenon known as the rise and fall of a particular historical epoch, a certain social system, involve? Well, a certain number of needs that are not being satisfied appear. The old system gives way to the new only when these needs intensify to such a degree that they render this change essential. The force of these needs has brought them into the foreground of social life; because it was specifically their satisfaction that was the 'social issue', accordingly the social change occurs in the direction thus indicated by them, and the entire superstructure of legal and political institutions, etc., is

---

7   The original wording of this law in the French lecture went: "Any movement aspiring for change in the fundamentals of the social system turns first of all to some distant or not so distant epoch from the past". I have replaced this with the above, broader and more precise [Kelles-Krauz's footnote].

cast according to the forms of satisfying these needs. They are the 'spirit of the laws'. But this 'spirit' is not visible to the naked eye; the real foundation of social change and new life is refracted, like the light in a prism, in laws and institutions before it reaches the spiritual gaze of people: these are noticed by people earlier than the foundation, and they begin regarding their development, application and broadening to encompass the entirety of social life as the most important thing. The inertia thanks to which actions in the field of psychology transgress the intentions causes in social life that the entire social life is sometimes forced into social forms cast according to a single category of needs; and the consequences of this inertia are all the more powerful as people cannot notice at a particular moment the incessant changes taking place in the social foundation, changes that are infinitely small, and they use only their broader or narrower integrals. This is because in the social sphere, as also in all others, one can ascertain the functioning of Hegel's general law, namely that quantity transforms into quality. Engels applies this law to sociology in his polemical book against Dühring. Just as in chemistry the addition of a few C and H atoms introduces a total change to the properties of a body, properties that we are only defining through comparison and in relation to other bodies, so too in social development infinitely small and unnoticeable changes, taking place in how sundry needs are satisfied, integrate and generate new qualitative categories that come into being in people's minds only through the juxtaposition of accumulated changes with some other pre-existing category.

But imposing upon the whole of social life forms brought to light by one category of needs, and that not-noticing of slow changes until they become serious changes, elicits the pressure of other categories of needs; when this results in signs of dissatisfaction the pressure grows, since the predominant system – fuelled by survival instinct – becomes increasingly exclusive, and steadily less tolerant. Minds wounded in their needs turn away from the ruling system and seek other forms of life. Let us recall here the law of posthumousness of the social form (the fourth of Weisengrün's laws that we cite): traces of the preceding system, indeed of numerous previous systems, are still alive, and their images are stored verbal or written traditions. Hopes and desires do not emerge out of nothing; there has to be factual material for them. When turning one's back on the present, one already has this material only in the past, and when examining it one discovers that the category of needs today predominant and repressing others was, in the directly preceding system, subordinate to others, while those others, then privileged, are similar to those repressed today. It is therefore clear that the forces dissatisfied with the present are beginning to desire a return of the past.

Not all desire this alike. The most conservative minds belonging to the first category of our classification, who have not yet managed to grow accustomed to the existing system, desire a simple resurrection of the preceding system. Still today one priest or another, or a Breton noble, prays perhaps for the Restoration of the Bourbons' kingdom from before 1789. But the minds of the third category have become too adapted to the current system, have adopted its spirit too greatly, for them to be able to dream of parting with it completely. Reluctant to abandon the present yet wanting to revive the past, they must resolve the puzzle of combining one with the other. The puzzle is resolved by life, just as the entire process mainly takes place unknowingly. When the infinitely small yet constant advancements of the social foundation and the simultaneous dissatisfaction, having reached a certain degree of accumulation, become integrated and supplant in turn the prevailing system – its achievements coalesce into a single new whole with the renewed forms of that preceding it. This is not a mechanical juxtaposition, but a genuine merging of the type of a chemical bonding: forms of the present, in absorbing forms of the past or being absorbed by them, generate totally new forms of the future. The Hegelian and Marxian formula proves true: 'thesis, antithesis and synthesis' become clothed in the body. Again, though, minds are seized by the momentum: actions exceed intentions, the conduct of the new institutions begins to be seen as more important than satisfying needs that never cease to change; and again certain needs are suppressed, which turns attention to the form recently abandoned in which they were satisfied; the pendulum oversteps the balance point yet again, and so on interminably.

One can see here that the approaching system is always, in some respect, similar to that abandoned, and that the sympathies of those who desire and sense it have something from the past. They differ from obscurants in that the latter desire retreat, while they – rebirth in a higher form. Such is the meaning of the law of revolutionary retrospection.

Let us take a couple of examples and applications. Karl Marx says in his essay *The Eighteenth Brumaire of Louis Napoleon*, which is a monograph of great value in the field of class psychology: "The tradition of the dead generations weighs like a nightmare on the brain of the living. At just when they seem engaged in revolutionizing themselves and things, in something that has never yet existed, precisely in such periods of revolutionary crisis they anxiously conjure up the spirits of the past to their service and borrow from them names, battle cries and costumes in order to present the new scene of world history in this time-honoured disguise and this borrowed language". There is in these words the brilliant intuition of the law of retrospection. And so further its shrewd application: "Thus Luther donned the mask of the Apostle Paul, the Revolution of 1789 to 1814 draped itself alternately as the Roman republic and as Roman empire, and the Revolution of 1848 knew nothing better to do than to parody, now 1789, now the revolutionary tradition of 1793 to 1795".[8] Let us add that the imitation of classic antiquity did not begin with the revolution of 1789; it is a characteristic feature of the developing bourgeois class and a symptom of the necessary reaction against the feudal system, which cared not of mercantile and industrial needs. The civic-mindedness of Greece, and particularly Rome, lent itself perfectly as a premise for equality in the face of the law and the gravity of law, so essential for the development of commerce and industry. It was nobody but the Renaissance that provided Revolution with its togas, lictors and curule seats, and its Gracchus brothers – in Babeuf skin.

There is no reason why such a renaissance should accompany the development of only one class and only one type of ideals. The 19th century also had its great renaissance. When society to which the year 1789 had given birth began in turn to neglect a certain category of needs, the classes turned with longing to the period of the past that preceded classic antiquity, from which Engels draws the Greek and Roman states – to the period of primitive community, the renaissance of which in a higher form is foretold by Morgan. Morgan, who did more than the humanists, as while they lived only in their thoughts in the Forum and beneath the Propylaea, he spent a dozen or so years of his own life living among the Iroquois – Morgan deserves to be called the Erasmus of that contemporary renaissance. And if, as Marx says, the ghosts of Roman days watched over the cradle of the modern bourgeoisie, then the godparents of the modern proletariat are the nameless heroes of folk legends, the monolithic throngs who lived identical lives or died of hunger together.

Currents that seem to go further reach even deeper into the past. For example, anarchism, fearing the shackling of the individual by the omnipotence of society, refers to the pre-gatherer and altogether pre-historical period of a complete absence of restrictions to personality. Besides, beforehand this was done by the bourgeoisie in the person of Jean-Jacques Rousseau, fighting the superfluity of mediaeval restrictions. And this kinship is not accidental either: anarchists today still most gladly cite Spencer.

Marx and Engels acknowledge, as we know, the Hegelian formula of development in contradictions, a formula from which derives the law of revolutionary retrospection. Another scholar who was quite close to Marxism, but too versatile (in various meanings of this word) to be able to accept it in its entirety,

---

8   See: Marx, Karl, 2008, *The Eighteenth Brumaire of Louis Bonaparte.* New York: International Publishers, p. 15.

namely Friedrich Albert Lange, considers the formula delusive. "The misleading appearance of an advance through antagonisms" , he writes in his *History of Materialism*,[9] "rests upon this very fact, that the thoughts which dominate an era, or which appear as philosophical ideas, form only one portion of the intellectual life of a nation, and that very different influences, often the more powerful because so little apparent, are at the same time in activity, until they suddenly become in turn the dominant ones, while the others retire into the background". But in another place he adds: "...without exactly resolving everything with Hegel into its opposite, it must be admitted that the operation of a great thought very frequently assumes an almost diametrically opposite tendency through a fresh combination with other elements of the age".[10] One can easily discern that these comments are consistent with our justification of the law of retrospection; Lange is also deluding himself if he believes that they prove the deceptiveness of the Hegel-Marx formula. On the contrary, in these conditions he is simply continuing the work of Marx and Engels, "putting dialecticism on its feet, since with Hegel it was walking on its head". This dialecticism could even be applied beneficially for the aftermath he demonstrated of philosophical systems (empiricism, materialism, sensualism, idealism, scepticism or criticism), which has already completed its merry-go-round twice in the history of humankind, and today is beginning its third circumvolution.

In examining the entirety of development in contradictions, and in the aftermath of theses, antitheses and syntheses, one could arrange sequences of periodically recurring expressions from the various social systems. Adding the constant epigenesis of needs to their evolution would entwine new sequences into this chain, sequences not beginning from a common starting point.

This would require a classification of the needs and social systems, which I have no intention of embarking upon here. I shall only point out that generally speaking, and leaving out numerous complex issues, one could differentiate two antagonistic principles that revolve around the dialectic consequence: individualism and socialism; and by these expressions I understand in this case: an advantage for the interests of the individual over those of society on the one hand, and on the other hand – the reverse relationship.

Let us take a look now at the social periods arranged in the successive layers, either drawing close to one of these two principles or moving further away from it: we notice that each already possesses in its past a certain number of

---

9   Lange, Friedrich Albert, 1877, *The History of Materialism and Criticism of its Present Importance*, Boston, MA: James R. Osgood and Company, vol. I, p. 57.

10   Lange, Friedrich Albert, 1877, *The History of Materialism and Criticism of its Present Importance*, London: Trübner & Co., vol. III, p. 272.

periods from which, almost like from portraits of one's ancestors, pointers and inspiration may be drawn. And so in the reformative aspirations of a particular period of modern times one sees the merging of components of diverse historical origin.

This is a very important fact. It will help us in investigating the real role played by the 'evoking of ghosts', those *Ancestors*,[11] in the psychology of revolutionary movements. In Marx' work cited above we find the following sentences: "Its [bourgeois society's] gladiators found in the stern classic traditions of the Roman republic the ideals and the form, the self-deceptions, that they needed in order to conceal from themselves the narrow bourgeois substance of their own struggles, and to keep their passion up to the height of a great historic tragedy".

"Similarly, at another stage of development, a century earlier, Cromwell and the English people had borrowed speech, passions and illusions from the Old Testament for their bourgeois revolution. When the ... transformation ... had been accomplished, Locke supplanted Habakkuk". "Thus the awakening of the dead" , he adds later, "in those revolutions served the purpose of glorifying the new struggles ... of magnifying the given task in the imagination".[12]

Indeed, the solemnity of a certain aesthetic delight is related directly, according to Spencer, to the degree of how far-removed it is from a species' fundamental life processes, from direct usefulness; Guyau again makes this aesthetic solemnity conditional upon the larger or smaller number of life components that merge into a certain feeling of beauty. Polish sociologist Józef Karol Potocki joined these two criteria, the first of which is based on leisure without effort, and the second the opposite, on the serious side of life, with the aid of a psychological definition of fun, which in his opinion is any pleasurable activity of a system, activity in which the perfect adaptation of attention totally excludes awareness of the effort and awareness of the non-aesthetic [since utilitarian – author's note] outside goals of this activity.[13]

The thing is that reminiscences from past periods of history, similar to the desired period in regard to their ascendant system, conform absolutely to the two conditions that, according to Potocki's theory, make a certain idea an

---

11   The Polish word used by Kelles-Krauz is 'Dziady', which is the title of the most famous Polish poetic drama, written by Adam Mickiewicz. The poem is considered one of the greatest works of Polish Romanticism. See: Mickiewicz, Adam, 2016, *Forefathers' Eve*, London, UK: Glagoslav Publications.

12   See: Marx, Karl, 2008, *The Eighteenth Brumaire of Louis Bonaparte*, p. 17.

13   Potocki, Józef Karol, 1894, *Ginekologia i socjologia*, Chapter IX, 'Głos' Warsaw edition, no. 12.

aesthetic delight. In regard to solemnity, they do not have a direct connection with the active struggles of the current moment, with the tangible goal of the transformation that involves the satisfying of certain needs hitherto despised; and as for capacity, they are closely connected to these needs because it is precisely the fact of their satisfaction that is their proper attribute, albeit of a lower, simpler form – and so they interfere with the most important issues in life. And so the task of these past recollections is to deliver an aesthetic element, the tissue of dreams, for future aspirations. What could possibly be more natural than them attracting artists of a particular movement? Honestly, only the short-sighted, enclosed within the moment of the day, might see proof of degeneration in this artistic atavism, atavism that is through-and-through progressive. Neither can I agree fully with Marx when he says later in his *Eighteenth Brumaire*: "The social revolution of the nineteenth century cannot take its poetry from the past but only from the future".[14] I understand this sentence on the tongue of a sarcastic historian, on the day of 2 December, which was not retrospection but simply parody. But the aesthetic components of the past have a totally different *raison d'être* in every transformation, under one condition only: namely, this past must be sufficiently distant for none of the contemporary factions to be able to appropriate it, so that the fundamental and real processes of revolution have no direct connection with it. However, I shall abandon this overly special issue in order to close the above arguments on the law of revolutionary retrospection and on the dialecticism of development in contradictions with a comparison, which – I must point out in advance – is meant to be no more, just a simple illustration.

The phenomenon of movement passing beyond the point of balance, or in other words pendulum movement, is fundamental and universal throughout nature. And the social spirit, one could say, vibrates between the turns of its metempsychosis. It vibrates like a plucked string. In a resounding string taken as a whole, schematically, a few simultaneous convulsive movements coexist; in other words, each of its fractions, thanks to the nodes that have formed, undergo a few complex actions and perform very complex movements. The nodes and partial vibrations that result from them may be compared to the dialectic transformations and retrospective turns that take place in the womb of some great, broadly-defined, separate historical era; just as with the extension of a string we would obtain new nodes and new partial vibrations, so too the further course of development introduces new needs and new sequences of partial systems into the dialectic consequence. Finally, the sum of the vibrations of the parts and the whole of the string delivers not only the raw sound,

---

14   See: Marx, Karl, 2008, *The Eighteenth Brumaire of Louis Bonaparte*, p. 18.

but also its resonance that is pleasing to the ear; likewise, those harmonic reso-
nances contained in recollections from the past could be said to give movement its aesthetic expression, which nobly consummates the whole.

An unavoidable question of great import arises here: does the vibrating
string stop at some point, does it pass into a state of repose, which would be
a total and ultimate synthesis, a harmonious satisfying of all human needs,
all without exception? Does the rising spiral line describe circles of an ever
smaller radius and eventually transform into a straight one? Quietists of various eras have dreamed of such a state. As for me, I do not believe in its arrival: an epigenesis of needs is sufficient to render it impossible. Nevertheless,
the constant pursuit of this synthesis by social vibrations – as of vibrations as
such – cannot be refuted; we may also acknowledge this synthesis, in the same
meaning as for a mathematician the asymptote of the curve representing these
vibrations would have.

The Law of Revolutionary Retrospection and the Theory of Imitation

In the preceding chapter I strived to demonstrate a sociological necessity – the
idealising of the distant past by propagators of reformatory ideas; I pointed
out that in this instance we are not dealing with the faithful recreation of this
past, as producing it would be impossible, but solely its idealisation, based on
the conviction or the feeling that the principles of the past rekindled will fuse
with the achievements of the current era, will give them new force, and in this
manner create a true synthesis, some kind of better equilibrium of mutually
contradictory needs. I would now like to return to the law of revolutionary retrospection thus formulated in order to further elaborate on certain aspects,
and mainly in order to juxtapose this law with the 'laws of imitation' and to
explain its relationship with Gabriel Tarde's sociological theory.

The connection between the law ascertaining the periodic about-turns of
minds towards examples conveyed by the past and the laws of imitation is obvious. When somebody portrays social life as the crossing of the rays of imitation, this law reveals itself to him to such a degree that Tarde, investigating
the transformation of fashion into custom, almost omits putting it into words:
he speaks of the grafting of tradition onto the blooming of novelty, inseparable
from the deepest of upheavals.[15] By ascertaining this kinship, I would also be
but fulfilling a simple duty, if I were simultaneously to be able to consent to

---

15   Tarde, Gabriel, 1903, *The Laws of Imitation*, New York: Henry Holt and Company, p. 173f.

the entire system which, with Tarde, seems to condition all of its laws of imitation and ingenuity, yet which as we know relies on acknowledging society as a great brain similar to the brains of individuals.

I believe that this concept – so long as it does not perform the role of an ordinary comparison, which would certainly not reflect the gravity attached to it in Tarde's works – is every bit as unjustified, every bit as insular and every bit as superfluous as the concept of society as an organism, so deservedly criticised by Tarde. Due to this difference in views, it would seem to me both useful and essential to clarify the premises from which in my view the law of revolutionary retrospection derives, and to what kind of systematic entirety they belong to – and in what manner and why this law merges partially with Tarde's laws and in what respect it differs from them. It is not possible for me here to carry out this plan other than by giving but the main contours. Let us therefore recall succinctly, yet precisely, and at the same time let us analyse the elementary notions constituting the basis of the said law.

Above all we have the formation of society, supposedly a casting, according to the predominant category of needs. The fact that the social system is never – or at least heretofore never has been – tailored to the totality of the needs of individuals, that on the contrary, one of their categories always shapes institutions in its image and likeness, while others are satisfied solely within the boundaries thus marked out – this fact is fundamental to our approach; in it rests the original cause of historical fluctuations, since it reflects the pendulum's first aberration beyond its point of equilibrium. This fact flows from elementary observation, which is easy to repeat in relation to any era in any society whatsoever. Tarde does not overlook it: indeed, he says that the spirit, i.e. the social mind, just like the attention of the individual, is overcome time after time by some aspiration that supplants all other pursuits. The phenomenon is thereby connected to the theory of the 'society of the brain', and finds no clarification other than the analogies that comprise this theory – superficial analogies, unless they require us previously to adopt such a risky and anthropomorphic conception as granting the dignity of members of society not only to the cell (in the organism), but even directly – in society – to the atom, to the molecule.[16]

---

16   Tarde's sociology is tied closely to his philosophy. Tarde is a disciple/adherent to the Leibnizean theory of monads – of molecules of matter brought to life by consciousness, and originally different. Once, in the times of natural creation, these particles joined into chemical atoms, which as we know are only chemically indivisible; these atoms later joined into physical particles, into molecules; and from these, in the same way, cells formed; from the cells – individual organisms; and from individuals – societies.

As for us, we accept the prevalence of one category of needs as the result of economic materialism, of a system according to which means of production is the basis of the social form. In historical society the creator, guardian and regulator of the means of production was always a single class of some kind, for which it was of direct benefit and which by transforming institutions or creating them for its own use, was concerned solely about its own interests, and in addition strived to weed out of them anything and everything that might harm the permanence of the means of production. But the historical means of production – capitalist (mercenary), feudal (serfdom – guilds), ancient (slavery) – are but successive periods of growth for the tree rooted in prehistory, meaning in the era preceding the formation of the proper (class-based) state. And so even then, though the economic factor had not yet vanquished other active factors and had not subjugated so totally all signs of social life, its formative influence was very significant. The means of production of those times – hunting, fishing, plundering, shepherding and farming (with their successive periods marked by inventions and technical discoveries), and the

---

For a monadist, the process of molecules forming from atoms is, in its nature, exactly the same as the process of societies forming from individuals. The molecules (if we take atoms as the final limit of the divisibility of matter) are the most ancient societies, and as such the most perfect and the most legitimate; human societies, as the newest, have not yet achieved a high degree of legitimacy; they have not even determined their contours yet. Differences between atoms boil down to the differences between their vibrations. The organisational force of these societies of atoms determined victory between abutting vibrations, and defined the attributes of the molecule generated. Fluctuation in the non-organic world corresponds to inheritance as such a force in the organic, and imitation in the social world.

Individual consciousness is the presence occurring at the foreground of the brain as the result of processes occurring within a single cell, and namely in them responsible for a given representation – i.e. the supremacy of a certain wave over the others that have become absorbed in it. Likewise social mood should at any moment be the victory of one imitative wave over others, which it could have absorbed. Hence society's acknowledgement for a supra-individual brain. If there is something in the life of societies that corresponds to an entire biological organism, then according to Tarde this would probably be the entire part of nature upon which a society's operations are based, like on a body: on the ground, the flora and fauna, the atmosphere, and cosmic influences. (See various positions of *Social Logic* and in particular the article *Les monades et la science sociale* in "Revue Internationale de Sociologie" 1893, nos. 2, 3). This entire "universally-sociological point of view", as Tarde puts it, alluring with its regularity – transgresses, apart from particular imperfections, above all in the transferring of difficulties to ground totally inaccessible to research, where one encounters beings primevally inspired by one's entire future [Kelles-Krauz's footnote].

first major division of work between men and women – held significant force of attraction for the social components, and out of them built institutions, or at least customs and habits, consistent with its own activity. The prevalence of each of these ancient means of production was a manifestation of the essentiality with which primeval societies had to adopt from surrounding nature such and not some other means of staying alive by satisfying such and not other partial needs, which in this manner became privileged; as such certain other psychological and perhaps even physiological needs, perhaps barely germinating yet nevertheless real and generated in the pre-social era by isolated or ultimately cave-centred life,[17] had to be pushed aside right away, had to give way to those that were essential for the survival of the species.

There was sufficient pushing aside for one of two things to happen: for these needs to vanish entirely through lack of cultivation, or for their pressure to be felt by the people, and that ever more sorely. This in turn sufficed for a succession of oscillations to begin from this starting point, a succession that perhaps continues to this day, enlarged by and crossed with a throng of others. "Never is man complete: nobody knows the number of self-amputations carried out", says Tarde at one point. These amputations, or at least the cases of muffling needs, are to be found at the beginning of evolution; they provide it with its yeast: an antithesis; while they are brought about by the difficulties of conquering nature by man. Where nature allows for the satisfaction of all originally existing needs, as for example in certain tribes concealed in the Amazon forests, there is no contradiction – but neither are there any changes; there is no history.

Here, however, I have entered the domain of another factor comprising the law of retrospection, that is, the psychological factor. The first explains only the wrong done to those needs still of secondary importance to a given era; the second should just justify their altercation with the prevailing needs.

This factor is the particularly important psychological phenomenon of the transition from consciousness to automaticity, which all functions succumb to. This is because the fact pointed out in the preceding chapter boils down to this: namely that customs, laws, systems, or in a word, institutions, turn from

---

17   In a speech at the first sociological congress, entitled *Elementary Sociology*, Tarde defined the elementary social fact and the elementary social group. In keeping with Le Play, as such he recognises the family, with the amendment that by family one should understand homestead (maisonnée), i.e. family members together with members of the household, household pets, the home itself, and means of existence. Such homesteads comprise the nation. Originally, prior to the emergence of nations, or rather societies, these were not maisonnées, but rather *cavernées*, or "cave-steads" [Kelles-Krauz's footnote].

the means they constitute at the beginning into the goals. When a particular institution is established, the goal of its repeated execution by the individual is, at the beginning, on every occasion, to satisfy a certain privileged need as perfectly as possible, while later – thanks to repetition of this action – this degenerates into accustomation, which commands people to execute the law for the very law itself, while forgetting not only that it was established to satisfy a certain need, but also that it has no value at all if it does not constitute the means for satisfying some fundamental need. In this manner upholding and applying the law becomes the goal to which leads one means, namely readjusting all manifestations of social life in order for their entirety to be consistent with the system of institutions. Satisfying needs, even those privileged needs that generated a particular institution, therefore falls from the rank of goal, as it initially held, to the significance of an ordinary means. It is precisely the transition of some function from its state of a goal into the state of a means that Tarde repeatedly points out; one can see from the above that it is identical to the transition from the state of a means to the state of a goal that we are talking about, but is only presented from the opposite side by Tarde.

One should note at this point that when the conduct of a particular social institution becomes its goal, it simultaneously gains a basis in the new need that emerged from the very action, and which in turn demands fulfilment. But this is a formal need, which itself – as results from the above – has its own source in another fundamental need. This formal need may further extract again another formal need of the second degree, etc.; precisely such an hierarchy of needs is expressed for example in De Greef's sequence.[18] Economic materialism consists in stating that the least formal needs, the fundamental ones, are material needs – and namely the needs of production and reproduction. Any modification in a particular fundamental need must inevitably bring about change in the appropriate formal need. Yet by virtue of the rule of transition from awareness to automaticity, the social form gains a certain independence from the basis, and this independence growing in the very existence of this form causes that the latter is always, with a certain resistance, obedient to the changes taking place in the relevant basis.

---

18   The Belgian sociologist De Greef splits social phenomena into seven categories, which
       he arranges in the following sequence according to two factors – rising complexity and
       decreasing generality: 1. economic phenomena, 2. reproductive, 3. artistic, 4. intellectual,
       5. moral, 6. legal, 7. political. I give this sequence of course only as an example, as one may
       have numerous reservations as to the actual order of its terms; I would think (without
       undertaking a broader justification for now) that moral and legal phenomena should be
       placed immediately following the economic, to be followed by political, with artistic and
       scientific at the end [Kelles-Krauz's footnote].

This resistance, together with the yearning for penetrating the social whole that we have already ascertained, as manifested by the form of privileged needs, will explain to us how and why certain needs come to contradict others, adopting the form of an antithesis. This is because somebody may easily opine that the entire evolution in contradictions depends upon the existence of some original association of principles in a state of involution, principles already as it were antagonistic since birth, which would appear as some kind of hard-to-accept social predetermination. This condition becomes superfluous in view of the fact that needs, which by their very nature are at the moment of the appearance of a later one totally indifferent towards one another, then become antagonistic through being brought together. The turns of this process have been brilliantly itemised and backed up with examples by Tarde in his 'sequence of historical logical states', or in other words, in the 'dynamic social logic' that he still calls the social dialectic, and rightly so, as this specifically justifies the Hegelian sequence of 'thesis, antithesis and synthesis'. Tarde's series demonstrates that between principles, such as for example knowledge and religion, or between aristocracy and democracy, there is no need in the least for the existence of an innate relationship of statement to negation, similar to the relationship that occurs e.g. between sleep and vigil, or between movement and rest, in order for these principles to be able to occupy opposite extremes. If we want this series to support our law of retrospection, then suffice for us to recall that precisely the two phenomena that we cite, and namely the resistance and expansive yearning of the social form, are the causes behind the first stance of the 'logic duel', which is expressed as follows:

A contradicts B, which does not contradict A.[19]

---

19   In order for some kind of idea to be able to form in the mind, there is no need at all, in Tarde's opinion, for it to derive logically from previously existing ones: it is enough for it not to oppose them, i.e. it may be heterogeneous. On this basis – let us note – an epigenesis of needs, apart from their evolution, is possible. Then two ideas, or rather two syllogisms, either having a conviction or a command of will as an object, enter the following sequence of phases in relation to one another:

1. A and B neither acknowledge nor deny one another; they do not support one another, neither do they fight (the phase of indifference).
2. A contradicts/negates B, which does not contradict A; A harms B, which does not harm A. Scientific research for example initially takes shelter itself under the wings of faith. Yet dogma, wanting to rule the entire space of intellectual life in society, receives it with suspicion, wants to displace the discovered area of thought (and this all the more so as it cannot immediately adjust to the socially fundamental changes that pushed

Two needs thus stand to fight: the string is taut, the vibration begins. A new factor adds impulsiveness to their wrestling: this is the insensibility of collective consciousness to the infinitely small changes taking place in the (relative) social base – until they merge into broader or narrower integrals.

In regard to the term 'collective consciousness', we have to halt by one of our statements from the previous section, namely that the entire process embraced by the law of revolutionary retrospection takes place 'largely unconsciously'. Now that it is becoming understandable, we withdraw this term in order to say, together with Tarde: multi-consciously.[20] Incidents of a feeling of grievance inflicted on the category of needs being born, of an agreeable recollection of the past, of the merging of its components with the components of the present – long are they scattered around the numerous individual consciousnesses ere they assume the form of a collective demand. This demand then turns via the agency of public opinion to society's legislative body, which may be either a monarch or the entire populace with a direct vote; and this body is what I call here the collective consciousness, without attaching any significance of some kind of supra-social personification to this name. However, I cannot equate this name with Tarde's uni-consciousness, since his term, particularly when juxtaposed with this thinker's other views (namely the recognition of the ability to make a precise plan for the individual in society), immediately brings to mind some future 'enlightened despotism' or pericleism. Were it not for this, there would be nothing for which one could criticise this law of transition from multi-consciousness to uni-consciousness, all the more so when we notice that

the human mind towards this discovery). Hence the further phases that Tarde continues to illustrate with eras of battle between knowledge and faith:

3. A and B contradict each other, and fight with each other.
4. B contradicts A, which does not contradict B; B fights A, which does not fight B.
   (Today religion itself wants to be based on science; but science rejects it – see phase 5).
   These three phases together constitute a period of discord, of logical or teleological duel.
5. A acknowledges or supports B, which contradicts or fights A.
6. A acknowledges or supports B, which neither contradicts nor fights A.
7. A acknowledges or supports B, which either acknowledges or supports A.
   The three final phases comprise logical or teleological concord.
   (See Chapter III of *The Social Logic*) [Kelles-Krauz's footnote].

20 See Chapter IV, § X of *The Social Logic*. In it, Tarde oppugns the supposition of a subconscious emergence of social orders from the chaos of novelty. It is only multi-conscious, i.e. fragments of the new norms are scattered in the heads of individuals. Along comes a Homer or Napoleon, merges them – and provides a code. This is the law of transition from multi-consciousness to uni-consciousness via the consciousness of a few [Kelles-Krauz's footnote].

any expression of collective will is always formulated by some individual, who for example presents a motion of his own redaction to parliament or a people's assembly.

And so this collective consciousness is incapable of sensing changes in social needs as and when they occur. For clarification of this phenomenon we are standing entirely on Tarde's favourite ground: on the position of the quantitativeness of desire. Growth and decline in the quantity of need, together with the continuity of these changes, leads inexorably to the notion of infinitely small growth, i.e. social differential; this in turn suffices, as in mathematics,[21] or in chemistry, etc., for understanding in what manner quality is born from quantity. Infinitely small changes in social needs (i.e. in the needs of connected individuals) are added up and integrate; and a certain integral, juxtaposed with another integral, constitutes quality, which can be noticed by the collective consciousness and begin its fray with its fellow contestants. However, it is clear that prior to its formation and appearance in a host of social realities, it left enough time for the other social forms that were battling with it for them to be able to become independent of their foundations and remain behind their progress. This retreat only increases the fierceness of the clash.

At this point I shall make a slight detour, so as to point out how much importance I attach to the evidence provided by Tarde of the quantitative character of desire and certainty,[22] and this precisely because of its result: the social differential; this is the name I give to the infinitely small change in a need. I believe this notion is essential for further development of the theory of economic materialism (which is also contained, indirectly, in the works of Engels), and namely – for explaining the moulding and dynamic impact of economic phenomena on the entire social superstructure.

In my opinion, what we have here is a sociological synonym of the concept of the atom. However, this issue could in itself be and probably, in time, will be the subject of a separate study, and as such I shall leave it aside.

Following the thesis and antithesis, all that remains for us to investigate is the synthesis: the merging of ancient and contemporary ways of satisfying needs – thus giving birth to new ways. The deep sinking in of the present day and material survival of the past are the factors behind this phenomenon. We will not be investigating them in greater depth here, and shall only stress that

---

21 Quality in mathematics: e.g. change in the direction of a curve [Kelles-Krauz's footnote].

22 This constitutes a cornerstone of Tarde's theory. He wrote about this a very long time ago in the 10th volume of *Revue philosophique*. He also bases his reform of logic on this quantitativeness; see the first and perhaps most valuable chapter of *The Social Logic* [Kelles-Krauz's footnote].

this synthesis constitutes a genuine logical reconciliation according to Tarde's definition, and as one of the most fertile.

We see therefore that the law of revolutionary retrospection derives both from economic materialism and from Tarde's theory of imitation. One may thereby conclude that there is no fundamental contradiction between these two systems; and indeed, such contradiction does not exist. Despite Tarde's repeated 'idealistic' assurances, he is perhaps less far-removed from economic materialism than he believes.

Let us take, for example, one of his main 'laws of imitation': the law of imitation proceeding from the inside towards the outside, *ab interioribus ad exterior*. What does this law mean? Tarde says: "imitation of ideas precedes the imitation of their expression; imitation of ends precedes the imitation of means".[23] We have already seen how easily one can reverse the relationship of goal to means; this also applies to the fundamentally identical relationship of idea to expression; then one needs to agree upon the starting point. Does Tarde want to say that any action, and therefore any satisfying of a need, must, even if for but a moment, be preceded by the sensing of this need and imagining of the action that will satisfy it?

That would be stating an acknowledged psychological truth. But his law could be translated otherwise: when one is dealing with an incident in which the social form has taken firm root in the minds, then one may easily fall prey to the illusion that the basic elements were actually the means for actualising the formal elements. For example one might, thanks to this illusion, regard an individual method of production as a means of actualising, as an expression only of the principles of liberalism: yet this would be establishing the wrong hierarchy of the idea above its own expression, the mistaken hierarchy of one idea (the idea of independence from one's fellow citizens) above another (the idea of using certain tools – tools that do not bring workers together).

Is it this reversal that Tarde had in mind? I cannot believe so, bearing in mind his application of the above law for the creation and broadening of legal provisions. "Legislative changes" , he says, "never precede, but at some distance the intellectual (in customs and in prevailing views is probably what he wanted to say) or economic".[24] These expressions go to show that Tarde cannot consider the method of production and appropriation the means for accomplishing some previous legal provision. For example, this means, in one country's laws being applied for imitation by another country, that if Napoleon's code could be introduced in Poland, then this was because capitalist production had

23   Tarde, Gabriel, 1903, *The Laws of Imitation*, p. 207.
24   Ibidem, p. 208.

already reached a quite high degree in our country – which history confirms. This does not mean, of course, that the introduction of this code, modelled on a more capitalistic country, was not to contribute significantly to an acceleration in the growth of capitalism in Poland, and this through the developing of a source of advantageous interferences between the base and the social form. There exists a reason for which Tarde's imitative system cannot be contradictory with economic materialism: in relation to the former, the latter is simply one storey lower down. Tarde arranged social phenomena in sequences, the expressions of which are joined by an imitative thread; however, he left the 'tangencies',[25] the initial expressions of these sequences, the foci of the imitative waves, to chance: he made them similar to those stars that occasionally make a sudden appearance in a certain point of the sky. He built further storeys on top of the house, if not in the air, then at least on a moving, capricious, unstable foundation. He did not want to seek the laws of invention.

In saying this I am only stating to which side the scales are leaning more; after all this issue, the correctness of innovations,[26] is very dark in Tarde's theory.

At one point he tells us that "the future will be made by as yet unknown inventors and no real law concerning their successive advents can be formulated";[27] elsewhere, that "successive inventions do not follow one another accidentally";[28] and again that this consequence, described to a certain degree by social logic, seems to him terrible, irreversible,[29] and he talks of the partially random character of inventions and discoveries.[30] It would seem that here lies the solution to the contradiction saying that the laws of invention, as opposed to the laws of imitation, "belong essentially to individual logic";[31] there, in the chapter entitled 'Laws of imitation', he lists the external conditions, irrefutably

---

25   One of Tarde's favourite thoughts, dating back to the time when he used to write verse (see his work *Les possible* in *Contes et poèmes* of 1879), is that what has happened constitutes but a fragment of what could have happened; but possibility – that for him is a conditioned necessity. Thus a certain line avoids a curve, but at certain coordinates must meet with it. Thus existence is the tangent of nonexistence. This is an old, Aristotelian thought; a purely logical construction, and not actually explaining anything; and yet Tarde seems to relay on this for understanding whatever is new, vibrational and organic (new forms), as well as social (inventions) [Kelles-Krauz's footnote].

26   I use this term as the more general, embracing inventions and discoveries. Tarde constantly says: *inventions* [Kelles-Krauz's footnote].

27   Tarde, Gabriel, 1903, *The Laws of Imitation*, p. 137.

28   Ibidem, p. 381.

29   Ibidem, p. 235.

30   Ibidem, p. 238.

31   Ibidem, p. 382.

social, of the emergence of inventions.[32] Among these conditions there is one, in our opinion the most important, that must logically lead to economic materialism: it is the one that Tarde, confessing to the term's uncertainty, calls the difficulty of invention.

An invention (any novelty) encounters a lesser or greater difficulty in hacking out its path for radiating among a certain people; beyond any other secondary causes, this difficulty depends on the degree to which novelty rises above the standard of a particular people – such is the quintessence of Tarde's thought. But what is this standard? It cannot be anything other than the entirety of the institutions functioning in a given society and stacked one above the other, according – as we already know – to their degree of formality. First of all, an invention or discovery (we have to run a little ahead here) may only emerge from the mutual joining of pre-existing components, or with some kind of external influx. Components of one and the same degree of formality – let us take the legal area once again as an example – gain (and we now know why) a certain degree of independence that allows them to join in people's minds, arbitrarily so to speak; but should such a connection, and so in our case a legal novelty, prove in contradiction with the state of phenomena in the field directly fundamental in relation to law, then this novelty will not radiate. On the contrary, the change that has occurred in the fundamental category will soon entail an invention in a directly formal field, while the radiation of this invention will ultimately overcome the resistance that we already know. This is also right in regard to novelties with foreign components. Thus the change, or – which amounts to the same thing – generation of fundamental needs evokes and defines innovations in the social form of these needs. The development of methods of production that constitute the ultimate basis of social life then defines, more or less directly, all innovations.

Such is the law – in the general outline thus sketched – of invention of economic materialism.

At first glance this risks the following criticism: what therefore defines innovations in the ultimate social base itself? Is it not pure accident that brings into the world, 'from the abyss of possibility', inventions in methods of production, tools? Yet it is probably exceedingly obvious that in primitive society they are dictated by bare need and the type of resources contained in the surrounding nature, while the relationship between these two elements is defined by the points of least resistance; we are also far from the "feeble, wayward imagination scattered here and there in the midst of a vast passive imitativeness which

---

32   Tarde, Gabriel, 1895, *La logique sociale*, Paris: Félix Alcan, p. 169.

receives and perpetuates all its vagaries".[33] Later as well the very pursuit of as little effort as possible in order to achieve the greatest possible productive result develops a number of tool inventions and the methods of production corresponding to them, one deriving from another.[34]

As for those 'inventive currents in a particular single direction', appearing within all fields, Tarde ascertains them on several occasions: their cause is, as he says, that innovators themselves are imitators.[35] I emphasise this point, because this by itself suffices for the acknowledging of the possibility of grasping inventions within laws: we conclude here that the nature of the invention is of a sameness with that of imitation.

In this respect Tarde expresses himself very clearly: he brings any novelty down to a fortuitous crossing of one imitative current with another similar current, or with some powerful impression originating from an external nature[36] (in a society that has already reached a certain age, it would be hard to imagine such an impression absolutely free of imitation). If all invention is imitation, then also any imitation is a genuine invention: this results from the previous definition. When a particular imitative current permeates into an individual consciousness, it always finds there a chord of (imitative) vibrations, irrefutably different for every individual as this is precisely what characterises the

---

33   Tarde, Gabriel, 1903, *The Laws of Imitation*, p. 95.

34   See: Beltov, 1956, *The Development of the Monist View of History*, Moscow: Foreign Languages Publishing House, Chapter 3, p. 50 and later; Ch. 5, p. 144 and later, where he oppugns Saint-Simon's well-established view that the inventions of tools of work are made by human reason, and so this reason is the ultimate spring of history. Tarde, who frequently voices ideas akin to those of Saint-Simon – such as e.g. the differentiation of 'dictionary' and 'grammatical' eras, highly similar to the division into 'organic' and 'critical' – reluctant to acknowledge at any price the dependence of inventions on fundamental needs and economic conditions, is forced to totally renounce any rule of inventions and by yielding them to the mercy of some independent reason, standing beyond the sphere of determinism, return to the point from which Hegel's philosophy, later transformed into the philosophy of Hegelian leftism, deduced the old French sociology. After all, what other does he do when, in a brief answer to my remarks above (see *Annales de l'Institut International de Sociologie*, vol. 2, p. 342), he claims that it was not the change in economic needs that evoked ingenious ideas for their satisfaction, but that "if lower needs underwent change, this was because higher ideas appeared without any summons from outside, under the influence of cerebral fermentation" – and when all discoveries and inventions are attributed to curiosity as a sufficient cause, with no desire to investigate the factors lending this curiosity one direction or another, important only for the content of the development? [Kelles-Krauz's footnote].

35   Tarde, Gabriel, 1903, *The Laws of Imitation*, p. 344.

36   Ibidem, p. 43.

individual – and so it always refracts in some way. The resultant of two vibrations, which in this way constitutes an act of imitation if only it rises above
the threshold of consciousness (which is also an essential condition in the
case of the appropriate innovation), even always – or at least prior to further
investigation – adopts in relation to it the form of a personal idea; this fills the
individual with the same inventive pride and joy. If one were unable to grasp
novelties in laws, then out of necessity this would also be applied to imitation,
which is but a quantitatively lower degree of invention. Hence when one reads
a few of Tarde's 'laws of imitation' – such as the linguistic law of the softening
of vowels, or shortening of expressions, etc.[37] – then they tend rather to be
taken as laws of invention.

Admittedly, where the refraction of imitative rays in an individual is concerned, this also applies to the refraction of some historical current within the
womb of a nation that adopts it from outside: because the latter refraction is
but a collection of analogical individual phenomena. For example – taking one
more example from Polish history – was not the Constitution of 3 May 1791 a
genuine invention, although its intellectual originators, Staszic, Kołłątaj and
Descartes, were imitators of the prophets of human rights?

Imitation is innovation not only when occurring with distance in space, but
also in time, and if the law of revolutionary retrospection is, without question, a law of imitation, then simultaneously it is also the law of invention. As
such it is wrong for the conservative camp to constantly describe as retrograde
manifestations cases of the dialectic resurrection of elements of the past intended for the fertilisation of the sterilised present held in its march. Mr Bloch
recently committed this abuse and error in his fawning note submitted to the
Parisian Academy of Moral and Political Sciences, and regarding Westermack's
work on *The Beginnings of Marriage*.[38]

"By proving that our ancestors were not civilised", says Bloch, "the author
does not draw from this the conclusion, as done by some authors, that we
should move backwards. What bizarre arguments may be heard in our times!
Our ancestors knew not the family – let's establish free love; our ancestors had
shared possession of land – let us abolish private ownership; our ancestors
were monkeys – let us continue to make our bed in the forest! Yet at the same
time one discourses on evolution, one praises progress", etc.

These really are frivolous though academic jokes, but in these views one
sees a very superficial understanding of evolution and progress. Besides, it
is but a warmed-up old accusation levelled at Rousseau by Voltaire, that he

37   Tarde, Gabriel, 1903, *The Laws of Imitation*, p. 143.
38   See: '*Séances et travaux de l'Academie des sciences morales et poliques*', 1895, August, p. 297.

supposedly wants people to walk on all fours. In Tarde's dialectic series, before A and B – initially mutually indifferent and later fighting – finally reach mutual acknowledgement and support, these two expressions undergo deep change, though not immediately noticeable: no moment of their existence is similar to a previous one. When their 'logical reconciliation' finally occurs, we do not find there a recreation of the past, but its genuine adaptation to the new social accomplishments, which on their part have also matured to receive this seed. Who, for example, could accuse the engineers constructing the railroads (and this is an example I draw from Tarde) of having dredged up the viaducts and other Roman buildings, abandoned for centuries, in order to connect them to the invention of the locomotive, which also without the former could not have been brought to life? And yet it was a genuine revolutionary retrospection in a technical field. Because, once again: "what is an invention? It is a fortuitous crossing of separate imitations in the brain, i.e. a jocular idea involving the establishing of a relationship between the means and the goal between two previous inventions, which hitherto independent and alien to one another circulated separately among people, but from now on will retain a mutual connection and from this mutually draw new strength".[39]

The phenomenon of revolutionary retrospection occurs in all areas of human activity. Not that long ago it could be observed in philosophy, when according to such a characteristic utterance by Friedrich Albert Lange: "just as a defeated army seeks a defensive spot in order to regather and get into formation, so in philosophical circles that call rang out: a return to Kant!" Retrospection occurs in the fine arts, for example in the programme of Richard Wagner, which involves the repeated merging of all arts separated during age-old evolution. Retrospection, sometimes very distant, is discovered where one has difficulty presuming that it could exist, since the traces of imitation were well concealed, and the actual imitation was probably unknown to its doers – for example in the pre-Raphaelite school of painters. Specialists claim that Egyptian painting was born from writing, and was therefore conventional and cared not for perspective; Tarde epitomises their opinions in the following sentence: "Any picture, or rather any ribbon of narrative sketches, was a phrase, the goal of which was to serve the viewer's mind with an impression of thought, not of sight".[40]

---

39   Tarde, Gabriel, 1895, *La logique sociale*, p. 379.
40   Ibidem, p. 401. And to say here that Nordau attributes absence of perspective and neglect of form for content among the English pre-Raphaelites solely and exclusively to an illness of will of their coryphaei, bringing in a chaotic association of notions! One more sample

However, on this occasion we must forgo research into the strata[41] of retrospection in all formal areas of social life. We shall pause but for a moment at the dialecticism of one important field, also formal, but whose formality is closest to the economic base, and namely: the social system. (The undetermined social adjective that I use here in a particular meaning covers, in the given case, the political system as well as part of law and ethics.) We said in the preceding chapter that the two main antagonistic principles revolve around a dialectic sequence: individualism and socialism – understanding by these names "an advantage of individual over cross-societal interests, and the reverse phenomenon". Perhaps we shall succeed in throwing new light on this eternal sequence, which will probably be an everlasting oscillation, by juxtaposing it with one of Tarde's most important laws of imitation, which seems to contain all others within it: the law of transformation of what he calls 'fashionable imitation' into 'customary imitation', and the order of these two types of imitation. This law results from the need that arises at a certain point for the abandonment of boundless accumulation of novelties, in order to replace one with the other, to harmonise and reconcile them, or – explaining it with the Hegelian language of economic materialism – in order to resolve their internal contradictions. This is because this harmonisation is the first condition and, at the same time, an unavoidable presage of the customary determination of the pressure of accumulated novelties. Tarde compares this harmonisation and determination to the activities of a grammarian, who puts the relatively[42] chaotic acquisitions of a dictionary in order. Because novelties do not cease to gather anew following the harmonising, 'grammatical' era, it is clear that this movement will always exceed its point of equilibrium, and that as such it will in this case perform like a pendulum.

Further on, it is easy to discern that the era of harmonisation must necessarily bear some kind of principle applied to the entirety of the social system, and to all members of society. This principle (not necessarily the socialising of means of production in all eras) is beneficial for society as a whole, i.e. is beneficial for its further development, which although it may merge with what is beneficial for a greater or lesser number of individuals (increasing their numbers is another law), and although it unifies as few individual interests

---

of the value of the psychiatric method in the sociological teaching of ideas [Kelles-Krauz's footnote].

41   I would like incidentally to protest here against the term 'stratification', which recently began to appear in many of our sociological articles and books [Kelles-Krauz's footnote].

42   It seems totally chaotic to somebody who, like Tarde, presumes that novelties fall from the sky [Kelles-Krauz's footnote].

as possible (by leaving ever larger portions of human activities within the private sphere, free of the regulations in force: which again is a different historical law[43]), it nevertheless only takes the average, unified, schematic individual into account. Conversely, in the era of accumulation, in the 'dictionary' era, the social principle, jostled and undermined from within, holds no advantage of the unlimited interests (at least *in potentia*) of any individual. It is easy to imagine how many philosophical, juridical, religious and even artistic models derive from this, ones that with each return swing of the pendulum can be embroidered on this or that basic background; we are of course not going to wander off in these endless deductions. We shall only point out that one of the main cases ascertaining the law of revolutionary retrospection drawn from dynamic economic materialism merges with one of the most important laws of the theory of imitation.

Gabriel Tarde devotes a few heartfelt sociocritical pages[44] to the period of unharmonised accumulation that our civilised society is currently experiencing in all fields. Economic materialism is observing the same illness, ascribing it to the excessively resistant social form being blown apart by the development of the base – the system of appropriation by the system of production. The resurrection of a transformed original society is the rebirth that Morgan foretells, resolving contradiction and bringing with it an entire treasury of harmonisation, of astounding logical reconciliations. Who will contradict Tarde when he attributes harmonisation with the unheard-of prolificacy in the creation of new inventions? Who will still wish to see the halting of progress, or perhaps even a moving backwards, into retrospection, which today is synonymous with the disappearance of one of the most violent social conflicts?

---

43   This is why the terms orthodoxy and heterodoxy do not seem to me suitable general definitions for these eras. Because views are moving ever further towards the private scope, while actions are yielding only to legal commands, I would rather call the subsequent periods: orthopractical and heteropractical [Kelles-Krauz's footnote].

44   Tarde, Gabriel, 1903, *The Laws of Imitation*, pp. 181–184.

CHAPTER 2

The Golden Age, State of Nature, and Development in Contradictions: From Studies into the Sources of Marxism[1]

The thought of returning to the state of nature and historical cycle, a yearning for an idealised past serving as a starting point for criticism of the present day, and the belief that humanity and even the entire universe fulfil their lives as though on a merry-go-round – these two closely-related states of the spirit, though sometimes separate and differing in character, were known to classic Antiquity. Besides, they are so applicable to the whole of the historically known human spirituality that they are also to be found in the dogmatic Christian middle ages, in the form of a paradise lost, or millenarianism, etc. In more recent times, which the researcher of 18th and 19th century philosophy must take greater account of, in the post-Renaissance era from which uninterrupted threads of intellectual consequence extend to our day, when with the collapse of feudal economics private, individualistic Roman law appears again, then a rationalistic critique of the present, based on the presumption of an ideal state of nature free of injustices and antagonisms, also exists with full force and self-confidence. If one were to close one's eyes to the positive constructions adapted to contemporary political demands, then the theories of natural law of Grotius and Pufendorf have such a fundamental character; Cartesianism also shares their fundamental critical negation of universally acknowledged things. This dangerous element was divined wonderfully and all the revolutionary consequences of such a stance were detected by the last brilliant thinker of Catholic scholasticism, and at the same time the first brilliant precursor of modern historical realism, Giambattista Vico, and in wanting to forestall them, in wanting to establish traditional social authority on new foundations, he incarnated the plans of Providence in mankind as a whole, in every manifestation of mankind's history, in each reflex of collective consciousness, and in keeping with them he ordered mankind to climb with difficulty from the original state of animality up the rungs of ever higher civilisation towards the peaceful happiness conditioned by order and obedience to the secular and

---

1 Source: Wiek złoty, stan natury i rozwój w sprzecznościach (Ze studiów o źródłach marksizmu), "Przegląd Filozoficzny" 1903, vol. 3, pp. 313–320; vol. 4, pp. 414–426; 1904, vol. 1, pp. 19–33.

spiritual authorities, while threatening those peoples unable to appreciate this
peace with a tragic return to a pre-paternal savagery. Such is the meaning of
the notion *ricorso*, the historical cycle in historical philosophy in Vico's *The
New Science*, a philosophy starting the 18th century. At the opposite extreme in
the modern history of the development of the idea of a historical cycle stands
a second genius, Jean-Jacques Rousseau, who realising the nature of the consequences of a rationalistic natural law no worse than Vico, consciously drew
them out – right up to the last one. In this work I intend to illuminate the
significance of the Genevan philosopher's views in the history of the idea of a
return of the past, and cast a glance over the further transformation of this idea
in idealistic German philosophy, linked to Rousseauism via a common knot of
rationalism and a certain genetic dependence.

I   **Rousseau and the French Revolution**

The intellectual kinship between Rousseau on the one hand and Grotius and
Pufendorf – whom he frequently quotes – on the other, and between Rousseau and Descartes, whose underlying doubt he carries over into politics, is a
generally known fact, and as such we shall not dwell on it. We shall also remain
silent about the evident traces of Christianity's influences, of the idea of paradise lost which, as we know, can be found in any modern theory regarding the
natural state, as a surrounding atmosphere of bourgeois sentimentalism, or
the Swiss idylls of Gessner, etc.

   If we say a few words here about Rousseau's relationship with classic literature, it will only be for the purpose of questioning Pöhlmann's[2] presumption
that Rousseau had actually read Dicaearchus, one of the main idealisers of the
'state of nature' and critics of private ownership in ancient Greece. This is because he cites him (in the fifth footnote to *Discourse on Inequality*) for a trivial,
secondary reason (to prove that by his very nature man is a herbivore), and this
is only according to Saint Jerome. However, this is a matter of secondary importance; what is certain is that the theories of a golden age and regarding the
state of nature in antiquity were known to Rousseau, if only via Ovid and Ver-
gil; their distinctive quotations, particularly those of Ovid, testify adequately
to their influence on Rousseau's mind. However, ere we set about investigating
in Rousseau's system his views regarding natural law, original happiness and
its return, of interest to us is to know whether and what kind of relationship

---

2 Pöhlmann, Robert von, 1893, *Geschichte des antiken Kommunismus und Sozialismus*, Munich:
   C.H. Beckiche Berlagsbuchhandlung, vol. 1, p. 113 [Kelles-Krauz's footnote].

there was between him and Vico. Montesquieu knew *The New Science*[3] and this book influenced his theories. *The New Science* was reprinted in Geneva at the 'Ancient and Modern Library' by Vico's admirer, the erudite Jean Leclerc,[4] but it was through Salfi significantly later that it became known in France.[5] Rousseau does not seem to have read Vico; in any case, he takes a diametrically opposite stance from him in all issues, and if there exists at all any analogy between their theories, it may be explained by some circuitous influence, or even rather by some general tendency of the age, the drifting as it were of certain thoughts in the air.

Besides, this analogy is limited to but a few views on the original government, which according to Rousseau was also initially theocratic, while later on aristocratic, when family fathers began counselling together on public matters (*The Social Contract*, published by the National Library,[6] pp. 172–195). However, in his *Discourse on Inequality* (p. 116) he criticises those who deduce the entire social system from paternal authority, as "nothing in the world is further from the ferocious spirit of despotism than the softness of this authority". Which is no more contradictory than Vico's historical sense...

Historical sense, faith in a divine plan, respect for the fait accompli: with Rousseau we find an antithesis to all these social features of Vico's philosophy. No surprise. From Plato, whose thought of a return to nature joins and merges with the thought of returning to the womb of God, stretch throughout the history of philosophy two divergent lines of development, each of which is characterised by one of these two thoughts: the individualist-rationalist line, and the mystic-emanative. The former – among cynics and stoics, among communistic and millenarianist sects, among protestants and precursors of modern rationalism, such as Grotius and Descartes – always has deep within the character of a protest against the present and the entire hitherto course of history; thinkers occupying a place on the latter line, whether Plotinus from whom it starts, or the mediaeval mystics of the kind of John Scotus Eriugena and Hugh of Saint Victor, or doctors of the church subscribing to divine almightiness unbound by the necessary laws – naturally hold the opposite position. Because the entire course of the world is heading towards perfection as

---

3   Maksim Kovalevski, *The beginnings of European democracy*, vol. 4: *The fall of the Venetian Republic* (Russian edition), p. 103. "Against Franck's opinion", says the author [Kelles-Krauz's footnote].

4   See: Michelet, Jules, 1894, *Oeuvres choisies de Vico*, Paris: Flammarion, p. 103 [Kelles-Krauz's footnote].

5   Ibidem, p. 141.

6   This refers to the French edition.

the ultimate goal, every step of this march, every fact given and every fait accompli, acquires in their eyes a certain degree of value and superiority over the
preceding one; absolute evil seems a purely negative fiction; the actual, historical original state becomes the least perfect; history and the world have within
them a divine plan. And when in the 18th century Giambattista Vico represents
this extreme of the philosophy of history, Jean-Jacques Rousseau becomes a
mighty reviver of the opposite direction. Rationalistic protest finds in him its
highest and purest expression: fait accompli is his enemy; history and reality –
let them bow before the reason of the individual. And as for a divine plan – in
what can one know it?

Although Rousseau admits openly to according "the writing of Moses the
faith which every Christian philosopher owes them", but, he says, "religion[7]
does not forbid us to draw conjectures solely from the nature of man",[8] which
means conduct as if God had never become involved in the course of human
history. Most probably the candidate for distinctions from the Dijon Academy
was so cautious as he acknowledged the usefulness of religious sanction for
governments, as preventing them from being overthrown too frequently by
the people;[9] however, when he abandons declamation in *The Social Contract*,
he talks of these matters somewhat differently: Yes, yes, of course "all justice
comes from God, who is its sole source; but if we knew how to receive so high
an inspiration, we should need neither government nor laws. ... Humanly
speaking, in default of natural sanctions, the laws of justice are ineffective
among men";[10] this is also why it is about mapping out the march of society "as
far as these things are capable of being deduced from the nature of man by the
mere light of reason, and independently of those sacred maxims which give to
the sovereign authority the sanction of divine right".[11]

On the other hand, says Rousseau (and here we clearly see in him an heir
of the reformation, of religious individualism, always combined with faith in
God, who acts in accordance with the unchanging laws of reason and nature),
if divine will is manifested at all in human things, then it is manifested in our
inner feeling that allows us to distinguish "in the actual constitution of things,
the operations of the Divine Will from the pretended improvements of human

---

7   The Polish translation has 'God' instead of religion [translator's note].

8   Rousseau, Jean-Jacques, 1761, *A Discourse upon the Origin and Foundation of the Inequality
     among Mankind*, London: R. and J. Dodsley, pp. 10–11.

9   Rousseau, Jean-Jacques, 1920, *The Social Contract & Discourses*, New York: E.P. Dutton &
     Co, p. 229.

10   Rousseau, Jean-Jacques, 1920, *The Social Contract & Discourses*, p. 32.

11   Rousseau, Jean-Jacques, 1761, *A Discourse upon the Origin...*, pp. 181–182.

art";[12] and later this 'divine will' is frequently replaced by its synonym, 'nature'.[13] This reveals that while for Vico the entire course of ideal and eternal history is a part of and materialisation of divine will, Rousseau in the meantime resolutely does not want to acknowledge the hand of God in the entire 'hypothetical history of governments', which constitutes the object of his deliberations;[14] in other words, he sees nothing divine in anything that is not a state of nature.[15] If God marked his involvement at all in something in this part of human history, then – and such would seem, despite certain contradictions,[16] to be Rousseau's thought – solely in the correcting[17] of human devices, in soothing the consequences of human ignorance, in preventing too great a disorder and aberrance, and namely – with the assistance of reinforcing in human hearts their feeling of justice and equality flowing from the state of nature and constituting the basis of the social contract.

Therefore, while not totally granting divine origin to a fait accompli, the author of *The Social Contract* may sarcastically reproach the royalist Grotius, whose "method of reasoning in constantly to establish right by fact",[18] and precede the dialectics of the left-wing Hegelian, Lassalle, criticising the law of the stronger in the following manner: "For if force creates right, the effect changes with the cause: every force that is greater than the first succeeds to its right".[19]

We cannot refrain here from a rather long quotation from a letter sent by Jean-Jacques Rousseau to 'Mr Philopolis' (Charles Bonnet), in order to show how the principle of providential optimism of Vico (whom, incidentally, Rousseau most probably does not know and does not cite), namely that evil does not really exist, because even what seems to be particularly evil contributes to the common good – how this principle, taken, one could say, from the other end, leads even to the opposite conclusion, to granting the individual the right to step forward on behalf of their own views and desires, and to show how

---

12 Ibidem, p. lix.
13 Ibidem, p. 7f.
14 Ibidem, p. lix.
15 "Disasters that burden people, and which, I claim, are their own doing", *Letter to Charles Bonnet* [Kelles-Krauz's footnote].
16 Examples of expressions contradicting the above train of thought – p. 26: "If we strip this being, thus constituted, of all the supernatural gifts he may have received ... if we consider him, in a word, just as he must have come from the hands of nature"; p. 24: "Religion commands us to believe that ... [men] are unequal only because it is His will they should be so", etc. [Kelles-Krauz's footnote].
17 Rousseau, Jean-Jacques, 1761, *A Discourse upon the Origin...*, p. lix.
18 Rousseau, Jean-Jacques, 1920, *The Social Contract & Discourses*, pp. 6–7.
19 Ibidem, pp. 7–8.

Rousseau clearly identifies the revolutionary ferment concealed within this conservative formula, that 'everything, that is, is good'. This interesting paragraph reads as follows:[20]

> According to Leibniz and Pope, everything that is, is good. If there are societies, it is because the general good wishes it that way. If there are none, the general good wishes that there be none, and if someone persuaded men to go back to live in forests, it would be good that they go back to live there. We should not apply to the nature of things an idea of good or evil that is derived only from their relationships, for these can be good relative to the whole although bad in themselves. What contributes to the general good may be a particular evil from which we are permitted to escape when that is possible. For if this evil while it is endured is useful for the whole, the opposite good that we attempt to substitute for it will be no less useful as soon as it occurs. For the same reason that everything is good as it is, if someone attempts to change the state of things, it is good that he attempts to change it, and whether it is good or bad for him to be successful is something that can be learned only from the outcome and not from reason. Nothing in this prevents a particular evil from being a real evil for the person who endures it.

We see here that according to Rousseau social matters are considered in themselves when we consider them from an individual point of view. This point of view leads to negation in the history of everything that occurred against and to the disadvantage of the individual.[21] Once we discard this, what is left is the state of nature.

Rousseau accuses the natural law of his predecessors precisely of not being entirely natural. "All of them, in fine, constantly harping on wants, avidity, oppression, desires and pride, have transferred to the state of nature ideas picked up in the bosom of society".[22] Rousseau also criticises the manner of defining the state of nature: "The writers of these books set out by examining, what

---

20   Rousseau, Jean-Jacques, 2007, *On Philosophy, Morality, and Religion*, Hannover and London: Dartmouth College Press, p. 45 [translator's note].

21   Although Rousseau says that civilisation has enhanced the individual, it has mislaid the species. Yet when we examine the notion of this enhancement of Rousseau's, the first step on the road to this enhancement, the inequality of riches, and its end result, state oppression, immediately indicate to us that it is actually meant to mean the enhancement of certain individuals, but is detrimental to equality, i.e. harming the original, ideal individual [Kelles-Krauz's footnote].

22   Rousseau, Jean-Jacques, 1761, *A Discourse upon the Origin...*, p. 9.

it would be proper, for their common interest, men should agree to among themselves; and then, without further ceremony, they proceed to give the name of natural law to a collection of these rules, without any other proof of such a collection's deserving that name, than the advantage they find would result from an universal compliance with it".[23] Neither, of course, did Rousseau himself avoid this automorphism, since he ascribed man in the state of nature with two attributes 'preceding reason': not only the instinct of self-survival, but also the instinct of sympathy, from which he derives man's innate goodness. However, essentially he does not want to commit the mistake of Hobbes and others, since "it never came into their heads to look beyond the times of society".[24] This sentence poses a question of fundamental significance for us: is the state of nature for Rousseau the historical state, or only the logical state? Does it mean a certain past era of humankind or just a corner in the depth of the human soul, free of any encounter with society, a place of the Cartesian escape, from where the throng of social phenomena arranges itself before one's eyes into a geometric perspective and from where we then return to society along the avenue of syllogisms, trimmed as straight as the trees in the park of Versailles? In his expressive and succinct Latin, Jaurès splits the issue in two words, to the disadvantage of historical interpretation: *non primaeva, sed originaria.*[25] The advantage of such a solution is that it denies any *raison d'être* to critiques of counterrevolutionary scholars based on historical realism, and it is quite natural for Rousseau's defenders to lean towards it. To us, though, it does not seem consistent with the text and the spirit of his *Discourse on Inequality.*

One could most probably quote classic and well-known passages in support of this purely logical interpretation. In one place, for example, the task is worded as follows: "to distinguish between what is natural, and what is artificial in the actual constitution of man, and to make one's self well acquainted with a

---

23   Ibidem, p. liv.

24   Ibidem, p. 247.

25   *De primis socialismi germanici lineamentis apud Lutherum, Kant, Fichte et Hegel, thesim etc. Tolosae* MDCCCXCI. The passage in question actually refers to Kantian views, but those that passed to Kant directly from Rousseau, and as such can most certaintly be applied to Rousseau. It reads as follows: *Cum omnibus hominibus terra habitaculum assignatum est, et homines sine terra vivere nequeunt, communia est terrae inter omnes homines originaria. Nec ea intelligenda est „primaeva communia", quam poetae celebrant, nam ea in tempore fuit: ea est factum, non idea. Non de communione terrae historica et temporali, sed rationali, agitur, non de primaeva, sed de originaria* (p. 39). The French translation of this thesis, given by A. Weber in the 'Revue Socialiste', is at this point (1892, II, p. 19) too discretionary and not entirely accurate (mais de la racine originelle de la propriété rationelle) [Kelles-Krauz's footnote].

state which, if ever it did, does not now, and in all probability never will exist, and of which, notwithstanding, it is absolutely necessary to have just notions in order to judge properly of our present state".[26]

Elsewhere we read: "Let us begin therefore, by laying aside facts, for they do not affect the question. The researches, in which we may engage on this occasion, are not to be taken for historical truths, but merely as hypothetical and conditional reasonings, fitter to illustrate the nature of things, than to show their true origin, like those systems, which our naturalists daily make of the formation of the world".[27] And also in *The Social Contract*: "The clauses of this contract [...] although they have perhaps never been formally set forth, they are everywhere the same and everywhere tacitly admitted and recognised".[28]

However, on the other hand such an explanation cannot be reconciled in any way with the manner in which Rousseau describes the state of nature and the transition from this state to civilisation. It is quite evident that he is writing history: "The times I am going to speak of, are very remote";[29] the ability to improve oneself leads man – over the course of time – out of his original state;[30] the period of time between the state of nature and our civilisational era.[31] He describes to us not only the physical nature of the first people,[32] but even the state which the Earth was in at the time when people were in the state of nature ("the face of the Earth is not liable to sudden and continual changes occasioned in it by the passions and inconstancies of collected bodies"[33]), which may with difficulty only be explained as an abstraction. Ultimately, when in support of his descriptions of the state of nature he gives the Caribbean as an example, he speaks of real savages according to the tales of travellers.

In the passage closing the description of the states of nature,[34] the words "the assumption of this original state" are used as synonymous with another expression: "a picture of the true state of nature". Here lies the solution to the issue, the clarification of this ambiguity, of this constant transition from a logical point of view to a historical point of view, and the reverse, as spoken of by Rousseau's commentators.

---

26   Rousseau, Jean-Jacques, 1761, *A Discourse upon the Origin...*, p. xlix.

27   Ibidem, p. 10.

28   Rousseau, Jean-Jacques, 1920, *The Social Contract & Discourses*, p. 14.

29   Rousseau, Jean-Jacques, 1761, *A Discourse upon the Origin...*, p. 12.

30   Ibidem, p. 38.

31   Ibidem, p. 114.

32   Ibidem, p. 32.

33   Ibidem, p. 21.

34   Ibidem, p. 88.

Rousseau has a desire to write history, and he believes that he is writing it, but he justifies this saying that he is forced to write hypothetical history. "[...] the lost and forgotten tracks, by which man from the natural must have arrived at the civil state";[35] they should be sought; "on the impossibility there is on the one hand of destroying certain hypotheses, if on the other we cannot give them the degree of certainty which facts must be allowed to possess, on its being the business of history, when two facts are proposed, as real, to be connected by a chain of intermediate facts which are either unknown or considered as such, to furnish such facts as may actually connect them; and the business of philosophy, when history is silent, to point out similar facts which may answer the same purpose".[36] The state of nature must have existed, also for example as a nebula of physicians, as without this it would be impossible to explain today's social world. It is not Rousseau's fault that ethnography has not yet provided a certain picture of this state and of its distribution; hence Rousseau turns to travellers and scholars with a passionate summons,[37] "we would ourselves see a new world emerge from under their pens, and we would thus learn to understand our own". But the Morgans, Bachofens, Kovalevskys and an entire throng of prehistoric archaeologists, who were supposed to satisfy this need for a reformative spirit so generously, had not yet been born, and Rousseau, entirely against his will, had to resort to suppositions only regarding in what way the events engaging him may have occurred.[38] Obviously in these conditions, entirely as with the cynics and the Alexandrians, the unavoidable automorphism of the dissatisfied permeates all hypotheses with insurmountable force.

Let us therefore summarise in a few short words that hypothetical story; it made such a gigantic impact on the direction of thought to which we owe the discoveries of today's prehistory. This will allow us to define what it actually is with Rousseau that corresponds to the notion of the golden age; let us say in advance that it is not the first state of nature.

What corresponds to this first period of nature is man "wandering about in the forests, without industry, without speech, without any fixed residence, an equal stranger to war and every social connection, without standing in any shape in need for his fellows, as well as without any desire of hurting them, and perhaps even without ever distinguishing them individually one from the

35   Ibidem, p. 176.
36   Ibidem, pp. 94–95.
37   Ibidem, pp. 219–220.
38   Ibidem, p. 95f.

other, subject to few passions, and finding in himself all he wants".[39] Men mate randomly with women, depending on their encounters, opportunity and desire; and they part with equal ease. Children, fed by the mother initially for her own need, and later out of habit and by then for them themselves, soon abandon her, becoming independent.[40] This is, generally speaking, an animal life, guided – according to Rousseau – by the instinct for self-survival and sympathy. It is a happy life, because these people do not know any of the sufferings generated by reflection and social precepts. Contemplating man is a spoilt animal.[41] The moral side of love is also an artificial feeling, deriving from social intercourse;[42] people in the state of nature did not know it, and as such they did not suffer at all.

The stages through which man left this state behind were as follows (see the second part of *Discourse on Inequality*):

> The natural difficulties of life pushed him to invent tools, or rather to discover them, because they existed ready in nature in their original form. The usage of tools spawned contemplation, a certain development of the mind, thanks to which man began to enter temporary relationships with other people for the purpose of hunting, etc., and therefore conceived the first notion of mutual obligations.

The new progress in technology, brought about following an entire succession of centuries through progress in human reasoning, caused a great revolution: the construction of cottages created separate families and provided the first beginning of a certain type of ownership. Associated families turned into nations. The following appeared: marital and paternal love, the division of work between men and women; but simultaneously jealousy, discord, ambition, inequality, disgrace, desire, revenge and – their unavoidable companion – a certain type of morality, and certain social bonds. This state of society being born was no longer a pure state of nature; but for as long as every person was satisfied with "works only a single person could finish ... they lived free, healthy, honest and happy, as much as their nature would admit, and continued to enjoy with each other all the pleasures of an independent intercourse".[43] "Thus, tho' were become less patient, and natural compassion had already suffered

---

39   Ibidem, p. 86.
40   Ibidem, p. 24.
41   Ibidem, p. 39.
42   Ibidem, p. 81.
43   Ibidem, p. 119.

some alteration, this period of the development of the human faculties, holding a just mean between the indolence of the primitive state, and the petulant
activity of self-love, must have been the happiest and most durable epoch. The
more we reflect on this state, the more convinced we shall be, that it was the
least subject of any to revolutions, the best for man, and that nothing could
have drawn him out of it but some fatal accident, which, for the public good,
should never have happened. The example of the savages, most of whom have
been found in this condition, seems to confirm that mankind was formed ever
to remain in it, that this condition is the real youth of the world, and that all
ulterior improvements have been so many steps, in appearance towards the
perfection of individuals, but in fact towards the decrepitness of the species".[44]

Therefore behold the second state of nature, a genuine idyll of mankind, a
golden age in the proper meaning of the word, which immediately preceded
civilisation.

"[B]ut ... from the moment it appeared an advantage for one man to possess
the quantity of provisions requisite for two",[45] equality vanished and ownership appeared. Metallurgy and agriculture civilised the people. Constituting a
possible consequence of the appearance of surplus value, we would say using
today's language that they caused a division in work on a grand scale, the division and ownership of land, followed by inequality in riches, and thereby the
"infant society became a scene of the most horrible warfare",[46] which people
finally left behind thanks to the social contract.

Private ownership, says Rousseau, was the end of the state of nature.[47] At
this point the notion of state of nature embraces both first states of nature and
the entire pre-civilisational time. But between the appearance of ownership
and the social contract stretches also a third state of nature, the state of war, of
everybody against everybody for the riches.

It is precisely from this state of nature that Rousseau, as also Hobbes, Vico
and all theoreticians of natural law, deduce the state and slavery, though in a
different manner. Rousseau also has this state of nature in mind when he compares the mutual position of political bodies in relation to the state of nature;[48]
when he attributes the social contract and laws with a significant superiority
over violence and "primitive confusion".[49]

---

44   Ibidem, pp. 117–118.
45   Ibidem, p. 119.
46   Ibidem, p. 132.
47   Ibidem, p. 97.
48   Ibidem, p. 139.
49   Ibidem, p. 163, 251; Rousseau, Jean-Jacques, 1920, *The Social Contract & Discourses*, p. 37.

However, compared to the strides of inequality, constituting an essential result of the social contract, then this state of nature – no matter how unclean –
holds the advantage of being an era of people 'haughty and indomitable', free
and with equal rights (*Discourse on inequality*, p. 113).[50] It is to this that mankind reverts every time the social contract is dissolved through violation of the
law.

With Rousseau, the reversion to the former state should be considered in
two different forms: either as an ideal, or as a necessity; as a thing consciously
desired by people, and as a fatal consequence of the natural course of things.[51]

The first two states of nature bear the attributes of the ideal, and mainly the
second, as the first seems too far-removed and too hypothetical. However, in
general this return is considered in the past conditional mode: "you will look
out for the age at which, had you your wish, your species had stopped. Uneasy
at your present condition, ...you will perhaps wish it were in your power to go
back; and this sentiment ought to be considered ... the condemnation of your
contemporaries...".[52]

Rousseau advises those who could to "take up again, since it is in your power, your ancient and primitive innocence; retire to the woods".[53] But this does
not seem possible to him. The original simplicity of people has been once and
forever destroyed by passions; they can no longer live on grasses and rootlets,
or get by without laws and leaders. Moreover, if people never had left the state
of nature they would not have experienced so much evil, but neither would
they have fulfilled the sublime mission of their species.[54] A savage is not bad,
because he does not know what it is to be good, and he is not held back from
evil by a legal suppression or the development of education, but only by the
dormancy of passions and ignorance of evil.[55] It is from this absence of contradiction, of this lack of separation of good and evil in the original existence of
mankind, that Fichte and Schelling later deduce their dialectic consequences.
Rousseau only declares that "nations need art, laws and governments like the
elderly need crutches", and with full disdain for this aged community he recommends obedience to laws and "wise princes who will know how to prevent,

---

50   Rousseau, Jean-Jacques, 1761, *A Discourse upon the Origin...*, p. 182.
51   Certain shades of expression also correspond to these two different thoughts: (conscious)
      return to the state of nature, and (forced) return to the state of nature [Kelles-Krauz's
      footnote].
52   Rousseau, Jean-Jacques, 1761, *A Discourse upon the Origin...*, pp. 12–13.
53   Ibidem, p. 218.
54   Ibidem.
55   Ibidem, p. 74.

cure, or palliate this host of abuses and evils always ready to overwhelm us", as well as practicing the virtues.[56] In this, people have a kind of means for a personal, individual return to the state of nature, the traces of which (e.g. inborn sympathy[57]) still live within them, and may in this manner hold society back from stepping too quickly towards old age and decline.[58]

Here Rousseau presents himself to us as how he always essentially was, the most consistent of the Utopian conservatives. In reading *The Social Contract*, one should never forget the *Comments on Government in Poland*, the sole outstanding application of the practical principles of the *Contract* made by Rousseau himself; here he reveals himself a determined conservative, a defender of class hierarchy, of provincial freedoms and even of ancient dress, a suspicious adversary to centralisation and the monetary economy.

The bourgeois structure of the Genevan republic seems to him that "deviates least from the laws of nature and yet answers best the ends of society",[59] while the structure of the aristocratic Venetian republic is on the whole totally analogous to the Genevan.[60] That state of nature, the ideal of which is based on "consult[ing] your own happiness with as little prejudice as you can to that of others",[61] has evidently survived to the greatest degree. What fascinates Rousseau the most, what he most regrets, is the small, bourgeois republics, that former calm life of the peasants who were self-sufficient.[62] The object of his hatred and unqualified criticism is everything and anything that accompanies

---

56   Ibidem, p. 219.

57   Ibidem, p. 76.

58   Ibidem, p. 251.

59   Ibidem, p. iv.

60   It was proved (by Julius Buy, *Les Origines des idées politiques de J.J. Rousseau*), that Rousseau based his social-political principles on the democratic constitution granted to the city of Geneva in the year 1587 by Bishop Adhémar de la Roche (Fabri). In one of the manuscripts preserved in the Neuchâtel library, Rousseau says precisely because of this *chartae libertatum*: "In wanting to explain current governments, I have to return to the source and illuminate what exists with the help of what once was". One more proof of the historical (at least in intention) and not logical method of the author of *Discourse on Inequality* [Kelles-Krauz's footnote].

61   Rousseau, Jean-Jacques, 1761, *A Discourse upon the Origin...*, p. 77.

62   See e.g. the eloquent passage in his famous note 9 to the *Discourse on Inequality*, in which the author, talking of the "poverty into which wealth pushes the most glorious nations" – an antithesis that Marx and his school exploited in the 19th century – describes the downfall of the countryman under the burden of taxes necessary for upholding the exuberance of the capitals, and his wretched emigration to the cities "to seek in town the bread he should carry there" [Kelles-Krauz's footnote]. See: Rousseau, Jean-Jacques, 1761, *A Discourse upon the Origin...*, p. 215.

monarchical centralisation and the monetary economy, that contributed to the decline and disintegration of those republics and that rustic prosperity. It is their march that he would like, were it possible, to halt or delay, and with this goal he removes, through abstraction, everything that has occurred in defiance of his partiality, and the remaining features, those he finds agreeable, he attributes to original man. The real object of his retrospection is the social equilibrium of the Middle Ages; and if Vico wanted nations to rest in monarchy, Rousseau would desire them to be immobilised in the small, democratic urban republics.

Rousseau did indeed exert a genuine revolutionary influence, and this via the positive conclusions drawn from his critique by the French Revolution. Besides, the entire French Revolution (and by the adjective 'French' I mean here not the nationality, but its character) began from a similar pre-absolutist retrospection. "In the beginning it seemed to people that it was only about a certain type of rebuilding, that France had no need for starting out on new tracks, but should only return to the starting point, guided by the recollection of its past". "Humiliated by the present, terrified by the future, we had to move back into the past so as to draw hope for a national rebirth in the graves of our fathers", says one of his contemporaries.[63] Yet more distinct is that pre-absolutist retrospection among the theoretical precursors of the revolution: in the 16th century a certain François Hotman and 'Junius Brutus' (Hubert Longuet), who even before Grotius saw in the monarchs civil servants of the people, delegated on the basis of a contract and who could, in the event of not adhering to it, be removed from office (the Jesuits added: killed). These 'Brutuses' walked in the footsteps of the Mediaeval Marsilius of Padua, Nicole Oresme, sectarians with communistic tendencies, and even the righteous 'Angelic Doctors'; these in turn were not so far from the times when in the West, and not only in Poland, genuine *pacta conventa*, 'social contracts', were concluded with princes, when for example it was said at the enthronement of the Aragon kings: "We, each of whom is equal to you, make you king, with the condition that you respect our customs, but if not, then no".

It was the same in other lands engulfed by the 'French' revolution. Wherever the revolutionary winners of the revolution appeared, everywhere did they 'restore' freedom. For example the Venetians saw nothing new in the French doctrines, just a revival and broadening of the former foundations of their republic.[64] The 'civil constitution' of the clergy was presented as a return to the

---

63   See: Champion, Edme, 1887, *Esprit de la révolution française*, Paris: C. Reinwald, Chap. 3, pp. 70–71.

64   Maxim Kovalevski, *Padenlje aristokratii*, p. 102.

principles of the original church, and in Brescia the revolutionists even said: *il Cittadino Gesù Cristo.*[65]

However, it soon turns out that the forms of the past are insufficient for embracing the phenomena of the present; instead of negating the acquisitions of the present in favour of past forms, the senses create something new by merging one with the other. With this purpose, in order to be able to overstep both one and the other, the "nation shifts to the beginnings of society, recalls that human nature is the source of a higher law above written law, just as it is above customary law".[66] In this manner Rousseau's retrospection becomes genuinely revolutionary. A phenomenon of the same kind is occurring in Germany, where from the retrospections of Klopstock towards Arminius,[67] or of Stein and the Romantics towards the Holy Roman Empire, a new pan-German unity is slowly emerging.

Revolution accomplished Rousseau's retrospection in the political field; via the intermediation of Babeuf it conveyed to the 19th century an economic retrospection of him and its other publicists, who called ownership theft but were a long way from wanting to abolish it. Today's heirs to Babeuf, the socialists, find with Rousseau many points to which they can relate their views: starting from that sole and fundamental point of the social contract, which is based on the total subordination of everybody associated, together with all of their rights, to the community as a whole,[68] in such a manner that the populace, holding full authority, resolves what portion of freedom should be left to individuals,[69] while the right of ownership is only a concession granted by the community,[70] and ending in the emergence of ownership from personal work,[71] in the image of calamities diffused by ownership already established,[72] even in the main outlines of pre-history and the beginnings of the class state. However, what the Marxists will value above all in Rousseau's legacy are the elements of dialectic: if in Vico he sees Labriola (alongside Montesquieu and Quesnay) the only philosopher gifted with a historical sense among the rationalists of the 18th century, then Friedrich Engels venerates in Rousseau the sole rationalist whose

65   Ibidem, p. 160.
66   Champion, Edme, 1887, *Esprit de la révolution française*, p. 73.
67   Arminius (approx. 17 BC–21 AD) was the chieftain of the Germanic Cherusci tribe. The German poet Friedrich Gottlieb Klopstock (1724–1803) made him one of the heroes of his drama, *Hermanns Tod.*
68   Rousseau, Jean-Jacques, 1920, *The Social Contract & Discourses*, p. 47.
69   Ibidem, p. 91.
70   Ibidem, p. 19.
71   Rousseau, Jean-Jacques, 1761, *A Discourse upon the Origin...*, p. 134.
72   Ibidem, p. 107.

manner of thinking is not 'metaphysical', static. The best-known example of Rousseau's dialectic, quoted precisely by Engels in the 13th chapter of the first part of his *Anti-Dühring*, is the development of despotism, which begins with natural equality, passes through the mission of justice entrusted to the prince, reaches negation of this mission in the law of the stronger – and here completes the circle, returning to the starting point: to the new equality – of all slaves before the ruler, to a "new state of nature different from that with which we began, in as much as the first was the state of nature in its purity, and the last the consequence of excessive corruption".[73] The new state of nature leads to the expulsion of the tyrant and the conclusion of a new social contract. "The oppressor becomes the oppressed" , summarises Engels, and this oppression of the oppressor finds analogy in the Marxist 'expropriation of the expropriators'. Besides, even omitting such and similar historical applications, the dialectic already lies at the very foundation of the way of understanding Rousseau; his mind, just like the mind of Marx,[74] is dialectically formed. "The essence of the

---

73   Ibidem, p. 175.

74   The manner of reasoning with which Marx comes to explain the emergence of capitalistic surplus value, the conversion of money into capital, is entirely analogous to that used by Rousseau for explaining the law-making act or appointment of the first government (see *Contrat social* [*The Social Contract*], bk. 2, Ch. 7 and bk. 3, Ch. 17, and K. Marx, *Capital. A Critique of Political Economy*, vol. 1: *The Process of Production of Capital*, Chapters 5 and 6. *Hic Rhodus, hic salta*, is one and the same in both cases. We have two strictly demarcated zones: omnipotence and holding office, the same as the circulation of riches and consumption. The law-making function, also as a function of establishing a government, is neither omnipotence nor holding office. After all, the function of the lawmaker that constitutes a republic is not a part of its constitution. "How can the appointment of a government, as an act of government, take place prior to the existence of government?" Likewise, the production of surplus value cannot take place within turnover, because any exchange here takes place on the principle of equality of value, and that surplus value would have to have existed before in order for an exchange to be able to issue a surplus value. Yet surplus value cannot be produced elsewhere than in the sphere of exchange, because when entering the sphere of consumption, a commodity abandons for always the sphere of exchange and exchangeable value. Finally there is a special person and special functions that belong simultaneously to the scope of the people's omnipotence and the holding of office, and special commodity, labour force, that is consumed without leaving turnover.

There are also other deep similarities between the method of *The Social Contract*, that bible of political critique, and *Capital*, that fundamental book of economic critique, one of which reveals the "fetishism of the commodity", and the other – the artificiality of political institutions. Thus e.g. Marx brings various specific activities down to their universal equality via abstraction analogous to that which leads Rousseau to acknowledge the natural equality of people (see *Capital*, Ch. 1, § IV). The basic development of the form of

body politic lies in the reconciliation of obedience and liberty, and the words subject and Sovereign are identical correlatives the idea of which meets in the single word 'citizen'".[75] Here we have a fundamental and immediate reconciliation of the contradictions, which is found throughout idealistic German philosophy and whose impact on the formation of Hegel's triads, though perhaps not direct, will still be no less important than the influence of Kant's categories.

If we return to the dialectic structures whose expressions are split in time, we find all of their roots and forms with Rousseau. The first, which perhaps plays the most important role in Hegelianism and Marxism: for example we have consequence, which becomes the cause of its own cause, in the history of the initial development of mankind, where growth in education and attempts at consocation caused by the invention of tools contributes in turn to the emergence of family, and provides the stimulus for a new ascent of thought. And the third chapter of the 8th book of *The Social Contract*, in which Rousseau indicates that three forms of government – democracy, aristocracy and monarchy – are capable of becoming larger or smaller, and that within quite significant boundaries, and "there is a point at which each form of government passes into the next", with what principle is it permeated if not the principle of quantity passing into quality, a principle inherited after all from Aristotle, the first theoretician of transformations of forms of government and the master of all later thinkers, also revered by Marx? If we consider that these three forms of government remain antagonistic towards each other, then here we even have something more, something also known to Aristotle: the transition of a certain thing into its contradiction.

This can be clearly seen in the progress made by various institutions, for example in the vicissitudes of the power of the Roman tribunes, "which they

---

value (simple form, developed form, general form and monetary form, Ch. 1, § VIII) is a process simultaneously logical and historical, just like the growth in inequality. A certain Marxist-Benedictine would have interesting room for exploration here.

We also emphasise that a typically dialectic intellectual operation, entirely analogical to those of Marx and Rousseau quoted above, is to be found at the basis of the third great sociological system, with August Comte. Namely because no sequence of observations of nature can arise if the mind does not have some kind of point of view, some kind of theory, but then no theory can be built other than on the basis of previous factual observations, and therefore the course of the "dialectic of the history of human intelligence", as Comte says, cannot begin other than thanks to the existence of a state of mind which is both a direct observation and a general theory, and which in actual fact is neither one nor the other: 'fetishism', attributing all things in the outside world to man's own nature [Kelles-Krauz's footnote].

75   Rousseau, Jean-Jacques, 1920, *The Social Contract & Discourses*, p. 80.

had usurped by degrees, finally served, with the help of laws made to secure liberty, as a safeguard for the emperors who destroyed it"[76] – in the development of militarism: "We should then see the multitude oppressed by domestic tyrants in consequence of those very precautions taken by them to guard against foreign masters";[77] and this all on the strength of one general principle: "for those vices, which render social institutions necessary, are the same which render the abuse of such institutions unavoidable".[78] Here are examples of yet another kind: how the usage of a particular means leads automatically to something the direct opposite of the intended goal: "the more we accumulate new informations, the more we deprive ourselves of the means of acquiring the most important of all; and it is, in a manner, by the mere dint of the studying man that have lost the power of knowing him".[79] Marx uses precisely the same means of highlighting concealed internal contradictions when he demonstrates that the more capitalists perfect the technology of production, the more difficult it is for them to sell their products. Neither will we find anything new, unless perhaps metaphysics, in the Hegelian theory of punishment as negation of negation (innocence, crime, punishment), if we recall Rousseau's justification for the death penalty. "It is in order that we may not fall victims to an assassin that we consent to die if we ourselves turn assassins. In this treaty, so far from disposing of our own lives, we think only of securing them";[80] in dialectic language, or – if you prefer – 'jargon', this may be expressed thus: (a) saving the individual thanks to the safety of the whole, (b) threatening everybody's safety through excessive self-survival of the individual (because if one kills oneself, one gives testimony to one's instinct of existence); and ultimately (c) protecting all through annihilation of the individual.

However, until now we have only had a closed historical cycle, the automatic reconstruction of the past in a new form with the help of the negation of negation, in the case we already know: the return of the relationship of nature between individuals as a result of despotism; a second case should be added: the return of the relationship of nature between political bodies similar to the relationship individuals had with one another before the social contract was concluded; this return is also automatic, because its cause is the very fact of the formation of societies.

---

76 Ibidem, p. 107.

77 Rousseau, Jean-Jacques, 1761, *A Discourse upon the Origin...*, p. 171.

78 Ibidem, p. 165.

79 Ibidem, p. xlvii.

80 Rousseau, Jean-Jacques, 1920, *The Social Contract & Discourses*, p. 30.

Let us notice at once a certain fixed feature of such automatic return to the state of nature: it is evil, as here we are dealing with that third state of nature, the state of war of everybody with everybody, and in addition even this state does not recur in its purity, but bears the stigma of a surplus of that corruption that brings it about. As for the presumption that "such a state [of nature] ever existed among men, unless they fell back into it by some extraordinary event: a paradox very difficult to maintain, and altogether impossible to prove".[81]

Not believing in the possibility of starting history anew, neither does Rousseau sense that panic-stricken fear that Vico displays towards some kind of new savagery at the thought of the extermination of at least a part of the legacy of the past: there are, he says, "periods of violence and revolutions do to peoples what these crises do to individuals: horror of the past takes the place of forgetfulness, and the State, set on fire by civil wars, is born again, so to speak, from its ashes, and takes on anew, fresh from the jaws of death, the vigour of youth"; such was the case with Rome, Holland and Switzerland following the expulsion of the tyrants.[82] With Vico, violation of the monarchical equilibrium by the people could only bring it back down to the pre-social state and force it to once again take the painful way of the cross, of eternally identical history; with Rousseau it can have the consequence of the immediate conclusion of a higher, better social contract. Both one and the other speak in almost identical words of the rebirth of the nation from its ashes; but according to Vico this is a severe punishment that God retains for those unwilling to take the shorter road to the destination indicated by Providence; according to Rousseau, on the other hand, it may be a radical means for all evil. Nevertheless, even according to Rousseau these are rare exceptions, and this violent means that is good for some states may be dangerous for others, which "disturbances may destroy [...], but revolutions cannot mend".[83] Hence Rousseau by no means wants to break the social contract, but is rather afraid of it; instead of expecting a renewal of freedom from bringing about its negation, despotism, to its unavoidable repeated negation, he pays homage to the princes who not only know how to anticipate and cure, but even if only how to assuage abuse.[84]

As for the return of the first or second state of nature, of that 'youth of mankind', this Rousseau would desire, but he knows it to be impossible. Reason has ultimately belied nature and nowhere do we find with Rousseau the wish or hope for the negation of reason to be able to restore the state of nature. It is

81   Rousseau, Jean-Jacques, 1761, *A Discourse upon the Origin...*, p. 10.
82   Rousseau, Jean-Jacques, 1920, *The Social Contract & Discourses*, p. 39.
83   Ibidem.
84   Rousseau, Jean-Jacques, 1761, *A Discourse upon the Origin...*, p. 219.

reason itself, rational upbringing, the wisdom of governments that should "re-establish upon other foundations ... all the rules of natural right", when reason, perfection of the human family, "by a gradual exertion of its own powers it has at last stifled the authority of nature".[85] Thus the road leading to the ideal is not a curve closing the circle, but is a straight line. And in addition this future ideal will always be lower than the happiness of mankind in past times. An old man cannot become a youth anew.

There never was a golden age, God is leading us to the ideal, and let us beware of him ordering us to start from the beginning once again: such was the conclusion of Vico's historical realism.

The golden age existed in the past; since that time we have fallen ever lower, we are aware of the ideal, we would like its return, but it cannot return: such is the final word of Jean-Jacques' idealistic realism. A natural process, essential, progressive, without retrospection on the one hand; and inconsolable retrospection without awareness of progress or an essential process – on the other.

Only does German idealism, reaching its peak with Hegel and reconciling the fear of regression with the desire for progress, lend this the character and dignity of an internal purpose of history; from the clash between the acknowledged present and the late-lamented past it will strike the holy spark of the future.

If, however, we do not restrict ourselves to Rousseau alone, but take his disciples and adorers, then we will see that they have an inkling of this work of German idealism, and even look far beyond this proper idealism, right up to its extreme Babeufistic left wing. Mably believes clearly in the historical existence of an original communism, and regrets this state; Morelly believes in the possibility of rebuilding it in the future. Particularly noteworthy in this respect is the Benedictine Dom Deschamps. He distinguishes three states comprising the cycle, a type of Hegelian triad. The first – a state of wildness, the state of nature according to Rousseau; from its disintegration emerged the second state, today's legal state. This state has so many faults, that the original wildness truly would be better if not (and this 'if not' is very characteristic of the process of retrospection transforming into revolutionary) for the fact that this second state, by the very fact that it evokes in people a need for speculating over some kind of better state, gives them the hope – and hope not so chimeric as it seems to them – for passing from this state to a third, better, 'customary' state, an *état des moeurs*, in which there would be equality and genuine natural morality, a community of property and women, universal health, where antagonism between city and countryside would disappear – which, in a word, would be

---

85   Ibidem, p. lvi.

significantly better than the original state of nature. Because the latter was a
state of diffusion with no connector other than instinct; our current state, its
antithesis, in its ostensible coherence is the state of the greatest diffusion and
discord; and only that third state, the state of socialisation without binding
laws, will be a state of true connectedness free of dilemma. Weishaupt, founder
of the German 'Illuminati', speaks even more distinctly of this, that if the past
was as if a Christian state of grace for mankind living in community, equality
and freedom, then without excessive requirements the future will be a return
to this state, but a state significantly improved. Except that the writings of such
a Weishaupt and Deschamps were then totally unknown to the wider public.
The influence of the first goes no further than a few secret societies, the second
kept his correspondence with Rousseau, Voltaire, Helvétius and d'Alembert to
himself, so only after almost a century did the erudite Beaussire[86] seek it out
in the lumber rooms of the d'Argenson family. Besides, Deschamps himself did
not care about the broader public; he would have wanted to convince the rich,
also suffering much from today's state of humanity, while "as for the sheep –
do they need to know where they are going to graze in the meadow, as long as
they graze?" And this is the characteristic feature of this social dialectic, setting it apart from the later, democratic dialectic for which German philosophy
prepared the ground.

II   German Idealism and Hegel

"By granting everybody the freedom of interpretation and comment", said
Jaurès in the quoted treatise, "while at the same time giving the Holy bible
as the basis of this freedom, altogether acknowledging human freedom as determined, the reformation trained German mentality to embrace contradictions". In that case Rousseau recalled this lesson and transferred it to the social
sphere, declaring that he wanted "to live and die free, that is to say, subject to
the laws".[87] But the facts, the social condition, were what best instilled it for the
German burgher; because it was not only the growth in the bourgeois class in
Germany through the 18th century, and at the same time a respect mixed deeply
with the fear aroused by enlightened absolutism, that turned the German into
that creature spoken about by madam de Staël, saying that "he flattered with

86   Beaussire, Émile, 1865, *Antécédents de l'hégélianisme en France*, Paris: Germer Baillière.
87   Rousseau, Jean-Jacques, 1761, *A Discourse upon the Origin...*, Dedication to the Genevan
      Republic, p. vii.

all his energy, and was obedient with force"; but precisely at the moment when idealistic German philosophy began to develop, Germany underwent one of the deepest and at the same time most violent dialectic processes to have ever bothered the consciousness of nations. In view of all, in the space of but a few years, the most extreme cosmopolitism transformed into arrogant patriotism bordering on national vanity. Those who together with Lessing saw in the love of one's fatherland a "heroic weakness without which they managed perfectly", those who together with Herder wanted to be above all people, and in so doing be Germans, suddenly – as a result of the internal contradiction of the French Revolution that both liberated and subjugated them – repeated Fichte's words from *Speeches to the German People*: "Let us be above all German patriots, and thus we shall serve mankind", while with Görres they became Germans against the entire rest of the human race.[88]

There was no shortage of contradictions to be reconciled among the devotees of Rousseau, Napoleon's enemies and the friends of freedom, who to begin with had insufficient force to imitate the French Revolution, while later felt obliged to centre around the Prussian monarchy. Hence the German idealists are the first to add contradictions to the divine plan of history and the universe. For Schelling, history is an 'epic laid out by divine reason', just the same as for Vico. But with Fichte and Krause the 'eternal ideal history' is no longer entirely identified, as in Vico's case, with reality; the 'applied philosophy of history' accomplishes only a part of the 'pure philosophy of history'. This part of history, with Rousseau as well, is purely human and 'radically evil', or at least indifferent. Vico's direct influence was assuredly essential for exposing to the German idealists the thought of a divine plan of history. Theology, which they all practised and which they had in common with Vico, was entirely sufficient for them to be classed in this respect into one and the same direction of development. However Vico's direct or indirect influence on some of them seems obvious: the similarities occurring are too characteristic. Schelling in particular explains polytheism and the cult for heroes through the existence on Earth before man of a greater and stronger species; he compares the invasion of the barbarians to a new Deluge, following which new creation begins; he believes that in the beginning statehood and science, religion and art merged and mutually intermingled, and that this would also be so in the future: this all strongly resembles the *New Science*. Michelet says that Herder read Vico.[89] The

---

88   Compare to the excellent, substantive book by Lévy-Bruhl, Lucien, 1890, *L'Allemagne depuis Leibniz*, Paris: Hachette [Kelles-Krauz's footnote].

89   Michelet, Jules, 1894, *Oeuvres choisies de Vico*, p. 140.

description of people in the state of nature as savages, uncouth and impetuous, could have passed from Vico to Hegel via the mediation of de Maistre.[90]

The sole difference, but deep and fundamental, between Vico and German idealism is the introduction of gradually reconciling contradictions into the process of the manifestation and later – the very happening of the Absolute. With Vico this element was noticeable barely in an insignificant embryo. German idealism owes it largely to Rousseau.[91]

From the years 1751, 1755 and 1756, dates that saw the publication of Lessing's very complimentary reports of two of Rousseau's treatises and Mendelsohn's translation of *Discourse on Inequality*, Jean-Jacques' ideas became well-known in Germany and immediately caused significant agitation. Möser criticises above all his logical schematicism, and in the name of natural differences and local peculiarities protests against the simplification and generalisation of the principles of social life. His polemic against the author of *The Social Contract* is, as it were, a harbinger of Savigny's polemic with Thibaut regarding the issue of the standardisation of civil law in Germany. Historical realism, which opposes the tendencies of revolutionary rationalism, already occupies its future position.

Herder, author of a maxim known well to historians, "Strive to live the life of every nation under investigation", moves it an entire and significant step forward. The return to nature is something extremely likeable for this sentimentalist. The state of nature in no way seems to him as barbaric and repulsive as it was later presented by Haller. In keeping with the stories of the Bible, the good Christian believes that the history of mankind began from the patriarchate, and that this period of the patriarchate was, in its simplicity, a golden age. Just like Rousseau, he also deduces despotism from the transition to agriculture. But every nation has its own proper nature, and as such it no longer seems possible to Herder to apply one and the same criterion of perfection of the social condition to all. Every nation has its own specific condition of nature, and consequently also has its own particular ideal. Every nation has within itself a balance point of its own happiness, just like every ball has its own centre of gravity, and the development of each is presented as a sequence

---

90   Franck, Adolphe, 1893, *Réformateurs et publicistes de l'Europe au XVIII siècle*, Paris: Calmann Lévy, p. 113.

91   Compare especially: Flint, Robert, 1874, *The Philosophy of History in France and Germany*, Edinburgh and London: William Blackwood and Sons; Fester, Richard, 1890, *Rousseau und die deutsche Geschichtsphilosophie*, Stuttgart: Göschen'sche Verlag; the article by Lévy-Bruhl, 1837, *L'influence de J.J. Rousseau en Allemagne*, "Annales de l'École des Sciences politiques", which Fester also cites [Kelles-Krauz's footnote].

of eras of a successive drawing closer to or moving further away from this ideal point.[92]

This point is situated ever higher as the universal history of mankind progresses from one nation to another. The consequence of such guiding ideas in different peoples testifies to a certain constant progress, is a result of the 'rearing of mankind' and its ascension to the pan-human idea. However, Herder does not define such a centre of gravity for mankind as a whole, since the history of man is for him a "theatre of a deity whose game we discern, we, people, through rather scarce windows, and thus only in individual scenes".

Kant is more faithful to Rousseau, whom he exalts as the first to have discovered the science of man in general, deeply concealed beneath the diversity of human forms.[93] He has a "notion of universal history from a cosmopolitan point of view", and this notion is actually Rousseau's notion, except that it is higher, calmer and more balanced, because it is presented as a hidden plan of nature serving to create the perfect political system, capable of ensuring the comprehensive development of all the skills with which the human family is gifted. From the very outset human nature had certain general inclinations. In order to bring about their development, nature evokes reconcilable antagonisms between them: this is its tool of progress. The main antagonism occurs between two consecutive aspirations of man: between the aspiration to connect with one's fellow beings, and the aspiration for isolating oneself from them (Rousseau's self-survival instinct and the instinct of sympathy). This 'unsociable sociability' (*ungesellige Geselligkeit*) of man is reconciled in an organised society based on justice ("free – that means submitting to laws", said Rousseau). Therefore there exists radical evil, with which nature must constantly battle: this is precisely that essential anti-sociality of man, although only thanks to this can mankind constantly progress towards perfection. If not for the existence of this antagonism, social life might have never left the period of Arcadian shepherds, as calm as their herd, but also just as mindless and idle. The state of nature appears once again between political bodies, between states; but political bodies are also, one could say, gifted with 'unsociable sociability', which in the end leads them to a just community of nations, to a universal federation in which all the fundamental human inclinations achieve their highest degree of development. In this manner the perfection of artificial

---

92   Similarly as remarkable is Lelewel's view of grass-roots democracy – as a kind of ideal recurring and vanishing point of prosperity of the Polish people [Kelles-Krauz's footnote]. Joachim Lelewel (1786–1861) was a Polish historian and politician.

93   See with Fester, Ch. 1, how Rousseau approached the Kantian point of view in the theory of knowledge [Kelles-Krauz's footnote].

attributes revives the state of nature in its highest form. This is a major difference compared to Rousseau; there is also a second difference: together with
the rational plan of history, with Kant its essential consequence also occurs –
respect for the fait accompli, the very existence of which testifies to a certain
law; acknowledgement of existing authority, the very existence of which cannot but derive from the people's consent – and so the condemnation of any
dissent as quite simply senseless.

But Fichte, the passionate author of *Reclamation of the Freedom of Thought*,
did not share this Kantian respect for the Object, for outwardness, including
for the German princes. However, he did believe in the realisation of a certain
plan in history, and this belief in a plan of history not combined with respect
for the fait accompli was something new that was great and rich in consequences. It derived from Fichte's opinion that the entire history, just like the
entire objective world as such, was but a work and a reflection of one's own
'I' – of the absolute, identical with the noumenon, and just like it free and undefined from outside.[94] It is not a fait accompli that heralds a law to such an 'I':
it is the 'I' that realises its anticipatory law in the fact. If a fact is not consistent
with an idea, then quite simply it does not exist at all, it is an illusion, a passing
apparition. Only good really is real.

Therefore, if according to Rousseau the essentially indelible and enticing
picture of the state of nature exists within us because this state of nature must
have once existed in reality, and the transition to inequality and to the social
contract is a logical process because it could and had to have already been a
historical process, then there must exist for Fichte in the past and in the future
a state of nature split one from the other by a state of denaturalisation, because
such is the logical process of the self, because the self-generated 'I' establishes
itself, contradicts itself, and then once again establishes itself. Fichte disseminated this purely logical interpretation of Rousseau, according to which the
state of nature is the state of every individual person who, before concluding
the contract, before accepting any obligations whatsoever, acknowledges as the
starting point only the law of his own nature; and whether such a state of nature every existed in reality is a question that should never even be considered.

According to Fichte, therefore, Rousseau only wanted to place in the past a
picture of what we would one day be in the future. This would be in a manner
of speaking a double, fictitious reflection of a non-existent focus of light.

---

94   This philosophy of the 'I', according to which the 'I' creates the truth, may be compared to
      the following passage from Vico's *The New Science*: "Because the social world is the work
      of man, due to which the way in which it was created is to be found in varieties of the hu-
      man spirit, then he who contemplates social science creates for himself the very object of
      his contemplations" [Kelles-Krauz's footnote].

But Fichte lives and creates beyond the year 1789, which Rousseau was not to see. And the difference between these two advocates of a rationalistic natural law lies precisely in the fact that Fichte sees the revival of mankind and its march towards the ideal of perfection, while Rousseau, with a sorrowful resignation, reconciled himself with its agedness. Having posed mankind with the goal of aspiring for reason in freedom (*Vernünftigwerden mit Freiheit*), Fichte a priori deduces from this end point the preceding stages of development, which in regard to their main content must therefore read as follows: the absence of reason, and incomplete reason. At the same time he shows that the history of mankind accomplishes such development in the space of five periods. Does history realise such schema in reality? This question does not exist: it should, it must realise them. Therefore, since the very beginning, there has existed instinctive reason, which man is guided by like an innocent child. Yet in order for the development to be able to commence, this reason must encounter its contradiction. On the other hand, there has also existed right from the beginning a certain brutality of instincts breaking free from all laws of reason. In what way could it have become rational by itself? With Rousseau, one and the same mankind by its very self passes from the state of nature to civilisation. With Herder, as we have seen, every nation has its own appropriate state of nature. With Fichte there exist two separate states of nature appropriate to two different human species: on the one hand, savage sons of the Earth, timorous and uncouth, and on the other – a normal people, Israel in the past, and later, with the awakening of patriotism, Germany for the new times – a nation unwittingly yet perfectly rational, which imposes reason on the savages, and thereby begins the course of the development of reason.[95] This of course resembles the chosen people and the heathen from the Bible; also within it is a reflection of the dualism of Plato's formative idea and $\mu\eta\ ov$;[96] but what mainly strikes us here is the juxtaposition (though not yet reconciliation) of Rousseau's ideal state of nature with Vico's brutal state of nature, whose 'giant heathens' also begin to civilise under threat – and namely under the threat of a divine thunderbolt. The meeting in the minds of these two contradictory notions, an encounter that constitutes an important preparatory stage in the formation of the theory uniting protest against the reigning orders with a historical sense, is altogether characteristic of this historical moment. Schiller, a

---

95   In other expressions the dispute continues to this day between those who acknowledge the self-generated formation of the state within the womb of every people, and those who, like Thierry and today particularly Gumplowicz, cannot grasp it without a preceding conquest [Kelles-Krauz's footnote]. Augustin Thierry (1795–1856) was a French historian; Ludwik Gumplowicz (1838–1909) was a Polish sociologist and lawyer.

96   In English: 'not being' [translator's note].

poet and historian at the same time, as a historian is also unable to agree to the
ideality of original man's existence, and sees it rather as harsh and uncouth,
but as a poet sees the golden age of mankind in artistic Greece.

At the moment of a normal nation's contact with savages, reason rules
through power. The a priori structure develops further: now mankind must
free itself from authority, since it has cast instinct aside, and this through indifference towards all truth, i.e. through a state of total sin. Such is the present
condition. Thanks to a certain socialistic system of management and upbringing a period of taught reason is approaching (such as with Rousseau reason,
once it has suppressed nature, must rebuild natural law on other foundations)
and finally the time will come for artistic reason, just as unimposed from outside, and just as voluntary, as in the period of instinct. Thus the final contradiction disappears: science, as long as it is set against nature it is reconciled with
it in art, in such art about which Kant said that in it man exceeds the limits of
his own nature, which – according to the contemporary Schiller – is the highest morality. Mankind thereby recovered its paradise lost and returned to the
starting point, but how much greater and more noble, as enriched with the
achievements of its entire development! To such a degree that you could say
that for the whole time preceding the rule of artistic reason mankind does not
yet really exist: "it is just the embryo of mankind that time eternal carries in
its womb".[97] Marxists today say that only by man's mastering of the creative
forces, of the works of human hands, at the moment of transition from the
"land of necessity into the land of freedom" will there be an end to the "prehistorical period of mankind", and "the kingdom of the ignorant will be closed"
(Lafargue and others).

With Fichte we already encounter the point of the greatest decline right in
the middle of history, as if a swamp between two hills of unequal height. As for
Schelling, this thought, together with consolidation of the Christian dogma,
explicitly assumes the form of Christ's redemption of sinful mankind, while
with Schlegel, a philosopher of the Holy Alliance, there is an almost total rid-
dance of any non-dogmatic philosophical embellishments. This is because the
philosophical restoration and deposing of licentious individualism begins with
Schelling. The 'I' is not the absolute, because it is in itself insufficient, and for
self-knowledge it must set against itself its 'Not-I'. Besides, the Not-I is also not
the absolute, and for the same reason. The absolute stands above them, and
neither one nor the other yet exists in its womb. Neither is the 'I' an absolute

---

97   *Charakterystyka czasu teraźniejszego* [Characteristics of the present], cited by Fester,
      Richard, 1890, *Rousseau und die deutsche Geschichtsphilosophie*, p. 154 [Kelles-Krauz's
      footnote].

in regard to history; the juxtaposition itself rules out absoluteness. History is something more than the application and reflection of the individual's 'pure philosophy'. "The history of bygone times", says Schelling in his *System of Transcendental Idealism*, "exists for the individual only as a phenomenon of this consciousness..." Yet any individual consciousness is what it is because it belongs to a defined time, which is once again the result of the entire past history. We find a way out of this vicious circle in a higher principle, above the object and subject: in the principle of 'absolute identity'. Respect for the fait accompli is beginning to make a comeback!

So in what manner does a contradiction emerge with such a starting point? As with Plotinus: via emancipation. The first entity beginning to individualise already constitutes evil, but evil is essential for the manifestation of good, like darkness for the light. A return to the absolute is also a good. What degradation of the individual! The latter's very appearance on the stage of mankind and world history is acknowledged as the beginning of evil. The past or a future state, in which the individual does not oppose the whole, is the ideal.

As for nature, so too is mankind drifting ever further away from its ideal centre: from the sameness of opposites. This is also quite naturally why the primitive peoples in antiquity or the savages we know from the accounts of ethnographers have vague recollections of beautiful and greater ancestors. Here we may ascertain a significant step forward in the merging of legend, of 'retrospection',[98] with historical realism: the 'golden age' according to Vico and the golden age of Rousseau are no longer contemporary, as with Fichte, but the ideal precedes the animal. In this manner the savage peoples known to us may be brutal at the moment when we discover them, but this is no obstacle to the true existence of the ideal in the deep, hypothetical past. However, one can also see here that Schelling also needs an ideal, perfect state in the past; he did not go as far as to discern the germs of the ideal state, certain aspects of the ideal, in the brutal state itself of factual and not fictitious primitive peoples.

For Schelling, proper and known history begins from the era of fate, of the fateful play of unknown and invincible forces burdening mankind. Rome inaugurates the era of nature, the reaction of human will, the battle with doom. The era of Providence begins with the Christian Revelation. Unwitting obedience to nature, rebellion against nature, conscious conformity with nature – such

---

98   I shall take the opportunity to point out here that the character of this term, 'retrospection', appears very well in a certain sentence in Kant's *Anthropology*, which says of Rousseau that this is not what he wanted, *dass der Mensch wiederum in den Naturzustand zurückgehen, sondern von der Stufe, auf der er jetzt steht, dahin zurücksehen sollte* [Kelles-Krauz's footnote].

therefore is the cycle of human history. It is heading towards a total reconciliation of freedom with necessity, although never will it be able to reach this ideal.[99] It is easy to recognise what fragments emerged under the influence of Rousseau, Kant and Fichte. We totally avoid the well-known influence of Jakob Böhme, the Silesian cobbler-mystic, influence deriving from the depth of a simple people; after all, a separate study would be required by the question of whether and how the process – out of necessity close to his heart – of decomposition of archaic rural communism, that social state of reconciliation or non-existence of contradictions, affected the mentality of this child of the people, and whether in this case we are dealing with a process of the gradual transformation of the thought of a 'return to nature', testifying to regret for lost economic equality and social calm, into vague theories of a 'return to the womb of God', a process which we observe in antiquity when travelling in our thoughts from Antisthenes and Dicaearchus – to Plotinus.

Going back to Schelling, we already notice with him the thought of the recurrent return of a deity (the original centre from which man broke free and withdrew, the incarnation of Christ, the future reconciliation of contradictions) – although the return is in an ever higher form. "The manifestations of the deity in history" , he says, "do not follow one another in a mechanical gradation, but the same things always return, just in different forms or might, along the lines of a spiral crisscrossed by even lines".[100] Such is the picture so oft repeated since, which then led Goethe to contemplate Vico's *ricorsi*. However, both Schelling and Fichte emphasise above all one great cycle of history, one great reconciliation of contradictions. For Schelling's apprentice, Christian Krause, that remarkable mind whose sublime and most poetic mysticism draws the closest – at least in a historical and social sense – to scientific truth, and of whom Robert Flint verily not without cause said his understanding of worldly and historical processes essentially differed little from Spencer's, the cycle of

---

99   It would seem that one could say that in this spirit Edward Abramowski resolves the issue of the interdependence of the individual and society, about which there are such disputes, and in contemporary sociology, in his beautiful treatise *Les bases psychologiques de la sociologie*. This writer is remarkably engaging for the seeker of analogue between the totality of views of the school of historical materialism and idealistic philosophy. In the brochure constituting a continuation of the above, entitled *Le matérialisme historique et le principe du phénomène social*, he managed to combine the most poetic dreams of the mystics with the most positive deductions of the materialists regarding the sameness of the ideal and reality, regarding the merging of individual freedom with natural necessity in a dazzling future [Kelles-Krauz's footnote].

100   According to the *System der gesammten Psychologie* (1804), cited by Fester, Richard, 1890, *Rousseau und die deutsche Geschichtsphilosophie*, pp. 188–189 [Kelles-Krauz's footnote].

emanation and absorption becomes as it were an internal and omnipresent vibration, the final division of the constant becoming, of the history of the world and mankind.[101] According to Krause, the categories of the entirety, autonomy, and autonomy within the entirety (*Ganzheit, Selbstheit, Ganzvereinselbstheit*) constitute in their constantly recurring succession the essence of the incessant, uninterrupted, and countless cycles of all life. All life is divided into three ages: in the first – a being exists in the state of an embryo contained within some kind of whole or dependent on it; in the second – it differs from the whole, separates from it, opposes it, which is a source of evil and error; in the third – the being is once again reconciled with the whole, it enters a relationship with it, though maintaining its own individuality. This final age is the age of maturity; following this comes the decline, through which the being passes via a sequence of analogous states. Each age may in turn be divided into three subordinate ages. Each of them is preceded by lengthy preparation, yet at the same time none may be explained solely by the past, and each one brings with it something completely new.

Human history breaks down into three main ages: in the initial state, society is weak yet free of dilemma, and remains in relationships with all celestial bodies and with God, intuitively possesses the secrets of nature, but as the pursuit for autonomy, for individualism, intensifies, Providence abandons mankind to its own fate, and discord and divisions appear, the intuition of supernatural things vanishes. The savage peoples that are known to us are already in a quite advanced stage of this degeneration. The second age, the age of growth, is characterised by the destruction of unity in every respect, by the dispersal of the human family, and by the appearance of tribes and peoples, by the division of work, castes and classes. This is split into three small eras: those of polytheism, authoritarian monotheism, and the love of God and people in liberty. The final era happens to be our time, yet the battle is still being fought in it. The mature age in which unity of all returns, with universal solidarity, is approaching; the return to nature and at the same time to God will be completed. The original picture, the prototype of mankind, is not only its ideal, but simultaneously its unavoidable and immanent conclusion. Thus in antiquity did the natural cycle, conniving among the stoics with the thought of a return to nature, also lend the latter the attitude of innate necessity. A new Messianism was born. How many poets and dreamers succumbed to its influence?! Let us recall Charles Fourier, whose series of social states closely resembles the succession of Krause's ages. However, Krause's emanationism was not totally

---

101   Particularly: Krause, Karl, 1851, *Das Urbild der Menschheit*, Dresden: Arnoldischen Buchhandlung; delivered in 1811 [Kelles-Krauz's footnote].

reconciled with the acknowledgment of innovation in the eras of the return to past forms, of mankind moving towards an as yet unprecedented ideal, higher than anything known to the past. The present always did remain a point of collapse, a state of degeneration, lower than the past. After everything that Rousseau did, in order to restore its superiority over the past that had been acknowledged by realists, such as Vico, and thus to clear the way for the notion of a future in which the returning forms of the past truly embraced and contained within them all the acquisitions of the present, it was necessary to turn back to Fichte's thesis – antithesis – synthesis, but to make it the motor of becoming the Object. This was the work of Hegel, who proclaimed – in defiance of Fichte – that "a philosopher does not introduce ideas to history, but finds them in history".

So far we have carried out our main task: we have tracked the development of the historical dialectic, external and objective, in idealistic German philosophy; now we must devote a few words to the parallel development of the logical, internal, subjective dialectic, which – at least in our opinion – only reflects the former, but does not define or cause it. In order to do this we must return to Kant, to his twelve categories split into sets of three. Just as in human history unsociability is reconciled with sociability in justice, likewise in the 'schematism of pure reason' the gulf of contradiction between negation and assertion, that is to say reality (the category of quality), is filled by limitation; that between totality and plurality (the category of quantity) – by unity; between substantiality and causality (the category of relation) – reciprocity; and finally between necessity and possibility (the category of modality) – existence. As we know, these are with Kant purely logical forms of reason's grasp of the outside world. The outside world, conceived, imaginable, the noumenon, does not itself yield to these categories (among others the category of causality) at all. The human 'I' has no influence on it, yet itself shapes – as we can see – its own phenomenal world. However, Kant did not stop at the 'philosophy of pure reason'; in his 'philosophy of practical reason' he released our 'I' from the bonds of logical categories, and subjected it to the force of the 'categorical imperative', incapable of being judged according to the principles of necessity, of phenomenal causality. Fichte's entire pantologistic philosophy is known to have derived from this. As the German bourgeoisie, called upon by the governments themselves to defend and repair the fatherland, grew in social and political importance, as it overcame the external limitations placed upon it by the Prussian monarchy and other feudal governments, so too an appropriate philosophy formed, ensuring the greatest scale of reformative energy, "cutting the coat according to the cloth, not the cloth according to the coat" – the human 'I' also freed itself of limitation by the noumenon and by the categories of understanding. As not subject to the category of necessity, it became a noumenon itself; it opposed the phenomenon, i.e. matter, with action and not thought; only then did the synthesis, the limitation, occur. Schelling, as we mentioned above, deposed the 'I', took away its character of absoluteness, and transferred it again to the area of the outside, the object. He saw the absolute in the original and ultimate sameness of opposites. Hegel broke off from this emanationism, which we also saw in Krause. He considered it impossible for any kind of movement whatsoever, any kind of novelty, to result from sameness, from an absence of opposites, and this is why the Absolute was not a transcendental source of all things for him, but their immanent end, or rather the very process itself was the Absolute, the universal becoming of the world, therefore the common source of both the 'I' and the Not-I. With Fichte, when the 'I' identified in a manner of speaking with the universe, the Kantian categories of pure reason gained more importance than the logical, than the subjective categories; here, with Hegel, the 'I' is not the universe, but has the same nature as the Not-I; the reason in it is the same as in the universe; and so the Kantian categories are already emphatically of significance not only for subjective logic, but also for the objective dialectic of the universe. Their opposition and reconciliation is the same as the course of the theses, antitheses and syntheses in the life of the universe; in learning the 'genealogy of pure concepts' we are at the same time getting to know the process of the becoming of the universe, the Absolute. In this way the twelve types of judgment that were distinguished by scholastic logic, and which were reflected in Kant's categories, become – alongside the sociocritical ideas of a return to nature and a return to God – one of the distant sources of the Hegelian dialectic, which in turn exerted such an influence on Marxism.

We shall recall here, in but a few cursory sentences, what it is in general that this Hegelian dialectic involves, setting aside a closer inspection for a study of its later proponents, and in particular Friedrich Engels. The essence of the Hegelian dialectic is the resolution of the opposition between the content and the phenomenon, between the principle and the consequence, the cause and the effect, the force and the action, the factor and the fact, the content and the form – via the concept of action, the course of things, a process. In action these opposite concepts incessantly pass one into the other, a universal interdependence occurs in the universal variability – and only this leads to the concept of the whole. The subjective whole opposes the objective whole, while the absolute idea, which is the peak of the dialectic development of the concept of existence but which does not exist beyond the wholeness of its manifestations, constitutes their synthesis. The development of Ideas is manifested in the history of mankind; Hegel's dialectic development of humanity takes us closer.

With Hegel we encounter two philosophical-historical constructs: one, the earlier, applies more to the philosophy of religious history, while the second is ultimately fixed on the philosophy of general, social-political history.

The former is of interest to us because it is not actually a 'triad' but a 'tetrachotomy', it comprises four phases. In the first consciousness rules, in other words a simple sensing of the outside world, but not yet its negation or gaining control over it; in the second – self-awareness, which is a turn towards our 'I', and imparts a negative character to the sensed object; in the third – reason, in other words the certainty that one is the entire reality, which once again signifies a positive attitude towards reality; and ultimately in the fourth – the spirit, which admittedly differs from reason only in that the certainty of our reality is raised in it to the might of truth, which in a way makes it objectively considered reason. According to Barth[102] this gradation also reflects the influence of four types of judgment of scholastic logic: quantity – in awareness sensing the multitude of outside objects; quality – because of contradiction – in self-awareness; relation – in reason containing laws; and even the manner – in the phase of the spirit, which involves the certainty that one is the entire reality.

According to Hegel's second main historical-philosophical construct, the essence of the historical process, the immanent goal of history, is becoming aware of freedom (*Bewusstwerden der Freiheit*). From this point of view, there are three main eras in the development of the spirit in the history of mankind: the era of 'substantiality and infinity', that is of the eastern monarchies in which the individual is nothing and has no awareness of freedom; the era of 'individuality and finiteness', or in other words the Greek and Roman world where the blossoming of individualism is brought about by the imperial authority itself through its own abuse; and ultimately Christian Europe, parliamentary monarchy on divine law, in which substantiality is reconciled with its contradiction – individualism, the individual arriving at awareness of their freedom amidst and on the principle of state order. Each of these eras is split into lesser triads. This entire rising of the spirit towards the Absolute takes place within the state and through the state.

The first era obviously has nothing attractive about it. Although the individual is not yet opposing the whole, the whole itself is nothing ideal, and is but a shapeless shell in which the individuum is closed. This is assuredly not the first moment of life of mankind; but the entire life of mankind before the formation of the state, or in other words prior to the beginning of written history, is indifferent for Hegel, and does not preoccupy him at all as it does not belong to

---

102   Barth, Paul, 1890, *Die Geschichtsphilosophie Hegels und der Hegelianer*, Leipzig: O.R. Reisland, pp. 11–12.

history, but only to 'nature', to the field of randomness, because it is "still a non-organic existence of the spirit". Only when man, possessed by brutal passions in this state of nature, recognises in his fellow beings a consciousness similar to his own, and limits his own freedom with their freedom, only then does the existence of the 'objective spirit', which is to say society, begin. As for written history, the state – they only really begin when differences exist between classes, when there is quite a significant gap between the rich and the poor.

Therefore, as we see, the last word of German idealistic philosophy is denial of the golden age in the past. But what is the reason for this? Hegel himself explains: "Because freedom" , he says, "must be won, because it does not involve only negation of pain and evil, because in its essence it is affirmative, while its goods are the goods of the highest consciousness",[103] or in other words – because the original golden age must be devoid of attributes that the spirit of contemporaries longs for and wishes to attribute it with, in the form and degree that might correspond to this spirit. Yet if the future is to be a synthesis, if the present is the antithesis, then there must be the 'thesis' in the past; and because the Idea, reaching higher degrees of its development, never destroys completely the products of the preceding phases, then one has to conclude that the spirit of this thesis endures in the present, and that enhanced with the acquisitions of the present it will blossom again in the future. Establishing development in contradictions must therefore logically lead the successors of Hegelianism to search in the past for the germs of the future ideal.

On the other hand, Hegel ascertains in vain that the Prussian monarchy, "which does not suppress personal freedom as did the Platonic state, but in Protestant religion reconciles the independent freedom of self-awareness with the laws of the state", that this monarchy is the apex and final expression in development of the Absolute Idea. The gradual formation of the Absolute Idea, the dialectic destroying any hardened form – such is his legacy, adopted by his heir – Marxism; and together with it this heir to the entire German idealism inherited this belief of Krause, proclaimed in 1829, and as such in a characteristic moment: "We are living in the first light, not at the hour of twilight!"

---

103   Fester, Richard, 1890, *Rousseau und die deutsche Geschichtsphilosophie*, p. 272.

CHAPTER 3

Comtism and Marxism: Positivism and the Monistic Comprehension of History[1]

I

It is a long, long time now since anything has been written about Comte. In the days of 'Warsaw positivism' he drew much attention, but even then – from a special point of view. The theoretical side of August Comte's philosophy and sociology was of relatively little interest to our positivists of the time; they left us not only without a translation of the master's works, if we omit articles published in journals, of which there were few, but even a general exposition of his teachings; he who fulfilled this duty back then, Bolesław Limanowski,[2] cannot be classed within the camp of the 'Warsaw positivists', and his treatise – as far as I am aware – was not broadly disseminated and made barely a ripple. Our intelligentsia cared not then for philosophical and sociological theory, but rather economic practice; and the popularity of the catchword 'positivism' derived from it having been juxtaposed with political romanticism and economic helplessness, which Comte did not have in mind at all, and not (or at least not above all, as was the case with Comte) with metaphysics in its purely philosophical meaning. The theoretical tackling of certain sciences and a certain philosophy also no doubt corresponded to the era of 'organic work'; but these were the natural sciences and materialistic philosophy. And from the point of view of the natural sciences Comte was already by then doubtlessly outdated and devoid of significance, while from the point of view of Büchner's materialistic philosophy, that sharp, apodictic philosophy resolving all issues, August Comte's positivism may have seemed too bland and relative and could not have achieved such success in an era of battling the opposite – religious – dogma.

Then came the new wave of thought from Europe, bringing us Spencer in place of Comte, with his philosophy and sociology built not on the basis of mainly the physical and mathematical sciences, and that not brought to the

---

1 Source: Comtyzm i marksizm (Pozytywizm i monistyczne pojmowanie dziejów), "Głos" 1904, no. 18, pp. 283–285; no. 19, pp. 299–301; no. 20, pp. 314–315.

2 Limanowski, Bronisław, 1875, *Socyologija Augusta Comte'a*, Lviv: Drukarnia J. Dobrzańskiego i K. Gromana. It would be worth publishing this assiduous work again today [Kelles-Krauz's footnote].

final stage of development as with Comte, but on an impressive foundation of the latest spoils and theories of biology. It would be difficult to define in just a few words the difference between the philosophy of Spencer and that of Comte, while a broad investigation of this topic is not our task right now. Neither have our proponents of Spencer done so. We shall only point out a few of the most important points: the exchange of Comte's positivism for agnosticism – an exchange seemingly insignificant, that could pass by unnoticed, yet as a matter of fact very deep and momentous, and – in our opinion – setting human thought backwards, since instead of a simple repudiation of the search for the 'first causes' we have here a dogmatic justification of this abstinence through the acknowledgement of something Unknowable beneath the world of phenomena, opening the gates to mystical speculations; furthermore, apart from the paper mentioned above and the usage of biology, the elaboration and usage also of psychology, an area brushed aside by Comte; and in sociology itself – development of the thought only suggested by Comte of the 'social organism', although – and here, in our opinion, is the most fundamental difference – with Spencer the stance of the critical individual, unleashed but also left to his own fate, is quite the opposite in relation to society than with Comte, where 'mankind', a 'Great Being', not only moulds and creates every individual right down to its very deepest corners, not only looks after it but at the same time rules over and wants to rule over the individual's mind, yet unconditionally demands from them the sacrificing of all their thoughts, feelings and interests.

A third ideological wave reached us together with Spencer. In setting itself social issues to resolve, 'economic materialism' did not shift the centre of gravity of its contemplations beyond society, did not investigate the laws of gravitation or the life of organisms in order to transfer them directly to the science of society, but based this science on the genuine energy and social biology that economics is. From this point of view this theory could have been called social positivism. This is not syllogistic sociology deduced from the theory of the world and life constructed beforehand and supposedly altogether objectively, but sociology – and nothing more than sociology – beneath which there obviously also lies a certain general manner of grasping the entirety of the phenomena of the world and life. The creators of economic materialism also elaborated much more consistently than Comte the thought that philosophy today is not the 'queen of sciences' raised above them, ruling them and independent of them, preceding them, but is something mobile, variable, fluid, contained within each separately and in all individual sciences together, and which only now has to be extracted from them, crystallised, formulated. Considering themselves economists and sociologists, they did not feel appointed for this generalising activity, and they fulfilled it rather forced by circumstance, by some kind of challenge, such as Dühring.[3] However, it is quite natural that this work – of tying Marxism with a certain general philosophy and formulating the latter – proceeds slowly from here, via various techniques, and with varied success. In our opinion, defining how the theory under consideration relates to various others, past and contemporary, belongs to this work and has an important role to play. Therefore, once this ideological wave gains ever greater significance in the intellectual life of our society as well as all others, when this economic materialism is elaborated ever further, and when interest in theoretical studies finally awakes and spreads among us, then we believe that it will be high time for contemplating the philosophy and above all the epochal sociology of Comte in relation to economic materialism.

If we still have those faithful to and in favour of Comte's theory, they will probably meet this new sociology with the same reluctance displayed by Comtists abroad, mainly in France, during hearings regarding economic materialism at congresses and in sociological associations.[4]

At first glance this may be surprising, but it is in fact totally natural. After all, August Comte himself, with his characteristic depth of thought, observed that 'only what is exchanged changes'; or – if we want to explain more precisely, without resorting to proverbial phrases – one can only destroy something when this something is replaced; and so in the victory march of positivism, in the history of its conquest of all fields of contemporary thought, monistic sociology is the first and only opponent encountered by positivism that knows how to wield the same weapon, to rely on the same principles, and to satisfy – though in a more perfect manner – those same, unreflected needs. Being the heir to positivism, it had to become its enemy; and this is only applying one of the aphorisms of Comte, who at the same time agrees totally with the revolutionary spirit of the dialectic.

This reluctance sometimes reaches very far. After all, a certain brilliant writer did not hesitate to call Comte a 'degenerate and reactionary pupil of Saint-Simon': a flagrant contradiction with that truly filial, deep respect he has for another reactionary – Hegel; he too was overtaken by the monists, but they do not throw invectives at him. Yet, in the matter of philosophical restoration characterising the first half of the 19th century, did Comte not play a similar role for France as Hegel for Germany, and does his philosophy contain fewer elements capable of a dialectic transformation into revolutionary elements?

---

3   Friedrich Engels polemicised with his views in *Anti-Dühring: Herr Eugen Dühring's Revolution in Science* [Kelles-Krauz's footnote].

4   Compare the opinions of E. Delbet and A. Coste in "Revue de Sociologie", 1899, and in "Annales de l'Institut International de Sociologie", 1902 [Kelles-Krauz's footnote].

We shall deal with the investigation of this issue below; anyhow, one thing is absolutely certain, that historical monism owes Comtism nothing directly, that Comtism played no special direct role in its genealogy. It is arguably a positive sociology *par excellence*; but historical monism drew that positivism, that historical realism, those attributes opposing static rationalism and the ardour for a pure political form of the 18th century, directly from other sources and developed them entirely independently, just like Comtism, but in addition incorporating two fundamental elements: monism and dialecticism, brought to the final consequences, bequeathed to it by Hegelianism, which itself was the heir to and crown of the entire German idealism.

This is why social monism really was not the son of Comtism, and never did it want to be considered such. It even forgot that, ultimately, they were brothers: the sons of a single father, but of different mothers, born in different eras of community evolution. For the Marxists, Comte's students could then have been as it were stepbrothers; a handful of them, forming an extreme positivistic left wing similar to the Hegelian left, later also approached historical monism in a brotherly fashion. One of the most brilliant and best known of them is Wilhelm De Greef, author of *Social Transformism*, and rector of the New University of Brussels;[5] if these examples are scarce, this is because there are altogether few to have retained the name positivist Comtist in the full meaning of this expression, since they formed a kind of dogmatic church incapable of advancement.

Yet beyond these, as Lévy-Bruhl rightly observed, "Comte's philosophy is still functioning and flourishing even among those who fight it"; and the overall atmosphere of science generated by it, "which is breathed like the air, paying it no attention", is most definitely conducive to the development and spread of economic monism.

Above all this is because one of the most fundamental components of this atmosphere of positivism is the most precise social determinism as well as the grasp of the individual's relationship with society, the role of individuals in the march of mankind, entirely consistent with monism. Familiar is Comte's maxim that the individual should be explained by society, and not vice versa – society by the individual. A single person is, for Comte, an abstraction, as this person's entire intellectual and moral repertory derives from society, because from the very beginning the social state, and namely the family, was the natural state of man. We are people only through our participation in mankind. In the actions and thoughts of every one of us, the sum of actions of the past and the society surrounding us is expressed. Even science, that crown of human activity, is the collective work of mankind, the fruit of the shared action of

---

5   Université Nouvelle [translator's note].

all people, of the entire nation. Contrary to the rationalist aristocrats, Comte revives the beautiful and fertile tradition of Vico, who in many respects was his predecessor; his 'deep identification of scholars with the active whole' is equivalent to the 'discovery' by the Neapolitan scholar of the 'true Homer', meaning the people. His wonderful theory of speech and art, which he considers the work and intrinsic property of the entire people, also constitutes a continuation of the theory by the author of *The New Science*; it completes in, enriches it with a modern attribute: the demand and announcement of democratic art close to social life; economic monism has here a valuable source of arguments against those who strive to deprive social development of the attributes of unity and collectiveness, aggrandizing the factor of individual inventiveness and making it independent of all laws; nay, some even say 'the caprice of the individual', precisely in these fields: because by being still the least investigated and elaborated from a monistic point of view, they are the most suitable for these anti-deterministic variations. As for the role that individuals have, then not having Vico's faith in Providence that guides mankind, Comte was able to contemplate and define it entirely the same as done by monism. He said that the individual may only develop effective activity in the direction of 'progress', i.e. general social development, that great people seem to be but managers of society, while in fact they are only the first to yield to each collective evolution; this barely propounds all new issues, and only places them distinctly before human awareness when the means and manner of resolving are also given; in general, from a static point of view a person may only change the intensity, while from a dynamic point of view – the speed of social phenomena. But by limiting in this way the momentousness and very ability for individuals to take action, Comte by no means intended to contradict it; on the contrary, he placed identical emphasis on both sides of the statement given above, and namely that the march of mankind takes place in individuals and through individuals. The individual is only a crossing point of social forces, but social forces may only function through and on individuals in whom the products of other social forces meet. If, according to the concept of Comte's natural law, the entire order of the world is only a 'fickle necessity', then all the more so society, being very complex and thereby less perfect, may and should be changed, but can only be changed via the action of individuals. A very powerful, very resolute and very idealistic ethics flows from here, rejecting any indeterminism, but also any fatalism and quietism, verily no less full of contempt for egoists, those 'creators of manure', than the romantic calling of Mickiewicz's *Ode to youth*, leading man to a 'sublime revolution': to devote one's entire life to future generations – an ethics equally beautiful and certain while at the same time equally scientific and poetic as the ethics of stoicism and one other realistic doctrine, seemingly dry and hopeless ... When one reads a defence of the 'monistic understanding of history' written by Engels and then by those who never succumbed to the direct influence of Comte, such as Mehring, then in the matter of so-called fatalism, anti-individualism and 'amorality' or immorality of doctrine, one encounters deductions entirely similar to Comte's.

Admittedly, this similarity not only occurs between Comtism and Marxism. Undoubtedly there is not only some kind of general analogy between these two doctrines on this point, but almost a sameness, even reaching as far as a sameness in terminology; but the concepts of social determinism, of the dependence of individuals' actions on collective laws, and even the concept of individual and idealistic, conditioned morality, by no means ruled out by this determinism itself, is accepted today not only by sociologists as a whole almost without exception, but even by the larger portion of historiographers. However, some among the latter are still rebelling. Even when they are permeated by the scientific and positive spirit, it bizarrely seems to them that this spirit requires the evasion of generalisations, being content with the minutiae, and the denial of laws of history. After all, a certain brilliant historian, permeated – as he says about himself – with a 'liberal, secular, democratic and western spirit' (the reader here has recognised Seignobos) ended his *A Political History of Contemporary Europe*, recently published, with the following astonishing passage: "The revolution of 1830 was the work of a group of unknown republicans, who were helped by the inexperience of Charles x; the revolution of 1848 – the work of a few democratic agitators, who took advantage of the sudden fright of Louis Phillippe i; and the war of 1870 – the personal work of Bismarck, prepared by the peculiar policy of Napoleon iii". For these three unanticipated cases we find no general cause in the intellectual, political, or economic condition of the European continent. Three events determined the political development of contemporary Europe!

This abhorrence for generalisations, and exaggeration of the role of individuals, is not an individual case either; it flows from the instinctive fear that generalisations and laws will lead to the discovery at the bottom – of a resolving factor which unreflected leads mankind further – towards a future undesirable for the bourgeois historian; this is why his reluctance is aimed specially against the 'monistic' grasp of history.

Because today as well, in the fight against indeterminism in history, first place is occupied by monism and not Comtism, and sometimes, as we shall see further on, monism must call upon positivism and its proponents to fully and staunchly respect the principles of determinism, must resist the inclination incompatible with this principle yet almost irresistible, of placing the centre of gravity at the intellectual peak, in people of providence.

II

Let us take into account here another, closer, and singular similarity between Comtism and economic monism, namely the classification of social phenomena into a certain number of layers rising one above the other in an order dependant on the degree of declining prevalence and increasing complexity. Admittedly, we emphasise in advance that Comte applies this classification strictly and totally only to a certain category of social phenomena – to the sciences; in the meantime, in the womb of the new school, first of all Engels, totally independently of Comte, sketched out a succession of social phenomena, the higher rungs of which are defined by those lower down, while the first rung conditioning all others is the manner of production; this system was later better developed by a scholar-systematician who emerged from the left wing of positivism, De Greef; he accepted unequivocally, even retaining the terminology, the Comtean criterion of declining prevalence and increasing complexity, proclaiming the dependence of higher phenomena on the lower in the following order: economic, familial, artistic, intellectual, moral, legal and political phenomena. The order of the rungs in this series (with the exception of the first – the economic) is not fundamental; that proposed by De Greef does not necessarily have to be accepted by the monists, and we ourselves have proposed a different order.[6] However, what strikes the eye here is a sort of direct kinship at this point between Comtism and monism. De Greef passed with ease from positivism to economic determinism, and in broadening positivism in this way he believed, not without reason, that he was remaining loyal to it. That attribute of prevalence serving as the foundation for the classification of the sciences is indeed known not to be purely logical with Comte, but it actually signifies a certain relationship of dependencies: namely, any science may develop and even manifest itself in a 'positive form', meaning as a proper science, only at the moment and to the extent when the state of development of the science immediately lower and preceding, more general and less complex, allows this and demands it. On the other hand, Comte also considered other social phenomena, not only scientific, from this point of view, and even all cosmic phenomena in general: namely according to him the 'more subtle' among these phenomena, i.e. the more complex, are dependent in terms of the conditions of their existence on the 'common' ones, i.e. simply those that are more general. Admittedly, in regard to the spiritual phenomena of mankind, Comte

---

6   1st – Economics; 2nd – Morality and law: of ownership, family, and power; 3rd – Science and
    art; philosophy and religion. See the paper at the 4th Sociological Congress [Kelles-Krauz's
    footnote].

has them dependent on our 'organisation' and on our 'situation', which on the one hand should signify direct biological phenomena, and on the other – the period of development of science through which we pass, and the entirety of the civilisation dependent on mankind's spiritual phenomena; just like 18th century philosophy, the creator of positivism did not fully realise the primary significance of technology standing between the biological environment and man, and thereby becoming the nucleus of the crystallising of the whole of civilisation. Yet despite this, Comte many a time stresses the close connection between science, even the most sublime, and the elementary needs of human life. Opponents of economic monism, bent on proving its error and keen on protecting the 'noble independence' of the human mind from its 'brutal attacks', put forward as their final argument the innate, natural and primal curiosity from which the germs of relationships between man and nature, neither economic nor related to production, must have resulted right at the very beginnings of mankind. Comte treats this 'inborn curiosity' as it deserves; in his opinion, it is one of the secondary and later inclinations, one playing a very insignificant role in the first forming of the beginnings of science compared to utilitarian factors such as hunting, war, or in general the fundamental 'desire to avoid suffering and death', which as anybody would admit, after all, means exactly the same as Lippert's 'care for life' (*Lebensfürsorge*), as the production of usefulness. In specific cases Comte knows perfectly well, for example, that mathematics was given birth to by the art of measuring applied for the first time in dividing up land, and also understands, although does not express in precisely these words, that alchemy was the first attempt at creating a science applied to industry and intended for satisfying the emerging economic needs. And in general, far from believing in the Olympian impassivity of science, Comte always saw its deliberate connection to the needs of human life and its origin from the respective art or craft. At the same time Comte no doubt maintains that although science is utilitarian in its genesis and its goal, the condition for its development is the greatest possible forgetting of this origin, and particularly of this utilitarian goal, becoming a 'pure science', a goal for itself and in itself; and to confirm this he quotes such a striking example: steering ships in open sea would be impossible if not for the abstract and selfless speculations by geometricians in the field of celestial mechanics. However, one cannot consider this thought inconsistent with economic monism, or foreign to it. Engels already writes broadly and at length about this essential independence that science is acquiring. Let us also take this opportunity to observe that Józef Karol Potocki, in linking Spencer and Guyau, provided an aesthetic theory permeated with the same spirit entirely; in his opinion art always has a utilitarian beginning and purpose, but it only truly begins when all awareness of that element of usefulness has evaporated, when art has become a goal in itself. Generally speaking, the fundamental assertions of economic monism include the one that social 'forms', scientific, artistic, legal, political and others, dependent in their emergence on the social 'content' that is ultimately economic, acquire a certain independence once having emerged and formed, and this grows to the extent that a specific form is further-removed from the base, thereby succumbing to its influence more indirectly, via the mediation of a larger sequence of links; thanks to this acquired independence, the social superstructure temporarily resists changes in the base, and even if it is the furthest removed from it and ostensibly indifferent, it affects the fundamental phenomena.

According to Comte, sociology – the highest of the sciences – could only emerge at a certain quite high degree of development in biology, but once having shown up, itself it only supplements and only can supplement biology in the broadest and highest sense of this word; likewise according to the monists economic growth conditions the political and legal forms, but since only the growth of production adequately prepared the ground for the new law, only the formulation and implementation of this new law can bring about further economic development. Thus one can see – and he who reads the writings of Labriola sheds any doubt on the matter – that the monists acknowledge and proclaim the unity of development and social life, the mutual interdependence of all categories of social phenomena, with an equal if not greater force and clarity than Comte, since he thought that its prevailing factor, 'intellectual evolution', would ultimately also be conceivable without any others, and that the most general phenomena influence others while not succumbing themselves to their mutual influence. Economic monists declare a strict and deep clarity of society, but lead their monism to the consequence that is appropriate for them and that sets them apart from positivists and other sociologists: namely, they also proclaim unity in the general lever of society, claiming that social development is subject to the conclusive direction of the development of means of production to which all social movements may ultimately be reduced to. And if the positivists reproach us, saying that every transition from one row of phenomena to the next is an 'enriching of reality', demanding its own law; that the differences occurring between various categories of phenomena are qualitative, and that qualitative differences, despite the assertions of the Hegelians, cannot be boiled down to quantitative differences and as such higher phenomena cannot be reduced to lower ones, but at the most one may express the latter via the former; that therefore economic monism makes the glaring mistake of ordinary materialism, wishing to explain mental functions via 'corporeal' functions – then by no means negating the rightness and usefulness of special and partial laws, acknowledged as such in advance for every single field of phenomena, without entering just now into the dispute regarding the great abstraction of the Hegelian dialectic and not even tackling at all the accusation made to psychological materialism, our answer is that it is not about all that at all, since all social phenomena – whether economic, philosophical or artistic – are of one and the same psychological nature, and as such may be reduced to another, and that besides in the practice of sociological research – to reduce the political or religious superstructure to the economic foundation, or to express some kind of economic novelty through novelty in the superstructure – basically means one and the same. Therefore, in his practice, August Comte repeatedly voiced thoughts totally consistent with monism in regard to the meaning of the economic factor as well as specific dialectic of social development. For example when he describes the great social transformation that prepared the way for the modern society, the disintegration of the mediaeval system, he sees perfectly that this disintegration began with the homestead, and distinctly emphasises that economic evolution must precede aesthetic and scientific evolution, that the basis of a modern society's system is economic, and that this is the main attribute distinguishing this society from others. Comte also said that critical doctrines may only appear when the disintegration has reached a certain point, and that doctrines may only form at all, and above all float to the surface and exert an influence, when there is conducive social ground for this to happen.

He understood well that the raison d'être of any critical doctrine, for example the doctrine of the absolute right of the individual, is to serve as a weapon for forces striving under the pressure of economic conditions for disintegration of the former system, or in other words he well-nigh discovered the doctrines' class character of these forces; he knew that following the passage of this period of social development, they too must collapse.

However, they resist, and in general not only doctrines but institutions strive to endure for longer than the time ordained for them by the general march of the human spirit, and I say – for longer than their social usefulness and conformity with the economic foundation; they have a yearning for becoming relics. Hence the necessity of revolutions. Comte, in general, understands well their necessity and their legitimacy.

He is assuredly a realist; the principle of the conditions of existences tells him that everything that is essential is unavoidable, and that everything that has happened, that exists, since it was not excluded, is therefore essential; this thought is similar to Hegel's: *Alles, was ist, ist vernünftig;*[7] but for Comte ultimate perfection does not flow from the fact of existence, and according to him one should by no means identify 'the scientific autogenous order with the

---

7   From the German: Everything that is, is reasonable.

systematic defence of all existing order'. On the contrary, he sees a 'concrete dialectic of the intellectual history of mankind' in the fact that every condition through which mankind passes before reaching a pure positive state (as this constitutes an exception), and so both the original theological condition and the intermediate metaphysical conditions, contain within themselves the germ of their own disintegration, an internal contradiction, which man with his fundamental need for unity cannot bear, with his constant aspiration for 'perfect logical accord'; under the influence of this highest factor, every subsequent period removes temporarily the contradictions of the previous. In a word, Comte knows that the 'present is replete with the past and burdened with the past', and therefore there exist truths only relative, only temporary, which slowly, through the constant planting of new meanings, 'transpositions', and former meanings falling out of use, cease to be truths in relation to the general conditions of the social environment and give way to other truths, which become truths. All this is strikingly resemblant of concepts and even expressions that Hegelianism suggested to others, and which were developed and defined more precisely mainly by Kautsky.

This profound and all-penetrating dialecticism common to positivism and economism meant that both these doctrines came up against an entirely identical accusation from the Kantians: they say that both lack a theory of cognition, that one and the other neglect or even downright ignore the critical issue of the relationship between subject and object. And the interesting thing is that both doctrines have an almost identical answer to this accusation: 'proud *autarkoumen*'[8] – man is sufficient in himself.

Professor Lévy-Bruhl clearly demonstrated how greatly this accusation, insofar as it applies to positivism, is unjustified and testifies to a misunderstanding of the leading thought of August Comte's philosophy. August Comte proved the impossibility of supplying the subject that is learning with anything, even the most elementary qualities, that they could use in relation to the object that is being learned; he proved that this subject is absolutely beyond the limits of our observational and defining activity – and he used for this aim arguments very similar to those we encounter with Edward Abramowski, when he speaks of the 'intuitive self'.[9] Therefore the relativity of Comte's knowledge is

---

8   A combination of the words 'autarky' and 'noumenon' [translator's note].

9   Abramowski, Edward, 1897, *Les bases psychologiques de la sociologie* (*Principe du phénomène social*), Paris: V. Giard, E. Brière; in Polish: *Podstawy psychologiczne socjologii* (*Zasada zjawiska społecznego*) 'Ateneum' 1896, vol. IV, pp. 242–287; the text in 'Ateneum' with minor alternations for censorship [Kelles-Krauz's footnote].

by no means based, as with Kant and his students, on the acknowledgement of things in themselves, of some kind of 'unknowable', some logical earlier and invariable limits to the human mind. On the contrary, Comte is convinced that we can get to know everything that we really need to get to know, and that beyond the borders of our ability to discover there is nothing that would have any value for us whatsoever, that they are issues that in reality are non-existent. Because deep down in every issue to have stood before us there absolutely must lie something that influences our being in any way whatsoever; and this thing only takes on an existence for us through this influence. Therefore we discover an object in its entirety as it reveals itself to us; and the manner in which we discover it is defined by the consequence of the appearance of objects within the limits of our existence, and we may observe and investigate it only within the objective intellectual history of mankind, that concrete universal 'subject', but not with the assistance of the deceptive internal observation of some kind of abstract subject. Thus it is striking that professor Labriola, that monist who spoke so harshly of August Comte, when striving to defend himself from the same accusation voiced by proponents of a return to Kant proclaiming a crisis, occupies the same position and uses almost the same phrases: "everything that is knowable may be discovered and everything that is knowable will indeed be discovered ad infinitum, while what is beyond the knowable in regard to discovery matters not a thing to us ... We gradually get to know what we need to know ... discovering is for us important to the degree in which we truly are given to discover, and it is pure delusion to presume that the mind somehow acknowledge a truly existing absolute difference between the cognisable and that which per se is unknowable – unknowable, about which I state that I have come to know as unknowable!" A distinguished Russian author polemicised in a similar manner with the neo-Kantian Konrad Schmidt. The philosophy that lies at the basis of economic monism, that 'philosophy of the deed', is defined aptly and deeply by Labriola as a 'pursuit' of monism; however, this term 'pursuit' signifies the mind adjusting to the conviction that everything may be conceived as a genesis, and moreover, that what is conceivable is only a genesis; that a genesis possesses in approximation the attributes of continuity.[10] Our monist's 'genetic method residing within things themselves' probably seems to us bolder and more consistent than with Comte; one can see there the influence of Hegelianism 'put on its feet'; however, the dialectic character is basically the same in both, while the accord in such a matter seems to me, I shall say again, striking.

---

10   Labriola, Antonio, 1912, *Socialism and Philosophy*, Chicago, IL: C.H. Kerr.

III

The accord bursts, and Comte's pursuit of monism is upset at the moment when the dialectic motor is held in check.

We shall review Comte's contradictions regarding the role of the intellectual factor, contradictions similar in form and character to those which, on a different occasion and in regard to the kindred issue of inventions or novelties, we have demonstrated in another founder of the sociological school, that original and shrewd idealist thinker Gabriel Tarde.[11] We have seen that economic development had to precede scientific and artistic development, and therefore also the development of institutions, because in addition according to Comte politics is based on morality, and morality on philosophy. Meanwhile, in other passages, more fundamental, he says that institutions depend on customs, and customs in turn on beliefs; that resolving a social issue requires prior mastery of the new philosophy; and that altogether the 'leading thread' in the philosophy of history is the development of intelligence, that this is the most important factor on which all others depend, and which would ultimately be understandable on its own even without others. We have seen how deep and valuable Comte's thoughts are regarding the beginnings of mankind, regarding the initial relationship between concern for existence and science, regarding the autogenous emergence of speech. Comte, just like the monists, deals with the great issue of the transition from animal existence to mankind. He asserts that higher organisms are altogether better at resisting changes in external conditions, while people are the best at this of all the animals; he ascertains that enormous and sudden 'enriching of reality' or, as Weisengrün says, that "sudden and one-of-a-kind transformation of quantitative differences into qualitative", which occurs at the transition from the animal kingdom to humanity; and finally he asks himself the following fundamental question: "Why with such a small difference in the organs is there such a significant difference in the actions?" This all testifies to Comte having taken the road that led the monists to the beautiful and deep, though very simple, solution to the puzzle: that we consider the tools of production (and defence) artificial extensions of natural organs, as a miraculously malleable and self-improving armour that shields the human organism from the effects of the natural environment, changes it and adapts it according to man's comfort, and in this way almost relieves this organism from the necessity to make biological changes in order to adjust itself to the environment. We must stress that Comte was very close to

11   See: Kelles-Krauz, Kazimierz, 1902, *Pojęcie przeciwieństwa u Tarde'a*, 'Przegląd Filozoficzny' 2, pp. 168–183.

this solution, raising – though admittedly in a totally different train of thought and with a different goal – the tools' social character, which we consider an attribute distinguishing the human race. Were he to have taken this road further, placing this thought in the foundation of his sociology, then his concepts of the advantage that intellectual and moral actions specially acquire in the life of mankind, liberating themselves from the prevalence of animal and organic factors, they would have nothing in them contradicting determinism and monism and would in a certain respect be similar to that dialectic idea that in the future, when as a result of establishing society's conscious mastery of the manufacturing forces the 'prehistorical era of mankind' comes to an end, man will break free of the shackle of things, and pass as it were from the 'kingdom of necessity' to the 'kingdom of freedom'. But at its very foundation, August Comte's philosophy strays from the genuinely positive road and begins walking on its head. The resolute step from animality to humanity was taken not when the first tools were created socially, but on the day when man's mind passed from fetishism to astral god! In our opinion the creation of the first tools really did take man beyond the entire animal kingdom, while according to Comte this was done by the first great 'creation of the gods'! This suggests that religion is the foundation of any human society, and that the cycle of human history visible to the eye has no border posts within certain forms of production, but stretches from autogenous original religion to proven ultimate religion.

Ultimate – here lies the entire secret of the contradiction, where once again lies the fundamental similarity between Comte and Hegel. Each of these two thinkers had to have something ultimate, had to apply the dialectic of history to the past only, and halt at the point acknowledged as the peak of the rise of mankind: for one this peak was the Prussian monarchy – justified by Hegel; for the other, positive religion – proven by Comte. Comte, that merciless critic of doctrines of the past and even acknowledging the legitimacy of revolutions – does not hesitate to declare firmly that at the moment when society is finally ordered on the principle of positive religion, doubting this order or this religion will not be allowed. They will assuredly be established in a way none other than following unconstrained investigation and thorough discussion, after the consent of all is obtained, but afterwards it will never be possible to withdraw this consent, and apart from this the preceding investigation will not be able to be conducted by the people as a whole, but only by competent people, to whom others will transfer their highest right of investigation freely, voluntarily, convinced of their own incompetence. Positivism must unconditionally eliminate 'acrimonious discussion', the incessant rebellion of individual reason, that has already brought about the disintegration of so many social systems. The government, entrusted not only with the material interests of members of society but also their spiritual lives, will have the duty of guarding over this order, such that after the establishing of harmony there would no longer be new internal strife.

Comte is already imposing this obligation of organising on the present. He is revolting against the bourgeois economists who to the suffering of the people answer only with the 'merciless pedantry' of their all-too obviously self-interested dogma of non-intervention. In this and in his entire revulsion for the plutocracy and the anarchic condition of today's society, he is moving close to monism; and today, when the thought that some kind of revolution could in a single moment change all social relations deriving from the system of ownership has long been abandoned, the thought against which Comte rebelled in the name of a 'positive way of thinking', today, who knows, perhaps he too would call himself a monist – at least of the 'new method', as so many others suffused with Comte's spirit. In any case, he deserves respect for the courage and acumen with which he unveiled the spirit of the bourgeoisie, even foretelling their abandonment of Voltaireanism and reconciliation with dogmatic Catholicism – 'that true basis of the system, defended by it'. Yet still there is an entire abyss between Comte and monism. Concerned with the ideals of Bonald and de Maistre, he participated in the reaction of minds against the evil forces and the incompleteness of the bourgeois revolution being content with the change in forms, but he did not grasp this reaction as did others who wished to add to the revolution, drawing all organisational, creative and positive consequences from it, and he made do with criticising the bourgeois system – above all and mainly for its instability, leaving the bodies and, more importantly, the spirits of the proletariat in a state of 'vagabondage and camping'; and excited with adoration for the Middle Ages, he desired to resurrect their organisation, though without the theology. He no doubt wanted to regulate the execution of the right of ownership, seeing in it – more or less as Saint Thomas Aquinas, a social function and not a ruthless natural law, but at the same time he resolutely defended it against attacks by 'mad sectarians'. Comte defended ownership and the inheritance of property because, above all, he was attached heart and soul to the bourgeois family, and wished it to be retained unchanged. Here the stamp of class worn by his system, just like any other, is at its most obvious, at its brightest. This is that thought taken in advance, serving for the whole system as the subconscious core of crystallisation; we have here that utilitarian rationale of that system, as of any, a rationale that later forgotten and mainly totally lost from sight, allows all deep and lofty arguments lending August Comte's philosophy so much beauty, but which – though invisible – is always present, makes itself noticed and appears in phrases and at the crossroads, and a thought, which is always considered free, guards against taking the descent of dangerous conclusions at the cost of contradiction.

Yes indeed, at the cost of contradiction. Because Comte, who as a principle of sociology set the overall evolution of societies, never even posed himself the issue of evolution of the family.[12]

According to Comte, it was to woman that the role of moral soothsayer befell, the role of man's emotional guide, but she was not even allowed to be on a par with man in regard to intellectual activity; such a purpose for woman derived from the philosopher's deepest feelings, feelings he shared with his class. In keeping with these feelings, Comte considered the bourgeois family, the kind that existed in his day and which had also existed, admittedly, through a number of centuries without major change, as the natural, unchanging and inviolable basis of any social existence; he was opposed to even the most modest form of divorce. For justification of the immobility of such an important social factor, it was essential to assume that this factor corresponded to the original, primary and immutable qualities of man, and essential to think up some kind of 'fundamental nature of man'. Comte also genuinely believes in it; but of course he does not reach this demand along the deliberate road that we have outlined here in the most general of terms, but the deep and sincere feelings instilled in him by the economic and legal milieu secretly lead his thought and suggest the rationale of pure and sublime systematic philosophy, absolutely selfless rationale, like that perfect correspondence of the static and dynamic stance. This correspondence requires that the entire evolution of man be explainable by his original physical and spiritual build, that it develop like the curve fully contained in the equation representing it, that nothing absolutely

---

12　I know that this assertion is considered by Comte's followers untrue. They answer that Comte knew perfectly of the existence of polygamy and allowed for change to and improvement in contemporary marriage. Yes, marriage, but not family, is our answer to this, and by no means is it a random usage of the first of the two terms above in that passage of *Cours de philosophie positive* (vol. 4, pub. 1893, p. 445), where he says of them "inevitable changes". The limits to Comte's concept of the development of family are given in the following passage: "The fundamental spirit of the institution of family is based on that unavoidable, natural submission of woman to man, which reoccurs in all ages of civilisation, though in various forms, as an unobliterated attribute, and which new political philosophy manages ultimately to defend from any serious anarchic attack" (*Cours de philosophie positive*, vol. 4, p. 445). This is obviously not evolution in the proper meaning of the word, because it excludes forms that are shared or free, matriarchal or feminist, ascertained by contemporary ethnology in the human past [Kelles-Krauz's footnote].

new appear throughout the history of mankind, nothing that *in potentia* did not already exist in the fundamental nature of man.

And so thanks to this requirement for pure logical symmetry, which entails an entire sequence of consequences also logically pure, the entirety and changelessness of the ideal family is even better protected, and no longer can anything take it by surprise, there can be no unexpected attack.

On the other hand, when having such a precious treasure to defend, who would expose it to the mercy of dependence on 'the most brutal phenomena of social life', economic phenomena, changes in the tools and means of production, and in the division of riches, etc.? The brutality of these phenomena is manifested in the march forwards, constant, uninterrupted, just as human striving for greater productivity is unceasing, and simultaneously – blind. Never does one know what this march may call forth along the way, how 'vicious' its consequences may be and what harm they may cause to that philosopher's treasure, which also fears it, obscurely, unconsciously. In the meantime, the evolution of 'higher' factors, and in particular the intellectual factor, which namely is considered irrespective of the guiding influence of the economic factor, is after all always only more or less an arbitrary development in time of the logical, unchanging definition of so-called human nature, thanks to which one can always anticipate what will happen, and one knows what to expect and what to avoid. The intellectual factor always fulfils what it has committed itself to, what it has been obligated to. Therefore the philosopher entrusts the boat of evolution, bearing this inviolable Holy of the Holy, to its purposeful, conscious and certain direction, and not to the uncertain and deep waves of the economic ocean. Hence, whenever we encounter an unvarying rationalist concept of human nature, even if only under the neo-Kantian form of the 'category of understanding', we can be certain that here deep down is a more or less conservative social-systemic idea, or at least an ethical idea 'entrenched in the nature of man' (Friedrich Albert Lange), which must be defended, or some kind of 'eternal justice'. And always in such cases, whether we are dealing with the idealist Fichte or the positivist Comte, or even to a certain degree with Jaurès, who sees in history the 'unceasing protest of man against the inhuman usage of man', actual history is corrected deductively by conclusions drawn from the 'nature of man'. And Comte also believes that the historical method in sociology must be controlled by 'the positive theory of human nature' – although previously he claimed that one cannot practice history deductively. The irony of fate goes significantly further; it has been demonstrated (Lévy-Bruhl), that for Comte as mankind passes from the object of research that he was at the beginning to become the object of religious love, the social equilibrium changes slightly to the image of future mankind; even the title itself reads: "an abstract treatise on the order of mankind"; the possession of the definition 'unchanging human nature' inevitably leads Comte, that disdainful opponent of the utopians, to build his own utopia ... And only monistic sociology, in which the concept of human nature is absolutely and exclusively dynamic, because this nature creates and transforms itself constantly by the very fact of exchange with the environment, which represents the satisfying of man's needs – only this sociology allows for the avoidance of the above contradictions, and in this manner upholds the banner of positivism, and takes it to all logical consequences – sometimes despite August Comte himself.

A Glance at the Development of Sociology in the 19th Century[1]

Wallace called the 19th century the 'Age of miracles', and to support this laudatory name quoted an entire range of impressive and truly miraculous advancements in human thought accomplished in the course of the century, above all in technology and in the natural sciences most closely related to technology. At the close of his treatise, rendered into Polish in the supplement to 'Prawda',[2] this English thinker drew attention to the social system, to the way in which people used the abundance of treasures acquired, and having discerned the glaring disharmony occurring between the accumulation and deliberate ordering of great and useful new developments on the one hand, and disintegration, destruction and chaos on the other, he ended almost with his lips delivering the words: monstrous age!

A friend of Darwin, Wallace did not include sociology in the sum of achievements in the last century; it had not yet earned the title of miracle. Yet it is sociology that is crossing the threshold of the new century with an ever louder and ever more pronounced slogan on its lips: of harmony, applying a social form with technological content, the superstructure with this basis; of lending the universal battle for a livelihood forms worthy of and appropriate to human society, the genuine materialisation within it of a supra-biological organism, of the highest degree in the sequence of concentrations comprising the universe! Moreover, with similar-sounding exhortations sociology had already stood at the cradle of the 19th century, and to justify them before that recalcitrant, miraculously and at the same time monstrously growing and ruthlessly critical pupil, it descended ever lower, though in pain and reluctantly, from the clouds down to Earth, and from dogma and utopia became a science.

---

1 Source: Rzut oka na rozwój socjologii w XIX wieku, "Prawda" supplement, Warsaw 1901, pp. 65–104. Printed according to the volume Grabski, Stanisław and Kelles-Krauz, Kazimierz, 1901, *Rzut oka na rozwój ekonomii i socjologii w XIX stuleciu*, Part II, series 'Wiek XIX', Warsaw: Drukarnia K. Kowalewskiego.

2 Wallace, Alfred Russel, 1899, *The Wonderful Century*, New York: Dodd, Mead and Company; the Polish translation was published in 1901 in 'Prawda'.

§ 1

The existence of sociology is usually dated from August Comte, who devised its very name; yet in order to understand and properly assess the new science's character, present from the very beginning and piercing right through Comte's work, one must go back somewhat. Although sociology's arrival in the world belongs to the 19th century, the 18th bore it within its womb – and not that universally known and admired 18th century of rationalism, of Encyclopaedias and Revolutions, but another 18th century remaining more in the shadows: the heir of the centuries-long social thought of Catholicism, its system of order, law and hierarchy.

For the less prepared reader, the above sentence reads a little unexpectedly. We shall in a moment clarify. Above all, we emphasise that by no means are we dismissive of what the '18th century' achieved in the sciences of society and mankind, i.e. that pantheon of thinkers usually understood under this collective name. The philosophers of the Enlightenment and Revolution, without the slightest doubt, made great contributions in this area. The most general description of their activity, ignoring the differences and even disputes within their collective direction, may be enclosed within two sketches. On the one hand, in the field of psychology of the individual, it saw the flourishing and establishing of the principle of subordinating phenomena of the spirit to phenomena of the body; hereditary powers – to acquired attributes; mysterious, aerial and arbitrary forces – to noticeable, commonplace and valid facts; in a word, the principle of determinism and materialism. On the other hand, an entire host of great minds worked on the development and materialisation of the concept of law as an attribute of the individual intrinsically granted to the latter by the state of nature, in its manifestations and essence identical to the universally binding and above all genuine reason. Between this second principle, individualistic and rationalistic, proclaiming the autonomy of the individual, and the first, ascertaining the dependence and subordinate character of that individual, there was undoubtedly an internal contradiction; this was even manifested in those discords between philosophers, mainly rationalists, and others, mainly materialists; when these two directions met in Kant's mind, he strived to reconcile them with the assistance of his paradoxical 'critique of practical reason'. Yet the generality of thinkers then reconciled these currents not with the aid of such brilliant ideas, but simply – as most often happens – by not noticing their contradiction. After all, they both responded to the more fundamental social current, to the class needs of the intensifying bourgeoisie in the economic, political and philosophical areas. The first principle, deterministic-materialistic, undermined the authority and exploitation of the clergy, snatching from its hands the key to the arsenal of miracles, punishments and favours, while at the same time it was a consequence of the general flourishing of the sciences and natural methods, accompanying and favouring the development of trade and industry, and the growth in man's command over nature. The second – the individualistic-rationalistic basis of law and criterion of truth – allowed for the negation of all gravity and institutions lived through and inherited from the past. This second principle was, for the expanding and fighting bourgeoisie, the more important; and it also prevailed, took control of their intellectuality, and readjusted the first direction suitably for itself, and subjugated it. As such, ultimately the most prevalent tone of that entire current is, we might say, individuocentrism. The dependence of the human spirit on the laws of nature is often strongly emphasised, but not so the dependence of the functioning of this spirit within the individual on the laws of social life, on the masses, the collective, whether of generations past or that of today. Ideas, *opinions*, whatever their origin in the individual, rule the social world. In relation to society as an object, and to institutions in general, the individual is granted great creative force, the capacity for transformation. Critique based on an individual gauge of law and the truth condemns the entire past that has its continuation in the present. The whole believes in the possibility of rapid and unlimited progress – and this is the third characteristic feature of the intellectual trend of that time; entire extraordinary theories of progress emerge: after all, nobody has the right to forget the contribution by one such Condorcet to constructing the edifice of future social science.

Determinism and realism in the psychology of the individual, significant development of the fundamental concepts of law, and the idea of progress: rich indeed is the legacy left to social science in the 19th century following the Enlightenment and Revolution of the 18th century. And yet we know that the fully-equipped sociology present at the turn of the 19th century, Comtean, rejects this legacy, or at least its main component, the individual criterion of law and truth, and brings totally different attributes to the fore: social determinism, the subordinate status of the individual, and adequate assessment of the past and the present, or in other words the historical and realistic sense – these attributes were alien to the mind of the 18th century. Here as well, admittedly, we also encounter brilliant exceptions. Even in the inundation of French rationalism, Montesquieu and Turgot, representatives of the moderately reformative section of the bourgeoisie that did not take a stance of total negation in regard to existing forms but strived to gradually transform them, display a historical and realistic sense, an understanding of the law of continuity of development. Turgot even comes close to formulating before Comte a law of three conditions that human mentality passes through in history. Level-headedness, that essential condition for social phenomena to be treated scientifically, and disengaging from the violence of rationalism came more easily to the English bourgeoisie, who had already been through revolution at the turn of the 18th century. Thus Gibbon reaches such a high degree of grasping the interdependence and correctness of social phenomena, that a century and a half prior to economic materialism he splits them into three degrees according to their growing level of complexity and decreasing universality, placing on the first step – at the basis of social life – not ideas, but economic and technical phenomena as the most simple, the most general and the most enduring, because they are the most essential; further on there is legislation, politics, science, and trade in industry – in the sense of defined economic forms; and only on the third step, as the highest, the most laudable yet also the least enduring, least essential and exerting the smallest influence on history – poetry and philosophy. Realism, if not yet a historical sense, is also demonstrated and being developed by the economic science nascent in England and France. In Germany, where the revolutionary and nugatory blades of rationalism have been blunted by the long-grafted Protestantism, Iselin, Lessing and Herder are changing bold theories of progress for theories of the rearing of humankind by God, and this belief in a divine plan, guiding the history of mankind, allows them to grant relative value to any form of historical past, or in other words permits them to display a historical sense.

However, here we have everywhere mixed forms of intelligence. In the purest and most distinct form, attributes opposed to the entire materialistic and rationalistic current, attributes so characteristic of sociology in the early years of the 19th century, and namely the historical and realistic senses and the subjugation of the individual to the whole, occur naturally among thinkers of the camp most threatened by that disintegrative current: the Catholic camp. Catholicism – a term I use to embrace in this case the entire social and political system of the Middle Ages, of which it was simultaneously the sanction and the expression – did not feel threatened in its lastingness and omnipotence only by the revolutionary currents of the 18th century, but significantly earlier, in the 15th, 16th and particularly the 17th centuries, by the currents that prepared the Revolution. Apart from Protestantism in a purely church-related scope, this preparatory and disintegrative role in relation to feudalism and Catholicism was played by the direction of individualistic natural law in regard to social economics, and by critical rationalism in regard to philosophy. The threat they posed had long been understood by the most outstanding Catholic minds, despite the outward accord between the coryphaei of these directions, such as Grotius or Descartes, and the ruling church and political institutions. So long as the battle was fought on the stage of academic discussion, the new

emancipative currents began to be counteracted with the principle upon which
the entire feudal system stood: the principle of the individual's subordination
to the group, the multitude, the community, which was linked to old church
assertions about all authority originating from God, and about the weakness
and fallaciousness of human reason, demanding recognition among lawyers
and rationalists as a criterion of law and truth. It was on these foundations that
the philosophy of history by the likes of Bossuet was built; but, still constituting theology through and through, mainly aimed against heretics in the field
of religion, it can barely be classified into the prehistory of sociology. However,
at the turn of the 18th century, on the eve or rather the dawning of the very
day of the decisive battle, Catholicism gave birth to a truly great thinker for the
defence of its perspective: Giambattista Vico.[3] This last great and independent
theologian, who though not a priest and not raised to the office of a doctor of
the church, is worthy of a place in the history of thought alongside Thomas
Aquinas, as an apologist for the Catholic system alongside its codifier, must be
acknowledged by any impartial expert as the first sociologist. I say sociologist
as in the meaning with which this term has been tied since the days of August
Comte.

Vico exerted the entire force of his mind against the rationalistic-
revolutionary current that he knew mainly from Grotius and Descartes, the
further development of which he sensed, and – though this may seem odd –
from this derived all of his great sociological discoveries. In order to refute the
claims of individual reason for absolute authenticity, its inevitable variability
had to be demonstrated. Which is why *The New Science*, as Vico named his
work, constituting an encyclopaedia and synthesis of all sciences then known
of mankind and society, is a history of human nature. This evidently explains
why Vico formulates the law of three successive states of human mentality: he
calls the first stage 'divine' or 'poetic', and considers its characteristic features
to be family theocracy and – as we would say today – animism, the anthropomorphic animation of nature; the second – 'heroic' – bears all the signs of military aristocracy; and the third – 'human' – is civilisation based on law and legal
authority. There is here a very distinct germ not only of Comte's law of the three
conditions, but also of Spencer's binomial of militarism-industrialism. In order
to blunt the horns of pride in individuals who rose above the whole and felt
summoned to shatter its everlasting wonts, it was necessary to demonstrate the
total dependence of even the greatest people on the masses, to demonstrate for
example that Homer was simply the people, which applied also to Dante and

---

3   Not Vicon's, as ours erroneously write; in Latin Vico is spelled: Vicus, Vici [Kelles-Krauz's
     footnote].

all of their ilk. There was in this an echo of the democratic, demotic principle of mediaeval parishes and republics with which Catholicism had on a number of occasions strived to identify; this echo can still be heard in the 'sameness of the scholars with the thinking masses' of the anti-rationalist Comte, and in the 'environment' theory of the counterrevolutionary Taine. Furthermore, in order to deprive people of their zest for revolutionary outbursts, it was necessary to demonstrate that the elements prevailing within a particular society are always 'the best', because otherwise they would not have gained power, and that the course of history proceeds according to certain invariable laws, the controverting of which could lead only to society moving backwards: this was served by the theory of 'eternal ideal history' and conditional *ricorso*. The most brilliant of the counterrevolutionaries wanted, as he himself admits, to create a *New Science* in order for it to be a 'civil theology' – proof of the constantly present eye and governance of Providence, not only in inanimate and lower nature, but also in the history of mankind – and a 'philosophy of authority and ownership', irrefutable justification for monarchy by the grace of God. Yet the spirit of the time, rankled for three centuries already by the currents of the Renaissance, meant that this aim could no longer be achieved by Catholic thought, embodied in Vico, other than by creating at the same time – as the author of *The New Science* again states – a concrete 'history of human nature', based on an investigation of facts, and a 'new philosophical critique', which is to say a social-deterministic treatment of the functions of outstanding and, all the more so, average individuals. An ordinary, inevitable irony of the social dialectic meant that Catholicism, defending itself with its last rationale, had to establish the foundations for a genuine New, great Science, still its most dangerous opponent.

§ 2

The executor of this counterrevolutionary testament of Catholicism was August Comte. He was not literally and directly a pupil and follower of Vico: if the creator of positivism knew the teachings of the Neapolitan master, then only barely, and at the time of creating his own fundamental views he probably knew them not at all. But when that storm of revolutionary rationalism, 'cutting the coat according to the cloth, not the cloth according to the coat', blew across the entire world, then, in the age of restoration, of bitter memories, ruminations and entrenching oneself against the constant threat of new attacks by the 'satanic' force, the views pronounced a century beforehand by that brilliantly vigilant yet unjustly forgotten Vico became widespread.

The counterrevolutionary blades of these views were, appropriately to the changing conditions, quite naturally even more pronounced, but this time as well this was no obstacle for Irony, the creator of history in its gradual transformation into the principles of the new revolutionary science. Thus did de Maistre prove that society, its forms and its fortunes, could not be the doing of human will. Hegel demonstrated the legitimacy of all forms ever having existed as a manifestation of the essential evolution of the absolute Idea, for which people and even nations are but tools. Haller, author of *Restoration of the Science of the State*,[4] characteristic by its very title, having specially taken the embodiment of revolutionary rationalism – Rousseau – as the target of his missiles, and the refutation of this theory on the origin of authority either from usurpation or social contract as his task, conducted such a fundamentally sociological judgment, that the social state – by which he understood authority, at least familial authority – always was the natural state of man. Savigny, defending the old, traditional, local, provincial institutions and customs against the aspirations of the bourgeois Romanist-rationalists for the uniformisation of law in a direction favouring the development of new economic forms, creates a historical school of law with the parallel establishment of a historical school of economics opposing Mancunian rationalism, destructive for feudalism. The concept of 'national spirit' as a source of law, institutions and poetry forms in the womb of the historical school of law, idealism and romanticism – a concept which, above all, as Kareev rightly says, is the 'embodiment of traditional dogmatism, herd instinct, reflexive submission to the existing system and passive obedience to the existing powers'. Bonald proclaims that society is a being living its own life, with its own goals, for which individuals are but tools; that man only exists for society, because it is not he who creates and shapes society, but society that creates and shapes him for itself, according to its own visions, as a result of which he has no rights in society, but only duties. Counter to the 'I philosophy' proclaimed by people in the 18th century, he wants to create a 'we philosophy' and inoculate this in people's minds. Ballanche also demonstrates the powerlessness of the individual as such, and the individual's intrinsic dependence on the life of the masses, on the higher laws of social development. One could extend this list of names and citations ... Thus in the counterrevolutionary melting pot, under the guidance of the Holy Alliance, the fundamental principles of positive sociology of the 19th century are forged: social determinism, historism and realism. August Comte lives in this climate, calls himself de Maistre's disciple, and it is on these principles that he constructs his system.

---

4 Haller, Karl von, 1822, *Restauration der Staatswissenschaft*, Winterthur: Die Steinerische Buchhandlung.

Yet at the same time Comte calls himself a disciple of Condorcet, so is he heir to the entire revolutionary movement? Whence this kinship of his with the counterrevolutionary camp and – as this entails – this camp's mark on the sociology of the 19th century?

In order to understand this, we should contemplate for a while another gigantic figure, rightly priceless and – just like Vico – wrongly in the shadow of the brilliance of Comte: Saint-Simon.

§ 3

In the picture of the development of social theories sketched out by De Greef, "Babeuf closes the 18th century, while Saint-Simon, of the most aristocratic blood, is born, and in him socialism and positive sociology take their beginnings and are further mixed".

Truth be told, when 'Babeuf closed the 18th century' Saint-Simon was already approaching forty, and the fact is that it was precisely then – as he writes in his memoires – that the momentous thought of 'setting out a new, physical-political road for human intellect' took shape. And what a characteristic moment it was! Revolutionary rationalism, held back in its victorious onset by neither the prophetical warnings of Vico, to whom nobody listened, nor by the proclamations or cannons of the coalition superpowers, exploded in storm in the French Revolution, materialised in the thorough revision of the 'social contract', reached its culmination, and drenched with blood the cemeteries ploughed in the soil of the future just to halt there – before immediately reverting to the same bloody measures to impede the drawing of further logical consequences from the principles of its own criticism, in order to render impossible a revision of the social contract, no longer in the political respect alone, but also in the social and economic respect ... The work, which commenced with a noble impulse on the night of 4 August, ended with the 'Gracchus' trial and the abominations of the Directoire. With a symbolic coincidence, this tragedy had the same course and ending for Saint-Simon, a princely descendent, as for the bearers of work-worn hands who aided the 'third estate' in capturing the Bastille: initially an ardent participant of councils, writer of speeches, later a fortunate speculator, an intermediary in the parcelling out of the national goods, he ends up in jail as a suspect, and emerges from this stormy period cheated by his partner and almost ruined...

On the whole this new creator of sociology at the turn of the 19th century was a remarkable figure. His entire life is extraordinary, with fighting for the liberty of the American republic, a stint as colonel in the royal army, and the tough hired-writer's work in a pawnbroker's, working nine hours a day for an annual income of 1000 fr., all followed in rather rapid succession, one after the other. However, what we mainly want to pay attention to is his constant retrospection towards the Middle Ages, which his aristocratic lineage furthered in an original manner. Charles the Great, that genius standing at the threshold of the Middle Ages and recognised by Saint-Simon as his progenitor, apparently – according to his assurances – appeared to him in prison and commanded him to give mankind a new system, and prophesised that he would equal him in fame acquired in philosophy. In any case, such dreams testify to the mediaeval inspiration that enwrapped this great Utopian.

Vico was an admirer and defender not so much of earlier feudalism, in which he perceived a 'heroic', combative and 'irascible' spirit, like in the Greece of Achilles, as of the later blossoming of the Middle Ages – of legally organised monarchy sanctioned by the Church. Romantics from the times of the Bourbon[5] Restoration, philosophers of the likes of Schlegel, poets and even lawyers from the school of the 'national spirit', by no means ceasing even for a moment to worship the monarchical order granted by the grace of God, under whose vigilant wings they were free to live and think, strived to irradiate it with knightly traditions, and breaking free of the atmosphere of the battle for existence between individuals and between classes, a battle that was developing ever further, they searched deeper into the mediaeval past, extracting from it the jewels of faith, of heroism, love, sacrifice, harmony and consentaneous collective awareness. The revolutionary-rationalistic movement, intensifying in the days of Vico but seemingly arrested in theirs, was of a character destroying the objects of both their and Vico's veneration. Yet this movement, which at the same time was a bourgeois-capitalistic movement, also functioned in the same destructive manner on a different aspect of mediaeval life. Though by no means are we forgetting the class battles between the feudal lords and urban merchants, between merchants and craftsmen, between master craftsmen and apprentices, one cannot deny that within the natural mediaeval economy and guild organisation there existed a certain harmony between the interests of the different social strata, that the system of that day prevented within certain limits excessively acute social inequalities, and above all the fickleness and uncertainty of existence. Haller could also say, with a degree of legitimacy, that whereas in contemporary bourgeois society crowds of paupers camp only from one day to the next, like vagabond strangers not attached in any manner to this society, in mediaeval society paupers at least have their space beneath a shared

---

5   The original speaks solely of the 'Restoration'; I have added 'Bourbon' to avoid any confusion [translator's note].

roof, and this reaction against the consequences of the ruthless individualistic economics of the burgeoning capitalistic bourgeoisie, a reaction from which Christian and state socialism, as well as economic ethicism so closely connected to historism, continues to flow, is not something that thinkers of the Bourbon Restoration have come up with. In the second half of the 18th century, the Italian priest and economist Ortes was already defending the former economic traditions (not fencing off fields after harvest and other similar local easements) against the capitalists, aiming for greater productiveness. He refers to the rights of the poorest, and indicates the bitter consequences of their expropriation. In actual fact Vico too warns against becoming savage and moving backwards as the inevitable consequences of everybody fighting everybody – for riches; yet this constitutes a rather minor aspect of his critique of the new movements. In Saint-Simon's retrospection towards the Middle Ages this factor of justified social harmony, a concord between various states and the certainty of existence favourable for all parties, plays a very prominent role. Saint-Simon's mediaeval retrospection differs from Vico's pre-revolutionary retrospection (which was really simply clinging to tradition) and the post-revolutionary retrospection of the Romantics in the fact that it is not counter-revolutionary. This descendent of a famous memoirist from the time of the Regency, who is proud of his ancestor having been "the sole noble of his time to have retained his former feudal character and displayed authentic independence", is after all a participant of the Revolution: he himself redacts an address to the National Assembly demanding the abolition of noble titles; he is a disciple of d'Alembert, an admirer of Condorcet. The French Revolution could also have accustomed him to looking back into the past with intent other than that of the Romantics of the Bourbon Restoration: after all, it referred to the original church customs in order to justify the 'civil constitution of the clergy', the close dependence of leaders and princes on the collective at the dawn of the Middle Ages – in order to deny Bourbon absolutism the aura of legitimacy. The centralistic-monarchical order was a negation of this original mediaeval democracy; and the monetary economy tied to it – a factor of disintegration for this harmony and equilibrium. This is why Rousseau is the enemy of both the centralistic monarchy and the monetary economy. But Saint-Simon has grown accustomed to the capitalistic bourgeoisie, and is a proponent of the development of productive forces, an industrialist. His social-economic retrospection towards mediaeval harmony and order is expressed not in an aspiration for halting or reversing the development of productive forces, but only in 'new Christianism', in which society is organised in a manner most favourable for the largest possible number of individuals, in ensuring the best possible moral and physical existence for the most numerous class. Saint-Simon classifies labourers, working only with their hands, into the same useful industrial class as entrepreneurs, manufacturers, bankers and also scholars; he believes in a total harmony of interests between them all, and sets them all together against the feudal, military, parasitic class. Having been through the hell of revolution, having seen its bankruptcy, he only does not believe in total equality, which he considers 'bloody foolishness'. He believes the existence of power and authority essential to avoid the recurrence of similar convulsions; but when theological authority and brutal power, specific to a military period, have been irrevocably eroded, they must be replaced by power and authority based on conviction, on knowledge, on positive morality. The 'philosophy of authority and ownership' thereby adopts here a form different to that present with Vico. The individual's uninhibited criticism is no longer prohibited beforehand and totally excluded; on the contrary, the new industrial system is meant to fully redress it, and thereby capture people's minds. Sociology ceases to be a dogma. Its very name, 'political physics', testifies to Saint-Simon adjusting to one factor, making use of a single trend, which for the astute Vico was particularly antipathetic and for the traditional dogmas truly dangerous: namely – that of the natural sciences. Saint-Simon differentiated two types of social state: organic eras, in which all human thoughts and actions are coordinated according to one general principle, and critical eras in which there is no such generally binding principle, and people and tendencies oppose one another in chaotic battle. He also understood that western European society has been undergoing such a critical, disintegrative era since the times of the Reformation, and for leading it out of this and bringing it into a new, organic era, he has created his own industrial system. Such a stance already differed in a certain very important respect from Vico's position: it was the position of the creative individual, inherited from the revolutionists. Although Saint-Simon's intent was to discover the invariable laws governing social phenomena, these laws were no longer supernatural, imposed on mankind from outside; they were physical laws, the laws of social nature. With Saint-Simon, the subject-matter of 'political physics' is mankind, the collective being, which develops and matures according to the laws of its own nature, and not according to the arbitrary ideas of individual reason; however, the individual may in full measure influence this development. Except that this ability to influence is conditioned above all by precise familiarity with and thereby proper assessment of the past; only the latter allows one to draw conclusions on the probable future. Such is the philosopher's historical sense, which also immediately entails the demand for reforming historiography such for it to allow for this type of deduction, in order for it to become an exact science. This is coupled with a sense of realism: the concept of individual creativity is limited. Systems of social organisation – says Saint-Simon – do not form: one can only ascertain a new band of ideas and interests that has taken shape. "The social system is fact or it is nothing". A great system, if durable, must be an expression of its age, and namely – of the forces prevalent in society in a particular age. This is why revolutions and political changes are of only secondary significance; they must be preceded by 'civil' and moral revolutions, of which they are but an expression, a confirmation; and politics must be based increasingly on economics, must be guided by its pointers, become the 'science of production'. If we are to understand this economic foundation of political forms, then let us familiarise ourselves closer with Saint-Simon's thought that a "great political system draws its strength in the services rendered by the majority of society, in other words in the poorest class". This is the rationale of its – the political system's – existence; it is also the rationale of the victory that the new system achieves over it. Thus transforms Vico's thinking that the forces prevailing in each era are 'the best', because otherwise they would be unable to prevail. For as long as the feudal nobility really did fulfil the taxing service of defenders of the working people against invaders, for as long as the clergy really was devoted to propagating education and civilisation, the social system had to be built on the dominance of these classes. However, the development of military technology, the invention of gunpowder, etc., rendered the warrior-nobles superfluous, changed them into parasites, while the clergy, having become the defenders of privileges, began to hinder the development of knowledge and thus to belie their own purpose. At the same time the industrial class was growing, and the role of the class most useful for the whole passed over to it. Thus it is displacing and displace it must the feudal classes.

Simultaneously the theological way of thinking connected to feudalism and a military system is being displaced by the knowledge and positive philosophy corresponding to the industrial system. However, because the transition cannot take place right away, there existed and still exist transitionary forms in between theology and militarism on the one hand, and positivism and the industrial system on the other: this refers namely to metaphysics, which the work of lawyers corresponds to in a practical sense. They are paving the way for the industrial system, but are not yet standing on facts, only on abstract understanding. Not all sciences lose their theological character right away, then their metaphysical character, becoming positive sciences. They pass through these stages of development one by one, starting from the simplest: astronomy, chemistry, physics and physiology. Now is the time for positive philosophy, based on all of these previous sciences, which should at the same time and above all, as we have already seen, be 'political physics', the theory of the laws of social life, ensuring harmony to people obedient to it, preventing struggles and bloody outbursts.

§ 4

Such is the internal connection of Saint-Simon's thinking. August Comte is the direct heir to this thought, and – one may boldly say – its imitator. We see with him the same starting point, the same leading thought: the assertion of a serious crisis, of a state of harmful anarchy in which mankind finds itself, and the intention to lead it out of this illness. Both Saint-Simon and Comte are wards of the bourgeois revolutionary-rationalistic and natural-materialistic currents of the 18th century, although Saint-Simon was witness to the bankruptcy of revolution, while Comte, who lived for longer, observed the degeneration of the bourgeoisie admitted to power in the days of Louis Philippe, and the terrifyingly disintegrative action of capitalism. By reproaching bourgeois economists for their class-egoistic ruthlessness, he also reprimands bourgeois society for the state of 'camping and vagabondage', in which it leaves the proletariat in a physical and spiritual sense. So it comes as no surprise that Comte, just like Saint- Simon, moves closer to the likes of Bonald and Maistre, that even more than Saint-Simon he admires and praises the Middle Ages for their spiritual coherence and social harmony.

At the same starting point we also find with Comte all the same fundamental ideas as with Saint-Simon. Likewise sociology is initially called social physics. Likewise mankind is considered a collective being on which individuals depend, and which they should serve, because they are only secondary organs. The life and development of this collective being possesses continuity in the manner that each new nation comes into the possession of what the preceding nation achieved, and from this point it develops further. The evolution of mankind involves the transition through three states of intellectuality, three ways of thinking: theological (fetishism, animation and the epitomising of all things in nature), metaphysical (belief in abstract and general forces as the causes of phenomena) and positive (discovering the laws of phenomena, or in other words the fixed relationships between them, sufficient for forecasting and influencing, but not the initial causes). There is another strength that corresponds to these three states of intellectuality in two respects – spiritual and mundane: of priests and warriors, philosophers and lawyers (the 18th and preceding centuries), and finally of scholars and industrialists. Between one state and another there is always a critical, disintegrative era; the entire metaphysical period is really like a crisis between the theological and positive states. Each of these three states and each of the mixed, transitionary forms is, at its time, essential and useful; each also, up until the purely positive state, bears within itself an internal contradiction and the necessity of giving way to the next. Comte advances this historical sense, this justice for the past, to such a degree that he commands sociology to renounce the concept of progress and replace it with only the concept of development, free of any absolute criterion of superiority; he considers the relativity of such criteria, of truth, good and happiness, a fundamental feature of positivism. This incontrovertible and momentous social-scientific achievement is, here as well – just as we have seen in other examples with Vico – a result of the thinker's attitude towards the surrounding social currents; in the given case it is undoubtedly the display of scepticism in regard to such resolute rationalistic catchwords, a result of the disappointment caused by the Revolution. Also related to this is assigning a very subordinate role to changes and political forms, and – in general – to any influence an individual has on the course of social matters. Having made of mankind 'le Grand-Être', a godhead, Comte also 'transposes' an old fatalistic proverb, and says: *L'homme s'agite, et l'Humanité le mène*, which in English[6] would be 'man proposes, mankind disposes'. 'Man can only change the intensity or speed of social phenomena', but never their character or their direction. But with Comte, this historical sense and feeling of relativity, this social determinism, is not connected to such a highly developed – as with Saint-Simon – third characteristic feature of the emerging sociology: realism. In his contempt for economists and economics, in his inordinate understanding of the role of scholars, in this respect he pushes backwards the legacy received from Saint-Simon: he moves the centre of gravity of social evolution from the fundamental, elementary economic and organisational actions towards an intellectual factor, towards the process of developing the view of the world from theology via metaphysics towards positivism, and he considers this the leading factor, decisive in the development of societies. At this point one hears the echo of the powerful influence of pre-revolutionary rationalism, which Comte was never able to adequately exorcise from his mind. On the other hand, certain contradictions flow from this in regard to the view of the role of the individual and the impact of the individual's understandings and actions on the fortunes of society. Comte passes from an objective to a subjective stance, becoming a social-religious lawmaker, and in ascribing his discovery and his ideas extraordinary significance, as the only ones in history, and totally neglecting the issue of the external, economic and political conditions of their realisation, he stands in the same row as so many Utopians of his age; except that he remains a bourgeois Utopian. This lack of realism also means that his practical ideas regarding the resolving of the social issue, the organising of relations of

---

6   In the original Kelles-Krauz naturally wrote what it would mean in Polish; the Polish translation given ('Chłop strzela, a ludzkość kule nosi') means 'A peasant shoots, and mankind carries the bullets' [translator's note].

ownership, relationships between capital and work, though imbued with the same overall leading thought, a thought that is in any case traditionally Catholic, about the relative character of the law of ownership and the obligations of the owner towards the whole, are vague, timid and significantly weaker than Saint-Simon's.

However, we have already pointed out above that this shifting of the fundamental point of view in appraising the importance of various interdependent phenomena derives from the exalted perception of the role of scholars and science, while a consequence and expression of this is – once more – granting sociology its appropriate scientific form, which it lacked with Saint-Simon. Comte ascertains everywhere the utilitarian source and goal of any science; and with him the very formation of sociology does not result from a fondness of science for science's sake, but from a desire to serve mankind, to give it a means for leaving the state of intellectual anarchy. At the same time, though, he understood and stressed very clearly that any science may only develop properly and thereby fulfil its utilitarian purpose when it loses sight of that utilitarian goal, when it becomes a goal in itself, when scientists work and create animated by their selfless and frank love of science. And so too he himself laboured over sociology, and so too – although we either do not encounter or only encounter very few new ideas with him, and that in detail – whereas with Saint-Simon everything bears a chaotic, haphazard form, when the mind is constantly preoccupied by practical applications, Comte lends his ideas exact form, develops them according to scientific schemata, and creates a cohesive, harmonious system. It cannot be said that he possessed greater erudition than Saint-Simon, but his erudition is more systematic. He thoroughly mastered the mathematical and natural sciences within their scope at the time, and contributed to sociology a natural element to a greater degree even than Saint-Simon. He splits sociology into the static and the dynamic according to the formulae of mechanical physics (the main motive for which lies in his desire to reconcile – by designating the proper scope for each – the concepts of order and progress, such that in the future "the theories of order would not need to be, as they have till now, always reactionary, and progressive theories – anarchic ..."); he considers it essential to base sociology on the findings of the whole of biology. Taking as the foundation the social static, the so-called *consensus*, that is to say the interdependence of all component parts and factors of society in a given place and time, he discerns an analogy between this interdependence and the interdependence of the parts and actions of the living organism. Having ascertained that the higher the organism, the greater the interdependence of its parts, yet at the same time the greater the division of work and difference in actions between them, in this respect he considers society a concentration yet higher than the highest biological organisms, and social phenomena – as the most complex. The criterion of increasing complexity and decreasing universality serves for him as the basis for developing and elaborating in detail the historical series of sciences in the order in which they pass from the theological and metaphysical to the positive stage. He devises a detailed and systematic classification of the sciences, and within this determines the place of sociology as a theoretical science, but an unapplied abstract science investigating the laws of phenomena, and not as a specific science describing individual phenomena. He also gives much attention to the issue of methods of sociology, investigates the conditions and ways of applying methods in the new science: observational-experimental, comparative, historical....

If anything, it is probably precisely this formal elaboration of sociology, this introduction of content that he inherited and that was floating in the air within the exact sciences established earlier, that may give Comte the right to the title of 'father of sociology'. If with Saint-Simon social science ceases to be the dogma that it still was with Vico, with Comte – at least in the 'objective' section of his oeuvre – it also loses the character of dreaminess, of Utopia. It was this essence of positivism that struck and attracted so many brilliant minds. Many sociologists also devoted a great deal of work to developing Comte's methodological, classificatory and systemising thoughts, and this work continues in a variety of methodologies.

§ 5

We have neither the time nor the room for investigating and presenting this development of sociology in a formal and technical sense. Over the course of the 19th century the *consensus* of all sciences materialised and gained prominence; sociology also yielded to the influence of them all, and in turn also exerted its own influence on almost every one of them. Presenting these influences is not within the province of our task: otherwise, it would be enormous. For example mathematics had a large impact on how issues in sociology were posed, on its methods and techniques, and this through statistics; yet we can give but a cursory mention of the name Adolf Quètelet, who was influenced by the same social and ideological factors as Saint-Simon and Comte, and who – like them – pursued in his *Social Physics* the thought of the regularity of human phenomena, their social determinism, and their independence from the individual's whims. Likewise with the fundamental thinking of Buckle, who expanded upon Montesquieu's thinking of how society is influenced by external natural, climatological and geographic conditions, etc., and discerned outstanding successors in Metchnikoff, in Reclus and in others, successors exploiting the relationship of geography (in the broad sense of this term) towards sociology. Much could also be said of the influence of biology, psychology, history, law and economics on sociology, and vice versa, on the emergence and development of sociological anthropology and ethnology, research into animal societies, and criminal anthropology, etc., etc. As long as this would refer to the development of methods and sociological technique affected by this mutual influence, we must omit these topics; it will prove much more useful for the reader to familiarise himself for example via the appropriate chapters of a 'Teach Yourself ...'. Our task and endeavour in this brief sketch is, as the reader may perhaps have already noticed, to provide something else: a glance at the development of the leading ideas of sociology, at the consequence and relationship of schools of sociology – in connection with the social conditions – with the currents and class struggles troubling society of the 19th century. Here as well I believe it crucial to point out that this glance is neither even nor systematic. Instead of penning an abstract on the history of sociology, or rather of the books that to date have had to take the place of such a special history of sociology for us – such as Robert Flint's *History of the Philosophy of History*, Bolesław Limanowski's *Historia ruchu społecznego w XIX-tym stuleciu* [lit. *History of the social movement in the 19th century*], or Nikolai Kareev's *Introduction to Studies in Sociology*,[7] I prefer on these few pages to attempt to highlight certain factors in the development of sociology elsewhere given little if any emphasis, and its fundamental currents and the guiding ideas, although I have had to focus mainly on ground-breaking points. By thus grasping our task, we shall take into account the impact on sociology of only three new sciences, established in the 19th century: biology, psychology and prehistoric archaeology (pre-history). This is because each of these three areas corresponds to a certain breakthrough in the organisation and mutual relationship of the classes fighting for the form of social system.

§ 6

In the mid-19th century, seeing the end of Comte's activity and the beginning of that of his successors, the Western European bourgeoisie was totally different to that at the end of the 18th and in the first three decades of the 19th

---

7   I mention those books I have used here in part as indicators. The first, published in English, German and French, and which is one of a kind, and the third, possessing numerous merits, we have not yet seen in Polish [Kelles-Krauz's footnote].

century. In most countries of Western Europe its preeminent strata had ceased to aspire for power and influence on the social system; they already had them, and now had to defend them against the demands of new forces. They thus found themselves in the position of the ruling classes of the *Ancien Régime*: the agrarians and the clergy. Now they required a theory proving the groundlessness and fruitlessness of strivings to change the social order. Elements of social determinism such as those contained in hitherto counterrevolutionary sociology, directed against rationalistic reformers from the heroic age of the bourgeoisie, were used for establishing such a theory; however, they were lent new form by the usage of the results of the revolutionary work of these great predecessors: achievements in the area of the natural sciences. Such in essence was the genesis of the biological schools – organicistic and Darwinistic – in sociology.

Spencer is known to have developed and reshaped the germ of the idea of a social organism that was contained in Comte's sociology. However, less is usually remembered of the fact that the very grasping of society as an organism was already contained in the idealistic German philosophy contemporary to Comte and Saint-Simon.

This philosophy emerged from the trunk of Protestant rationalism, beneath its wings, as a result of which – as we have already proffered – even in its progressive critical-bourgeois beginnings, it was deprived the sharp blade of revolutionary negation. However, the conditions in which the German bourgeoisie lived and in which class awareness emerged, and its weakness compared to the monarchy, forced it to accommodate contradictions, meaning that in this philosophy if an individual opposed the collective there was then an immediate merging with this collective, a growing together. Thus the widespread pursuit at the close of the 18th and beginning of the 19th century for personifying society grafted perfectly onto the philosophy of 'the rearing of mankind by the Godhead'. Christian Krause compares society to an organism, while a presentation of the development of society as the growth of a being passing through the ages of childhood, youth, maturity and decrepitude is to be found with him as well as Fichte, Schelling, and with the almost contemporary Fourier and others. With the Bourbon Restoration, with counterrevolution, there is an even greater intensification of attributing one true reality to the collective being, the nation, the state, to the 'Objective Spirit', in whom the Absolute Idea is embodied with Hegel. When the German bourgeoisie later grows in strength and dares speak out in somewhat sharper terms against the might of the *Ancien Régime*, against the feudal lords and the Church, when it reaches for the weapon of materialism for this purpose and develops the natural sciences, then – as we know – numerous transitional forms of thought emerge, gradually transforming and modernising the ideas of the 'philosophy of nature' and the ideas of evolution that were contained in the idealistic dialectic. The concept of the social organism also undergoes such a gradual transformation; for example we see its transitional and even more philosophical (in the old sense) than natural form in the works of the Hegelian Konrad Hermann; it becomes modern, biological, though not totally devoid of German-idealistic remnants and stigma, with Lilienfeld and Schäffle. The bourgeoisie, on the whole, abandon 'idealism' and metaphysics: because in fighting the feudal institutions, they also wish to undermine the view of a feudal-religious world; however, they retain the concept of society as a collective being, dressing it only in modern garb and biological terminology, because this notion of a social organism serves them for reclaiming legitimacy from the new negational currents.

Spencer's concept opposes above all the mechanism. Thus the characteristic feature in his case is not only regularity in development and action, boiling down to the minimal significance of individual influences, but also self-development. The Comtean *évolution spontanée*: the organism bears the springs of its own development within itself, and they unwind by themselves. This is one more rationale for the superfluity and non-scientificity of any targeted, arbitrary intervention in the course of social development – intervention which, in a social-economic scope, when summoned by those wronged threatens the state of ownership among the capitalistic bourgeoisie, and the need for this was, conversely, acknowledged by Comte. Spencer recognises Comte's principle, that when passing from one category of natural phenomena to the next, to a higher one, 'reality is enriched' and a greater degree of complexity emerges, meaning that the same methods cannot be applied, a total analogy cannot be conducted. He also calls the area of social life 'supra-organic' and indicates himself the differences between a social and a biological organism; these differences are characteristic because they fully favour Spencer's anti-interventionist stance, his aversion to the growing demands of solidarity and conscious social organisation. These differences are namely – firstly – discretism, which is to say a lack of coherence between the particles of the social organism. We shall at this point forestall a remark most probably occurring to the reader: there is a certain individualism contained in this, but this individualism differs considerably from the revolutionary individualism of the belligerent, ascendant bourgeoisie. There the individual granted itself the right and power to influence society, to transform its system, while here the individual is denied the possibility of such influence, the need and legitimacy of which is excluded by organic self-development, but the individual is granted the quality, right and duty to organise their life on their own, in external conditions created and imposed on them by the course of social life, and to not meddle in what is happening beyond this sphere of their interests. Especially since the second, 'supra-organic' feature of the social organism is the absence of a collective *sensorium*, a news centre, a 'social soul' as other organicists would say. This is because the organicist school has numerous varieties. In other countries more faithful to its philosophical, counterrevolutionary and anti-anarchic – in all meanings – origin, it is connected to a certain type of state socialism. These organicists consistently personify society and find within it not only a soul, but a brain as well. In any case, they stick to the biological scale of development set by Spencer, and even, as we have seen, by Comte in a less precise form, a scale that passes from homogeneity to heterogeneity, to an ever greater differentiation of the parts with their ever greater integration into a whole, and from this division of work in the social organism they deduce not only the groundlessness of aspirations for economic equality, but also the legitimacy, essentiality and need for members of society to be divided into muscular 'cells' and brain 'cells', the specialising of a certain section of society in the actions of thinking and governing. We shall say again, many are there various theories of the social organism; their proponents, in expounding their analogy, have devised many a methodological question and thrown light onto certain specific issues of social life. By combining with other currents, this theory too has transformed, as later we shall see. But in its beginnings, in its original underlying idea, it is justification of the class-based ruling of the bourgeoisie by designating for the working classes the roles of lower organs necessary for the functioning of the whole, and indirectly availing of the prosperity of the higher organs (entirely as in the old tale of Menenius Agrippa) – and in this form it has also been propagated most by popularisers pursuing easy erudition.

A similar apologetic role in the service of the bourgeoisie was played in a slightly different manner by the sociological school of Darwinism. We emphasise right away that the introduction of the concepts of natural selection and transformism to sociology brought a much greater scientific yield than could be brought intrinsically by the concept of the social organism. Because where in the latter one was dealing with a general, formal analogy, the former shone a bright light on certain actual phenomena occurring in people's lives as in the life of any species of living beings. Thus when scholars, free of the tinted bourgeois lenses (by no means am I saying all of them), understood and took into account in this area the meaning of the 'supra-organic' factor of socialisation and technology, an entire anthroposociological literature developed, impressive, brisk, fruitful and authoritative, investigating the issue of selection in society, of the differentiation, enrichment and regression of individuals, and later – of groups of institutions. We also emphasise that the great authors of theories known under the general name of Darwinism understood the differences that the fact of belonging to a society and possessing technology made to the individual's position in the biological fight for existence. Alfred Russel Wallace perfectly observed the attributes differentiating man in the highest stages of social development from animals and primitive people: socialisation, collaboration, solidarity, and the division of work – attributes allowing for the maintaining of the weak and development of altruistic tendencies, not in spite of but in keeping with the laws and demands of natural selection; attributes also transferring the action of selection from the physical ever more into the intellectual and moral. But sociologists became possessed by the ideas of Darwinism with a determined class-based and bourgeois pursuit. At the same time these were thinkers of that section of the bourgeoisie, that shade, that in the footsteps of Malthus and Ricardo no longer believed in the possibility of harmony between different, contradictory interests, between the battling social strata and nations. Admittedly there are dilettantes of vulgar biological sociology of the ilk of Novikov, who in their gluttony for the delicacy of natural 'scientificity' digest simultaneously the theory of the social organism and the theory of the battle for existence and selection – always ensuring the victory of 'the best' in society. Yet on the whole, these bourgeois sociologists (or perhaps it would be better to say mainly columnists), who resort to the stalwart antidote of social Darwinism, no longer entertain themselves with the poultices of 'social organism' or Agrippa's tales of the stomach and members. They rebut the grievances of the weaker, of the vanquished – races, nations, and strata – simply with the disdainful argument that, since they are the vanquished, then obviously they are worth less, are less well adapted, etc. And here the individual is unleashed and recognised as much as, feeling the strength for it, he wants to get his own over the backs of others; on the other hand, the zeal of idealist reformers is held in check not with the help of 'eternal ideal history', the dialecticism of the Absolute Idea, or the self-development of the social organism, but with the help of the now thoroughly fatalistic concept of the development and improvement of the species, of the race, to which those who 'have been weighed and found to weigh less' are sacrificed. Entire theories of race are emerging, of the Le Bon type, although they are nurtured mainly in 'high' literature and in belligerent journalism, and are in a manner of speaking a continuation of the theory of the 'national spirit' (Kipling, Drumont, etc.). The youngest representative of the Darwinist school in sociology, the Englishman Benjamin Kidd, raises to the might of a dogma the assertion that the progress of some takes place through the regression of others; yet because only one religion may induce individuals with their own interests and drives to renounce them and their own lives for the higher interests of the species, he considers religion the most significant social link and a condition for the existence of society.

This is an original closure to the development cycle of the bourgeoisie. And vice versa: from idealistic German philosophy, that daughter of Protestant theology, came at a certain point a transition to social Darwinism; this occurred namely in Hartmann's *Philosophy of the Unconscious*,[8] where the blind battle between individuals and races gradually accomplishes human progress – progress that is always relative, bearing this battle's bloody and bitter stamp.

They usually class Ludwik Gumplowicz's system, and not wrongly so, as connected to the current of sociological Darwinism. Not wrongly so, although – not entirely rightly so either. This is because it is an original system that one might sceptically call counterrevolutionary; the bourgeois order within it cynically disparages itself, yet essentially contradicts the very possibility of transformation. This system is linked to the tradition of counterrevolutionary sociology – via philosophy and German law – by the absolute and most strongly accentuated social determinism, bringing the individual down to the role of a cog in the machine, a non-independent molecule in the group, which is only a sociological reality, such that the individual lives, thinks, feels and aspires only with material supplied by the group, and therefore its thoughts and aspirations are relative and subordinate in the extreme. But at the same time the collectivity, the states, society, their precepts and their needs, do not have any internal justification either: they are always the result of fighting between races and groups, results of the victory and ruling of the stronger; and there is no progress, there is only every greater integration between the fighting and winning groups. When taking into account the individual's affiliation in a developed and varied society with numerous groups and circles, which in every individual you could say meet and intersect, there flows from this stance a fertile direction of research into social structure and psychology, while its critical sobriety may also be used by the forces free of the helpless pessimism of the bourgeoisie, which in addition has come to know and lost faith in itself.

§ 7

August Comte recognised development of the way of thinking as the fundamental factor of social development, and as such constructed his system on a psychological grounding; despite this, in his sequence of sciences he placed not psychology but biology immediately before sociology, believing that positively understood psychological phenomena fully belonged to it. Spencer filled this gap, placing psychology between biology and sociology, which is widely

---

8 Hartmann, Eduard von, 1884, *Philosophy of the Unconscious*, London: Trübner.

acknowledged today, although he rectified Comte's view in that he attributed emotional factors with a much more important impact on the course of social issues than intellectual factors, which is to say the way of understanding. In the latter half of the 19th century psychology was continuously developing as an independent science, enriching and embracing ever more issues, e.g. mass psychology. At the same time all sorts of sociologists, distantly or closely related to and honouring Comte, introduced psychological deliberations to sociology. Worth noting and constantly bearing in mind is that this psychological direction always was and often is connected with the rehabilitation of the individual, their rights, consciousness, will and influence on society, which is related to the social, class-based foundation of this direction.

Namely the bourgeoisie, though almost entirely taking part in the reaction against the revolutionary, disintegrative rationalism at the turn of the 19th century, was not after all in its entirety in the position of the *beati possidentes* in the middle of the century. On the contrary, a significant part, and namely the petite bourgeoisie, remained beyond the doors of the capitalistic palace, and were by no means satisfied with this, especially as the development of capitalism was mistreating their certainty of existence. Having then a battle ahead of them, they also had to form the foundations for it; with this goal they returned to the rationalistic tradition of law and fundamental justice expressing itself in the consciousness of the individual, and understood the sociological and philosophical counterrevolutionary thought of the inner necessity and correctness of social development as materialisation of this individually experienced criterion. An example of this connection of dialectics and rationalism is Proudhon and his numerous epigones all the way to Jaurès. On the other hand, in certain countries the bourgeoisie or the professional intelligentsia, which preceded the appearance and stronger development of the bourgeoisie and temporarily substituted it, found themselves in the position of the pre-revolutionary French bourgeoisie, and had similar tasks to fulfil. For these forces it was important to restrict the autonomy of the individual in relation to the existing 'objective spirit' of both institutions and the mass mood, and to attribute an independent and decisive role to the initiators, to 'the heroes' as says Bruno Bauer of the Hegelian left. In his wake a similar stance was taken by Mirtov, and a kindred stance – by the so-called subjective Russian school in sociology. In his works, Mirtov draws attention mainly to the significance of individual thought as a disintegrative factor for existing civilisational forms; he investigates the degree of independence of various members of society in relation to these existing forms, and the degree of their participation in the changing evolution of these forms. Mikhaylovsky investigates the impact of the 'heroes', the initiators, on the 'throng'. Kareev formulates the momentous 'principle of the individual': "the individual is the sole real significance that sociology deals with". Those of ours belonging to this direction include Józef Karol Potocki. In America – Lester Ward, supplementing Comte with research into the 'anthropoteleological' side of social phenomena alongside the genetic side, and Giddings, drawing special attention to social processes depending on will. In sundry fields and countries one observes this striving to push the functions of defined, specific individuals into the forefront, instead of the previous characteristically sociological usage of collective beings, which is linked entirely naturally to the research of social psychology, which is to say spiritual phenomena occurring in individuals in their mutual influence on one another. Thus Tarde – a contemporary of Mikhaylovsky – investigates the phenomenon of imitation, simultaneously apotheosising the role of inventors, almost removing them from the laws of social determinism and vehemently protesting against 'ontology' in sociology, against the objectivising and personifying of collectives and institutions. Jhering corrects the errors of the school of the 'national spirit' in law, demonstrating that law only exists through individuals and for individuals, i.e. for specific, living people. Fouillée creates a 'psychology of the idea-forces' and attempts to reconcile his ideological stance with the theory of the social organism, introducing the concept of 'contractual organism' (*organisme contractuel*), which the youngest of the organicists, Worms, almost agrees to. Besides, one more attribute of these sociologies in general is that they strive not to reject the acquirements of natural-bourgeois sociology, as the application of biology in sociology also had, in its essence, a social-revolutionary significance that they are endeavouring to highlight and cleanse of its bourgeois conservative tint given it by the original organicist and Darwinist schools. Thus proceed Mirtov, who places the emphasis on the meaning of solidarity, transforming the battle for existence in society; Mikhaylovsky, improving Spencer's formula of progress through differentiation such that the individual is required to aspire for the greatest possible integrity, while the division of work should be at its greatest between the organs of each individual, and at its least – between individuals; and Potocki, highlighting the significance of the consciousness of social 'cells' as the condition for a social bond. Here those slogans of transfiguration of the social organism and of the battle for existence within it are elaborated, into truly supra-organic. Besides, even there where the individual's independence is not emphasised, and where the traditional concept of the collective being is not being fiercely fought, a psychological tint is appearing. Lilienfeld adds this to the theory of the social organism; De Greef develops Comtism in this direction; and from the school of the 'national spirit' unfolds the direction of research into the so-called 'psychology of peoples' of Lazarus and Steinthal.

As we can see, this psychological direction is enormously mixed – which also corresponds entirely to the character of the strata that form it. The dualism of the petite bourgeoisie has already been ascertained on many an occasion, whereby it must simultaneously assault and defend the individualistic-capitalistic order, which means that as in politics in practice, and as in theoretical sociology, on one occasion it is original, brisk, perceptive and discovering phenomena's new relationships, yet in the very next moment it abides by the most outdated of platitudes. A general attribute of this direction (though by no means to an equal degree in all of its participants) is also a predilection for inconstant equilibrium, for a position not entirely clear and defined, always leaving oneself the possibility of restriction and choice, eclecticism expressed in a reluctance to search for and the fear of finding a lasting and decisive *primi agentis* of social development.

§ 8

Economic materialism is a manifestation of the aspirations and worldview of a class that not only has no reason to fear the overwhelming, elementary action of such a fundamental factor, but for which, conversely, recognition of a similar factor has the significance of the same kind of Archimedean foothold as for the revolutionary bourgeoisie of the 18th century had belief in the unchanging criterion of reason expressing the state of nature.

Economic materialism grew from the womb of Hegelianism and Saint-Simonianism, and at the very least emerged beneath their crossed influence. Because class, of which it was an expression, attaining consciousness, had to by the very nature of its position take a most definitely active part in the reaction against the destructive action of the bourgeois forces. This reaction is very evident among the very first exponents of this consciousness, Owen, who sent projects for organising society to the congress of monarchs of the Holy Alliance, and Fourier, who foretold the arrival of a period of 'guarantism'. Both of them, despite their utopianism, already acknowledged the significance of the fundamental, economic factor. Economic materialism also inherited from 'social physics' and counterrevolutionary philosophy their antirationalistic and anti-individualistic attributes: the historical sense, a feeling of the relativity of truths and institutions, realism, the principle of regularity of social life, and the subordination of individuals to its will and consciousness. At the same time, though, a special role in the worldview of such a class had to be played by the necessity of transformation of existing forms; this is why economic materialism assimilated with such fondness the Hegelian dialectic, pouring into it (Engels) modern, natural content drawn from the revolutionary bourgeoisie:

the concepts of evolution, transformism, etc. That is not all. The tasks this class had before it required the individual to be granted rights and the ability to take a critical stance towards the surrounding social reality, and to have a reformative influence on it: it is not for nothing that economic materialism proudly places Kant and Fichte alongside Hegel in its genealogical tree. Through them on the one hand, and via Owen, Fourier and even Saint-Simon himself on the other, another heritage reached Marxism: the legacy of the 18th century's critical-disintegrative rationalism. A particular attribute of Marxism is the performing of a synthesis of critical and reformative rationalism and individualism with the most exact and realistic relativism and social determinism – ascertainment not only of the right and the possibility, but at the same time of the conditional necessity of an active role for individuals, an active role determined in its scale and quality by the social conditions themselves. This is expressed pertinently and briefly by one of the most brilliant practitioners of this school (Beltov), saying that economic materialism "indicates for the first time how we should cope with the social necessity". In him therefore occurred the ultimate descent from the clouds, the transformation of constructive sociology from a Utopia into the science that we spoke of at the beginning.

In its character, economic materialism, using such collective beings as society, nation, class and group, marking their determining influence on individuals, always remembers (or at least such is its tendency) that these are conventional beings, comprising living individuals, within whom exclusively social processes take place. Thus social-psychological studies lie in its nature, and it has many touchpoints with various forms of the psychological direction, just as in practical life the appropriate class sometimes goes hand in hand with the petite bourgeoisie and the intelligentsia taking its place. Some critics belonging to this psychological direction, proud that official bourgeois science, related to it as we have seen via natural nodes, takes this direction into account, in a manner of speaking shame economic materialism and reproach it for its pettiness, in that in such solemn salons of science as are the auditoria and studios of Wundt or Bernheim they know and say nothing about it.[9] Admittedly I do not know who should be ashamed. Besides, the fact is that indeed for a lengthy time economic materialism had no contact with sociology or bourgeois science in general (with the exception of political economics). While sociology proceeded from a common, Saint-Simonian source along one channel, increasingly convenient and evident, marked with the names Comte and Spencer, a second stream flowed simultaneously from the same source – underground, it foamed at the columns of ephemeral writings, gushed in the

---

9 N. Kareev, Ch. IX, X [Kareev, Nikolai, 1896, *Starye i novye etiudy ob ekonomicheskom material-izme*, Petersburg: Tipografiia M.M. Stasiulevicha].

jolts, flowed over into the brilliant utopias. Finally, coming ever closer to the surface, it also pushed ever closer to consciousness the active, unprivileged section of the bourgeoisie, and it was largely under the pressure of the latter, frequently unaware of this, that reformative forms of 'psychological' sociology emerged and continue to emerge. Today this current flows along an ever broader channel, and perhaps not too distant is the time when 'economic materialism' will cease to be a school, and become the atmosphere of sociology as a science. Of course this will happen as long as economic materialism absorbs and acquires – and this will happen when it totally absorbs and acquires – the achievements of previous and contemporary schools – biological, and particularly psychological, which as we have already pointed out is undeniably an active laboratory of valuable ideas and discoveries.

Among other things, particularly momentous was the convergence and mutual permeation (though hitherto not yet entirely accomplished) of economic materialism with the science of prehistory; by the latter I understand here the entirety of research into forms of social life that preceded Greek and Roman statehood, already known to and exploited by social currents and bourgeois science since the times of humanism, and thus I have in mind Maurer, Laveleye and Maine, as well as Morgan, Tylor, and he combining both the ancient-legal and ethnographic directions: Maksim Kovalevsky. At the transition from the humanistic classicism seasoned with the legal philosophy of the 'national spirit' to research into the pre-classic past stands the interesting and noble figure of Bachofen, whose *Mother Right* is published in 1861. The significance of this direction of prehistorical research and its encounter with economic materialism flows from the discovery of the original commune of ownership, which was already sensed, idealised and identified with the 'state of nature' by the rationalist-individualists of the 18th century, with Rousseau at the forefront, and later by the utopians of the first half of the 19th century. That economic materialism and the worldview amalgamated with it was, by its very nature so to say, predestined to merge into one with the emotional-intellectual currents issuing forth from these prehistoric studies and discoveries, is testified to by that telling fact that Karol Fourier, as one of the first, understood and emphasised the meaning of anachronisms in social life, and formulated a division of the history of mankind into periods very similar to Morgan's, while Saint-Simon anticipated the comparative-historical method, proclaiming that the state of the most highly developed nations in the various eras of the past was to be found in the present state of various uncivilised peoples.

How exactly the discoveries of prehistoric archaeology could be utilised by economic materialism we may best understand with the words of one of the greatest authors of these discoveries, Henry Sumner Maine, uttered due to the analogical impact of faith in the original state of nature on the people of the 18th century. Pascal – recalls Maine – observes in his *Thoughts* the kind of subversive impact that is exerted by a comparison of some existing institution with something that is considered a 'fundamental and original social right'. This remark, in Maine's opinion, was probably suggested to Pascal by the disturbances known as the Fronde, during which the Parisian parliament referred – against the king – to the 'original and fundamental laws' of France. Let us add that these were also cited at the beginnings of the French Revolution; and in regard to the social and not purely political order, such a role was played by the concept of the state of nature. The entire individualistic-reformative criterion, the entire eternal reason, law and justice was based on this concept; and essentially from this also derived the Kantian categorical imperative – although perhaps awareness of the source has become lost. Yet these elements reside still under diverse figures in the displays of aversion shown by sociologists of the 'psychological' direction and 'subjective' school in regard to the strict social-deterministic tendency of economic materialism. When social determinism and realism appeared for the first time in counterrevolutionary philosophy and sociology, the concept of the state of nature and the individualistic-reformative criterion based on it had to yield in the battle, because they were but previsions and held no real historical-realistic justification. The prehistorical archaeology of the 19th century discovered the real 'state of nature'. Economic materialism, that reformative form of realism and social determinism, had to assimilate such a discovery, and assimilate it did. Hence at the threshold of the further development of sociology in the 20th century, I dare say that in this manner economic materialism provides a genuine basis, an explanation and justification for the undeniable, critical-reformative and incapable of being reduced solely to the surrounding contemporary conditions, independently negational and initiatory relationship of the individual to society – and that this will be one of the paths making it possible to achieve the mutual permeation of economic materialism and the psychological direction, bringing sociology closer to the state of a real science, a state in which it will not be split into schools, or at least where alongside the schools there will exist a certain number of fundamental and widely acknowledged truths and laws, as in mathematics, chemistry or even biology.

§ 9

The conclusion to which we arrived above is nothing other than the essence of the law of revolutionary retrospection. And therefore to conclude we shall thus summarise our view of the development of sociology to date:

The ideas of the 18th century, the ideas of revolutionary rationalism, were – as we know – characterised by retrospection towards classical antiquity, dating from the origins of the growth of the bourgeoisie, from the Renaissance and Humanism.

Sociology came into being at the turn of the 19th century, emerging from the retrospection towards the Middle Ages, i.e. post-classical antiquity.

And the developmental momentum of sociology, with which it crosses the threshold of the 20th century, coincides with a retrospection towards pre-classical antiquity, retrospection giving birth to a new, strengthened, 'synthetic' – if not rationalism – then idealism.

The Crisis of Marxism: On the So-Called 'Crisis of Marxism'[1,2]

A great deal has been said in sociological circles over the last few years regarding changes taking place within the womb of the Marxist school. Andler, a professor at the Normal School and College of Social Sciences in Paris, long ago announced a book on the 'disintegration of Marxism', the interesting contents of which he roughly informed his students about at the above college in 1896 and 1897. In 1898 a professor of the Czech University in Prague, Dr Tomáš Garrigue Masaryk, was the first to appear in the Viennese 'Zeit' with the word we have in the title of this chronicle, and which took hold so perfectly; in the brochure entitled *Die wissenschaftliche und philosophische Krise innerhalb des gegenwärtigen Marxismus* (also translated into French by Włodzimierz Bugiel) he attempted to embrace in one go the entirety of this 'crisis', listing off its

---

<blockquote>1   Source: Kryzys marksizmu O tak zwanym „kryzysie marksizmu", "Przegląd Filozoficzny" 1900, vol. 2, pp. 87–94; vol. 3, pp. 80–99.</blockquote>

<blockquote>2   Bibliography: Masaryk, Tomáš Garrigue, 1898, *Die wissenschaftliche und philosophische Krise innerhalb des gegenwärtigen Marxismus*, Vienna: Verlag Die Zeit; prof. Kareev, Nikolai, 1896, *Starye i novye etiudy ob ekonomicheskom materializme*, Petersburg: Tipografiia M.M. Stasiulevicha; Abramowski, Edward, 1898, *Le matérialisme historique et le principe du phénomène social*, Paris: V. Giard; Croce, Benedetto, 1898, *Essai d'interprétation et de critique de quelques concepts du marxisme*, Paris: Giard et Brière and Croce, Benedetto, 1896, *Les theories historiques de M. Loria*, 'Devenir Social'; prof. Labriola, Antonio, 1897, *Essais sur la conception matérialiste de l'histoire*, Paris: V. Giard, E. Brière and Labriola, Antonio, 1899, *Discorrendo di filosofia* etc. (Lettere a G. Sorel), Paris: V. Giard, E. Brière (*On historical materialism; From conversations about socialism and philosophy (Letters to G. Sorel)*), [in: Labriola, Antonio, 1912, *Socialism and Philosophy*, Chicago, IL: C.H. Kerr]; Engels, Friedrich, 1895, *Lettres sur le materialisme historique*, 'Devenir Social'; Kautsky, Karl, 1896, *Die materialistische Geschichtsauffassung und der psychologische Antrieb*, 'Die Neue Zeit'; Belfort-Bax, Ernest, 1896, *Synthetische contra neu-marxistische Geschichtsauffassung*, 'Die Neue Zeit'; Kautsky, Karl, 1896, *Was will und kann die materialistische Geschichtsauffassung leisten?*, 'Die Neue Zeit' 15:1; Belfort-Bax, Ernest, 1896, *Die Grenzen der materialistischen Geschichtsauffassung*, 'Die Neue Zeit' 15:1; Kautsky, Karl, 1896, *Utopistischer und materialistischer Marxismus*, 'Die Neue Zeit' 15:1; Loria, Achille, 1893, *Les bases économiques de la constitution sociale*, Paris: Felix Alcan; Kudrin, N., 1896, *Na vysote obiyektivnoy istiny*, 'Russkoye Bogatstvo', etc.
This paper comprises mainly sections of lectures by the author at the Free College of Social Sciences in Paris [Kelles-Krauz's footnote].</blockquote>

symptoms in regard to: political economics – and so mainly the theory of value
(the third volume of *Capital*, the works of Konrad Schmidt and Sombart, moving closer to the Viennese school), political tactics (the issues of agriculture,
reform, and nationality), historical materialism (polemic between Kautsky
and Belfort Bax) and sociology in general (the revision that has commenced in
views regarding the beginnings of family and ownership, Heinrich Cunow and
others), in regard to views on ethics, aesthetics, philosophy and religion.[3] The
French, who of course read translations and not the originals, encountering
in the translation's title the term *la crise du marxisme*, laconic yet somewhat
overstepping the thinking of Masaryk, who strictly understood internal crisis
and adopted it without hesitation – have their fates and terms. The matter was
tackled in greater detail by Jerzy Sorel, author of interesting studies regarding
Vico and *New Metaphysics*, from which there is much to learn for the supporter
of economic materialism, an original thinker yet a genuine *dilettante* in philosophy, bereft of clear guidelines – the most zealous contributor to date of the
materialistic (in sociology) monthly 'Devenir Social' – and in an entire series of
articles in French, German and Italian journals – articles of very uneven value –
he set about announcing a 'crisis'. In Italy Saverio Merlino even founded the
special 'Rivista Critica' for this same purpose. In the meantime columnists in
other camps welcomed with joy this – as put wittingly by Labriola – "Ninth
Thermidor of Maximilian Carl Robespierre Marx", and unable to make do with
a 'crisis' informed their readers explicitly of the 'bankruptcy' (a term only recently popularised by Brunetière in regard to knowledge as a whole) or 'agony'
of Marxism.

In my opinion, all of this may be blamed (if I may use such a term) on ... on
the old Friedrich Engels, the very *Pontifex Maximus II* of economic materialism. He made an inexhaustible contribution to the development of Marxist
doctrine in general and in particular its sociological or let's say historiosophic aspect, which is all we are interested in in this paper, mainly in his *Anti-
Dühring* and *The Origin of the Family, Private Property and the State* – the latter

---

3   This brochure – which, as is usually the case when an affordable leaflet, will play a greater
    role than my book in the history of "crisis" – was but a forerunner and at the same time a
    summary of the work that was published this year (in 1899) in Vienna, *Die philosophischen
    und soziologischen Grundlagen des Marxismus* (also simultaneously in Czech). This work
    unconditionally deserves a more thorough critique; as such, I do not include it within the
    scope of this chronicle. For precision, I shall indulge by just pointing out an interesting and
    jocular critique of this work by one of today's most outstanding representatives of scientific
    Marxism, professor Antonio Labriola at the University of Rome, entitled *A proposito delia
    crisi del marxismo* (in the May edition of 'Rivista Italiana di sociologia' 1899) [Kelles-Krauz's
    footnote].

an attempt at outlining the entire development of the institutions of property, family and state to this very day loses nothing when compared to equivalent but newer synthetic attempts by Lafargue, Letourneau, and even Kovalevsky – not to mention e.g. Adolfo Posada. Yet admit one must that 'our' Abu-Bekr[4] also had less felicitous ideas as well. Not only did he introduce a new, independent factor to Marx's monistic view – alongside 'production', the so-called 'reproduction of life', which is to say development of the family crucial in the first period and taking precedent at that time over economic development – against which both Tugan-Baranowski and Henryk Cunow are currently reacting in their latest studies on the 'economic foundations of the matriarch', etc., which provided a motive for Weisengrün and Nikolaev to formulate the mistaken theory of three successive decisive factors, or 'normal concepts': the familial, economic and intellectual; but still in his outspoken letters written in 1895 to one of his German correspondents he accused the "young Marxists of ascribing too much importance to the economic aspect", whilst to a certain degree he accepted the blame for himself and Marx for not always, in the fire of polemic, giving back what their 'collaborating factors' deserved.[5] Both accusations proved a critical and anti-dogmatic spirit, all the way to suspicion and severity towards oneself, though entirely unfounded: after all, Engels probably did not have in mind any popularisers for whom the theory is not responsible, while as for the proper 'young Marxists', the 'disciples': Kautsky, Mehring (also applying to our scientific representatives of economic materialism), they on the other hand always treated the economic factor with great caution and with all reservations, yet quite unfairly acquired the opposite reputation – as any who has read them in the original will admit (e.g. Mehring's *Lessing-Legende*[6]). Let us take, for example, that point usually most focused on by critics of economic monism – the role of the individual in the historical process: in my opinion, in his long and important polemic with Belfort Bax[7], Kautsky was emphatically inconsistent and groundlessly limited the scope of the economic factor's action, using it only to explain what is common to all people in a given age and society, while leaving beyond the confines of its reach individual differences,

---

4   In saying 'our' Abu Bakr, Kelles-Krauz is referring to Engels [translator's note].

5   Cf. F. Engels to J. Bloch 21–22 September 1890 [Kelles-Krauz's footnote]. The letter was published in: Marks, Karl, Engels, Friedrich and Lenin, Vladimir, 1972, *On Historical Materialism. A Collection*, Moscow: Progress Publishers, pp. 294–296.

6   Mehring, Franz, 1938, *The Lessing Legend. The Origins of German Middle Class Culture*, New York: Critics Group Press.

7   Not published in German in a separate impression; French impression published by Bellais [Kelles-Krauz's footnote].

which determine – for example – poetic creativity, etc. If that were so, if economic materialism also stumbled on this kind of *principium individuationis*, it would thereby have essentially refuted the explanation of changes taking place in society, the entire social dynamic. This – in my opinion – is not the case, but this kind of mistaken interpretation of Marxism, which I would call excessively conciliatory and submissive, is unavoidable with the prevailing inclination to which Kautsky himself confesses, an inclination to explain the phenomena of the present above all – if not only – with the aid of the fundamental conditions of the present as well – an inclination that again derives from the constant and exclusive concern for the immediate practical utilisation of research and scientific deliberations. This same practicality, otherwise entirely understandable, legitimate and essential, commands Engels *de minimis non curare*, and thereby to discern 'pedantry' in attempts at using economic factors to explain, for example, all 'prehistoric stupidities' or the history of some small German statelet. Thus we see that contrary to widespread opinion, Marxists do not perchance want to reduce this or that to an economic basis, which I believe only testifies to their conception being as yet insufficiently elaborated, or they fully realise the multitude of intermediate links existing between a particular phenomenon and its economic foundation – which again is entirely consistent with this conception. We shall say the same regarding the acknowledging of the great significance of ideas as motors of development – conditioned, of course, like everything; he who would deny this of Marxism may simply be inundated with quotes – from *A Contribution to the Critique of Hegel's Philosophy of Right*, Marx's work as a youngster, right up to the latest works of Labriola. Besides, this might not help since the 'crisis of Marxism' frequently involves Marxism being attributed some kind of cramped view that is not and was not there, while later on it is discovered that only now is the theory shedding this narrowness of views and 'acknowledging other factors as well'. Even critics of such scientific value as Sorel, Andler and Masaryk – not to mention lesser critics – are not free of this peculiarity.

These critics had a predecessor not only in Engels, but also a more appropriate and direct one – and I wish now to discuss precisely this. When writing recently in French and German about Stanisław Krusiński,[8] I took the opportunity to point out that had Polish sociologists such as Józef Karol Potocki or Ludwik Krzywicki published their works in one of the international languages, they would certainly be well-known in academic circles. The same applies in

---

8 Cf. *Un sociologue polonais Stanislas Krusinski*, 'Annales' 1896, vol. 3, pp. 405–440; *Stanislaus Krusinski Anschauungen von Sozialen Organismus*, 'Die Neue Zeit' 1898–1899, vol. I, pp. 453–461.

the case in question to professor Kareev. He is well-known in western Europe as a conscientious historian of peasant relations, while nobody mentions him as the first proclaimer of a 'crisis in the womb of Marxism'. Yet it was in his book, entitled *Starye i novye etiudy ob ekonomicheskom materializme*, published in Petersburg back in 1896, that probably for the first time one finds the following stance in regard to economic materialism, a stance characterising all the critics mentioned above: one should acknowledge that contribution of economic materialism, that it put the emphasis on the economic aspect of history, hitherto overly neglected, and one should shell and store that healthy seed from it, but resolutely condemn the 'excesses' that Marx's disciples commit in their unrealisable and unscientific pursuit of reducing the entire course of history, its entire fabric, to an economic 'factor'. Neither does it seem to me by any means too late for a brief assessment of this book by prof. Kareev, since within it I also discern many other points in common with the western-European proclaimers of the 'crisis'.

On three hundred and four pages of fine print, prof. Kareev familiarises the reader with the views of the creators of economic materialism – Marx and Engels; of their immediate and most faithful disciples – Kautsky, Mehring, Lafargue, Kraus, Beltov, Struve and Baranovsky; of the more distant Weisengrün and Nikolaev; of the related Rogers, Lacombe and Loria; of certain economic historians: Łuczycki and Vinogradoff; and finally of the critics of economic materialism – the German Barth and the Russians Mikhaylovsky, Yuzhakov, Kudrin, Zak, Obolensky and a few others. These summaries, though interspersed with the author's constant comments, are generally precise and scrupulous, based on familiarity with the entire related literature and on good faith; as such, with the absence of another this book may be useful as an introduction for working on economic materialism, as a means for finding one's bearings within this world of thought as a whole and within related sources – and this is its greatest strength. We say 'in the absence of another', because its drawback is the stance unfavourable for the theories laid out, the unsystematic nature of the interpretation, and in addition – its incompleteness. The book is a collection of lax articles and lectures, and this is reflected in it. It would be fair to say that the author warns readers of this fact, and calls his work but a collection of "materials for the history and critique of economic materialism", and draws attention to it lacking an explanation of the views of, for example, Stammler. But then Stammler's work, also containing a critique of economic materialism, was published almost simultaneously with the book in question – also like Lafargue's study of the origins and development of property, which proving that this disciple of Marx is no less capable than Maxim Kovalevsky at dealing with scientific material, would most probably have allowed Kareev to speak of Marx with less disdain. Following the publication of Kareev's book, much of interest and import occurred in this field: there was Kautsky's polemic with Belfort Bax, and both of Labriola's books were published as were Abramowski's treatises. If we find nothing of them in Kareev's *Etiudy*, this is not the author's fault, although under their influence more than one of his views could have, if not changed, at least been worded differently. However, what we must find surprising is the total omission – in this otherwise so detailed review – of works then already known, and known broadly, of a certain Julius Lippert, who in reducing the entirety of civilisation, even together with language and religion, to *Lebensfürsorge*, to concern about existence, is so close to economic monism that I believe he deserved a space alongside Rogers,[9] and even more so – next to De Greef, whose sociological system, even connected genetically to Marxism, would have probably made it hard for professor Kareev to posit more than one unjustified accusation.

However, before we proceed to polemicise, we consider it our duty to point out that by no means does Kareev belong to that numerous host of fanatical and obtuse opponents with whom any discussion is impossible. On the contrary, even despite the many errors that a greater desire to grasp the fundamental thought of Marxism could have protected him from, his good faith and civil courage is appealing. He emphasises on several occasions that although economic materialism does not, in his opinion, have a future, the various aspirations usually linked to it are entirely independent of its fortunes, and he subscribes to Marx's economic theory as the "most authentic of those existing".[10] From professor Kareev's point of view this is undoubtedly much, although certainly neither Labriola nor Kautsky for example would agree to such mangling of the internal and genuinely existing unity of the doctrine in question. Kareev also considers economic materialism independent of the old-fashioned dialecticism removed today from science; Rogers, he says, a brilliant proponent of the economic interpretation of history, has nothing in common with the Hegelian dialectic, just as Hegel has nothing in common with the economic understanding of human development. I shall not at this point initiate polemic regarding whether a dialectic, such as Engels lays out in *Anti-Dühring*, may be considered *Hegelian* and excluded from sociological teaching. Such a polemic would have to be too extensive for the framework of this article, and besides – with the further elaboration of the law of revolutionary retrospection it would be more relevant to consider whether and what Barthow's critique of the idea of 'development in contradictions' is worth, an idea which,

---

9   We find but a four-line mention of him on p. 252 [Kelles-Krauz's footnote].

10   Kareev, Nikolai, 1896, *Starye i novye etiudy …*, p. 57.

unfortunately, Kareev agrees with so easily, and – whether without this idea economic materialism is capable of resolving the issue of the genesis of ideals and anticipations of the future, Beltov's soloistic solution of which Kareev undeniably rightly criticises. Whatever the case, although I acknowledge the entire profound difference that, in regard to how economic factors have an impact, there must be between an atomised society and a society consciously governing through production, I believe that one has to agree with Kareev to the criticism of that abuse of dialectic operations that led to Engels' thought of a 'jump to freedom', a thought that Weisengrün has in the sharper form of some kind of 'kingdom of independent intelligence', in which economic determinism would cease to play its leading role. Therefore, as we can see Kareev's criticism and remarks are entirely or at least partially pertinent, and may contribute to the illumination and development of an economic understanding of history. Everybody will agree that this theory still really needs more work, and that despite there being several in existence one is still particularly aware of the shortage of mono-economistic monographies, and for example Labriola puts great emphasis on this, calling upon this theory's proponents to work on remaking the entire historiography using its methods and from its point of view. On the other hand, the fact that one has to search sundry circumstantial writings by Marx and Engels for the wording of the main principles of economic materialism, and that economic materialism – which Nikolaev accuses him of – does not possess such a 'grand book' that, according to Littré, every great doctrine must possess, cannot be considered a circumstance derogating them. Too far is this conception from any dogmatism, and all the more so – from any stigma of 'revelation', too much does it live by only facts, which it emerges from the more they are investigated, for it to envy positivism its Comtean *Quran*. As for the second example, in which professor Kareev cites following Nikolaev, then Darwin's *On the Origin of Species* likewise contains a set of facts from which a certain general theory emerges, and it too cannot be considered some kind of entire code for this theory, just like *Capital*, only seven years later, and preceded by *A Contribution to the Critique of Political Economy*, which was published in the very same year (1859). The analogy between the two geniuses here is complete, and besides attention has already frequently been drawn to it (Lafargue, Krause, Ferri and Labriola, etc.).

The genesis of economic materialism itself, which was written about in detail by Engels, Beltov and Labriola, is undoubtedly among the most highly elaborated sections of general history understood economically. And in Kareev's *Etiudy* the relevant Chapter 2 is among the best, and deserves credit for drawing attention to certain points previously left in the shadows: the possible influence of Ludwig Blanc, the almost contemporary and symptomatic birth of the historical school in economics, and in general – the significance of the general disappointment at the turn of the last century with purely political revolutions, disappointment that shifted the centre of gravity to economic matters.

Every proponent of economic materialism will also agree with professor Kareev that Loria commits no end of excesses and mistakes, that his theory is cramped and insufficient; but criticism such as that he applies to Loria is by no means sufficient for disproving it. One cannot accuse Loria of totally overlooking the 'factor of altruism and sense of duty' in ethics, and seeing only 'awe'; on the contrary, Loria strives to explain by what strange paths in a system based on abolition of the unconstrained occupying of land the special category of 'non-productive', intellectual workers must lead both social classes to be guided by altruistic feelings, since only the limitation of egoism, appropriate to normal human nature solely in a system without contradictions, may prevent here violent confrontations between hostile classes – and he even distinctly says that in a slavery system fear is sufficient for this goal, while in a feudal system – religion is essential, and in a mercenary system – public opinion. Thus, in a manner of speaking, Loria considers altruism and morality as some kind of beautiful, intoxicating lotus flower growing only from and indispensably on the battlefield of the class struggle; likewise law and 'binding institutions' in general, maintaining social connectivity, which in a system based on 'unconstrained land' are entirely superfluous, since there is nothing there threatening this connectivity. This is where his cardinal error lies – in the fact that the phenomenon of the sprouting of ethical, legal and political forms from an economic foundation is limited solely to societies based on class struggle, and by this he sees the only cause of this phenomenon in the struggle of class interests. There is undoubtedly some truth in such a view, truth expressed by economic materialism and which Kareev does not want to acknowledge at all, thereby making it impossible for him to effectively criticise Loria; but such a total view, and one that indeed is consistent to the absurd, is precisely what differs Loria profoundly from the Marx school, which reduces the very class interests to the forms and tools of production, and acknowledges the autogenous and not the deliberately Machiavellian emergence of ethical-legal forms based on forms of production both in class and classless societies. Engels disclaimed Loria as an economist; and Peter Struve disclaims him as a sociologist (perhaps insufficiently pertinently – but that's another matter); Croce demonstrated[11] how in Italy Loria wrongly passes for a representative of Marxism, and mocked – in my opinion even unquestioningly too much so – this 'blond-haired Marx';[12]

---

11   "Devenir Social" 1896, no. 11, in Italian – earlier [Kelles-Krauz's footnote].

12   Benedetto Croce tells of how he knew in Naples a certain veteran who assured him, that at
      a certain meeting he had once seen Marx opening and hosting the proceedings. This Marx

Loria himself emphasises the differences between his own views and those of the mathematical-economic school – while Kareev absolutely insists that this school is supportive of Loria and responsible for Loria's excesses! A similar insistence is reiterated in other cases as well, and faced with Kareev's irrefutable good faith it testifies to how difficult it is for professional scholars to understand this conception, engendered according to Mikhailovsky's phrase, "beyond the confines of science", science – let us add – practiced behind the desk! For Kareev – economic materialism is a kind of doctrine according to which "spontaneous economic evolution is by its very self (!) progressive",[13] a doctrine that attributes ideas and individuals with no influence on social development, and which, if only it attempts to seek the reason behind any phenomenon not within a direct economic fact, becomes at once Kareev's 'psychologism' and contradicts itself. Thus when the author of *Capital* demonstrates the impact of political factors – of the colonial, taxation and customs systems – on modern economic development, by no means is he contributing to a justification of his monistic view,[14] while when Beltov declares that without knowledge of the state of minds in a previous era one cannot understand their state in the era concerned, he is contradicting a statement voiced by one of the creators of the professed theory – a statement which, after all, is purely aphoristic – that one should seek explanation of a given era not in its philosophy but in its economy![15] Then professor Kareev may quite naturally call: "Try to understand Roman law without the influence of stoicism!" and thereby deduce that "law has a dual kind of foundation: economic and moral".[16] And if the cosmopolitan rationalism of the stoics flowed in turn from the economic conditions of its time, from their rebuilding effect on earlier ideology? And if the adoption of this incoming seed on Roman ground was conditioned by a conducive economic system?[17] Kareev deals in a similar manner with the economic connective tissue of the Reformation, indicated by both Kautsky and professor Lubowicz: can you explain – he asks – the economic reasons behind the appearance e.g. of anti-trinitarianism in Polish Calvinism? Naturally, I am not about to undertake answering this question, one that requires a specialist;

---

was tall and fair-haired. Applying this anecdote to Loria acquires 'Attica salt', [the term means quick wit – editor's note] when one considers that Loria is just such a tall blond, while Marx – whom some take him for – was a short, dark-haired man [Kelles-Krauz's footnote].

13   Kareev, Nikolai, 1896, *Starye i novye etiudy* ..., p. 180.
14   Ibidem, p. 60.
15   Ibidem, p. 227.
16   Ibidem, p. 221.
17   See regarding one and the other: A. Labriola, *Le matérialisme historique*, Ch. VIII, p. 228 et seq. [Kelles-Krauz's footnote]; see: Labriola, Antonio, 1908, *Essays on the Materialistic Conception of History*, Chicago, IL: C.H. Kerr.

but I do know that when anti-trinitarianism appeared for the first time in the
11th century in the writings of Roscellinus of Compiègne, it was one of the uses
of nominalism that was also emerging, and which by exchanging all abstract
unities for *flatus vocis* was the first manifestation and tool of the revolutionary
aspiration towards making secular power independent and for the formation
of nations, and was fought against by Anselm of Canterbury, William of Champeaux and the Councils of Soissons – in the name of real Church unity; I know
that mediaeval Church unity was a very serious economic reality, and that roy-
alty supported by the burgeoning bourgeoisie gained subtle apologists in the
nominalists; that in the chain running parallel to the continuous economic
growth of the bourgeoisie and royal governments at the cost of feudalism and
papacy, Ockham was Roscelin's successor, and the Reformation – Ockham's,
and that certain favourable economic conditions, and a certain at least partially similar arrangement of the fighting forces – could have extracted the anti-
trinitarian 'heresy' from the scholastic dust. Finally, I know that in no way is the
principle of economic monism opposed by seeking the constituent parts of a
certain ideology, brought about by a certain economic system, in the ideolo-
gies of bygone centuries or distant countries (allochronic and allotopic) – even
if in this ascending genealogical series it would go as far as to take 'philosophy'
or original 'mythology' as a base, by which it is always easy to recognise the
moulding action of Lippert's *Lebensfürsorge*.

Having at this point reached not the individual but the fundamental issues,
the core of Kareev's critique, we must turn our attention for a while in another
direction, which will bring us back to the same point. Masaryk claims that the
general course of the 'crisis in the womb of Marxism' involves the abandoning of materialism in all of its forms; Kareev – on the contrary – demonstrates
that philosophical and historical materialism are by no means inseparably
coupled. Philosophical materialism might not be economistic at all in history,
but idealistic: ideas are states of the brain, but they rule mankind – proclaimed
the encyclopaedists. Naturalistic materialism does not specially distinguish
the economic side of social life, but mixes it with other aspects and renders the
whole dependent directly on either the conditions of the natural environment
(Buckle), or on conditions of physiology and race (Lapouge). Is there really
nothing in common between these two materialisms apart from the name? Or
do they differ from one another solely in the former being 'static' and the latter
'dynamic', as believe Engels and Beltov? Once again, this is an issue too capa-
cious for it to be possible to find room for considering it here.[18] In any case, they

---

18   See in this matter the collection of letters from Labriola to Sorel, published in Italian
      under the title *Discorrendo etc.* in 1898, and in French (V. Giard et E. Brière) in 1899,

do share one general point of view, and this could be illustrated with that reply by the first materialist monist, Diogenes of Apollonia, to Anaxagoras's νοῦς αὐτοκρατής: "When you deny man air, his soul ceases to exist, so it is not the soul that creates the air, but the air the soul". This, to use Lacombe's term, the iron antecedent of the 'fact', is tied to the name 'materialist' chosen by Marx, and evidently Kareev senses this common feature, because the fundamental arguments that he gives against historical materialism, despite the dividing line he himself applied, are such as though it were about psychological materialism.

The only real thing in society is the individual (*lichnost'*) – writes professor Kareev. And this, irrespective of this or that, of any metaphysics, experimentally – comprises two sides: a physical and a psychic, of the body and the soul. Reducing the whole of history to one or the other is one-sidedness. Psychological idealism did the first, and this was the 'thesis'; the second is being done by economic materialism – the 'antithesis'. Each is real within its scope, and they can supplement each other beneficially, but the more one ventures into the scope of the other, the more it reveals its inadequacy. It is therefore now time for their 'synthesis', time to abandon the monistic fantasies. What belongs to people's psychic influence on one another on the one hand, and to the exchange of material services on the other, should be restored.

Such is Kareev's fundamental view, faithfully summarised according to the 'introduction'. He adds to it sporadically in other places. Particularly when Peter Struve gives the following formula (aphoristic again) so reminiscent of the words of Diogenes of Apollonia in its spirit: "Economic materialism subjugates the idea to the fact, and consciousness and duty – to existence"; Kareev declares directly that he "does not intend to criticise this thesis, because he does not understand it at all, and he cannot imagine how facts can give birth to ideas, reality – to ideals, and economics – culture: it's beyond the human mind".[19] In response to Beltov's opinion that economic materialism does not ignore the role of reason, but strives to explain why the action of reason was precisely as it was in each era, and not otherwise, Kareev answers: "Why did reason function thus in each era, and not otherwise? After all the manifestations of reason, just like all phenomena, are subject to their own laws, the laws

---

particularly V–VII. This is an extraordinarily vivid, deeply considered and engaging work; I have already cited it above a couple of times. If in 1895 Mikhaylovsky could have written (though paying too little attention to *Anti-Dühring*) that economic materialism does not have its own philosophy, that it had not taken a position regarding philosophical issues, then Labriola's splendid *Discourse* is the first conscious step towards filling this gap [Kelles-Krauz's footnote].

19   Kareev, Nikolai, 1896, *Starye i novye etiudy ...*, p. 204.

of psychology and logic, the laws of spiritual development ... There are laws governing the birth of ideas from ideas, and there are different, separate ones according to which facts give birth to facts ... The history of ideas and history of forms of production each has its own laws".[20]

Therefore, for the respected professor, 'idea' and 'fact', or the physical and spiritual sides of man, are two entirely different things and isolated from each other by some kind of impenetrable wall. The former is arguably an attempt at applying agnosticism to an economic numen, but never mind. If a critique of economic materialism is reduced to this, then honestly the answer is easy: quite simply, it transfers all social life to one side of the wall. This 'social phenomenalism' was worded the most clearly, in the most scientific manner, by Abramowski – but he was always in all the writings of proponents of economic materialism. And we understand perfectly well that man is the sole social reality, but we cannot acknowledge as right Kareev's opinion that "economic materialism seeks the basis of all social development in something lying outside of man",[21] because it does not seem to us that man's economic activity lies outside of man. Neither can we accept the concession professor Kareev kindly makes for us, claiming that if the "economic explanation of various types of relation between theoretic man and the external world and himself" is unscientific, then it would be an equally unscientific thing to "search within the inner psychic life of the individual for the reasons behind the emergence of hunting, pastoralism, agriculture, the processing industry, trade and monetary operations".[22] So should we therefore seek clarification of these things beyond the confines of the 'psychic life of the individual'? No: beyond the confines of this life there is nothing for sociology, just as beyond the confines of objective investigation and monistic rule lies the undefined psychic life of the individual to which Kareev's 'psychologism' could be applied, but only an unknowable subject, escaping one's grasp, an 'I' without any attribute.[23] Therefore the issue should not be worded as: "By what means does a fact give birth to an idea?" but differently: psychic manifestations involving natural (phenomenal) forces adjusting to human needs (also phenomenal), i.e. forms of production, evoke, 'give birth to' and adapt for themselves other categories of psychic manifestation, involving the definition and understanding of man's attitude towards man or the universe. Of course, when the issue is thus posed, that the birth of

---

20   Ibidem, p. 219.

21   Ibidem, p. 114.

22   Ibidem, p. 3.

23   Abramowski, Edward, 1897, *Les bases psychologiques de la sociologie* (*Principe du phénomène social*), Paris: V. Giard, E. Brière.

'ideas' from 'facts' does not surpass the limits of human reason, and that 'ideas' have the property of experiencing the 'facts' giving birth to them (the reasons of which we shall not stop here to contemplate, as this in itself constitutes an entire section of economic materialism) – thus we reach the above-worded solution to the issue of the ascending genealogy of 'ideas' in a constant relationship with the economic relations maintaining their existence and processing them – in case of need – right up to the original states of humankind.

If that exceptionally erudite and impartial critic, Kudrin, were to now reproach us, saying that in original society as well the production of material goods does not exhaust man's entire attitude towards nature around him, that alongside the 'utilitarian' there has also been, since the very beginning of mankind, an 'emotional' attitude of man towards nature, generating the germs of art and philosophy,[24] then our answer will be twofold. Firstly, there is no doubt that practically nothing has been done yet in this field, although studies, for example by Lippert, allow one to presume that all those conceptionally ideal psychic manifestations do not occur randomly and independently in primitive man, but fall into place so to speak, accumulate around the core – of economic actions. Secondly: if man at the moment of his appearance on the globe already brings with him certain skills and inclinations, independent of concern for existence, and thus of the production of material goods, then this fact as well does not violate economic monism. Because if man, as Franklin says, is an animal using tools, then these tools are but an artificial modification of the organs, and mainly the limbs, of his predecessors, from whom he inherits these emotional inclinations and intellectual capabilities; the action of organs with which animals, though not producing them, grasp material goods is of course animal economics; while it is the anatomical structure, and primarily the development of the limbs, as Darwin stated and Helvétius before him, that determines the intellectual development of animals.

But I shall stop here, because although the author of the study *Holbach, Helvétius und Marx*, one of the most outstanding proponents of economic materialism writing in German, has already drawn attention to it, similar comparisons may seem eccentric. In this manner we could descend all the way to the oysters, as was so wittingly put by Kautsky, who in his constant practicality and sobriety answers Bax – that by no means does the materialistic grasp of history aspire to explain 'the entirety of human life', but only history, or in other words only what changes in it over the course of time. And it is not nature and the human organism that change, but his artificial organs, his tools, his forms of production. All other social transformations can only be reduced to their

---

24   'Russkoje Bogatstwo', May 1896 – contra Beltov [Kelles-Krauz's footnote].

changes. Nature and the organism (and so also certain 'laws of thought') are permanent (if they do change, the change is minimal, and caused by changes in the artificial environment) – and are givens. Naturally many things in society boil down to them, where science is at all capable of boiling individual attributes down to something. Man, living in society, does not cease to live in nature and to receive impressions directly from it – says Labriola. With such a more empirical, if not eclectic, positing of the issue, the response to Kareev's fundamental objection is even easier. Because it is not a question of the very genesis of ideas – as this is primevally given – but is about its change. No matter what kind of wall the dualists would erect between 'body' and 'soul', they have to acknowledge the parallelism of their changes, and therefore – the right of economic materialism to explain changes in ideology through changes in economics. In which case the form of production will not be a source of forms of social superstructure, but will in every case be something more – as professor Kareev wants[25] – than their passive condition: it will be the definer of these forms, the frame within which they fall into place, the mould into which they must be poured.

Besides, it would be impossible to stick to the position taken by Kareev. Between the areas of 'soul' and 'body' thus separated, an unavoidable osmosis immediately begins – and so in this respect there is no shortage of contradiction in his *Etiudy*. "Who denies", asks the author, "that economic ideas (exactly, economic and not others) depend on economic facts?"[26] To what end such degradation of Adam Smith's 'soul' and part of Aristotle's soul, because they opted for this subject and not some other? And politics? Is that to be classed under economics (fact) or philosophy (idea)? But here we have the most general self-contradiction: "Processes of thought and creativity are necessary for man to be able to acquire means for existence. Man's psychic life goes hand in hand with his physical existence, one cannot be separated from the other. In this lies the source of the identical laws of economics and psychology for the explanation of historical phenomena".[27] So no longer is it: hitherto – economics; hereupon – psychology. Belfort Bax, who adopts a similar assumption, escapes contradiction thus: spiritual evolution and economic evolution are largely interdependent, but to a certain degree, within a certain part, up to a certain point – are independent of one another ... One could probably proclaim that dualism of this kind really does go beyond the confines of scientific thought.

---

25   Kareev, Nikolai, 1896, *Starye i novye etiudy ...*, p. 167.

26   Ibidem, p. 223.

27   Ibidem, p. 113.

Absolute Cartesian dualism also sought an exit from the cul-de-sac – in oc-
casionalism. Kareev's 'experimental dualism' is as well like a certain kind of
sociological Cartesianism: but the difference between them is that whereas
Descartes had not yet presumed to speak up monistically regarding human
psychology, and on the basis of animal psychology paved the way to a bold and
fertile monism, professor Kareev is in the meantime reverting, unfortunately,
to stances taken long ago ...

Of course in every social opposition it is sometimes difficult to differentiate
the resistance of past forms being supplanted from aspirations for transcend-
ing the present; the difficulty lies in the former gradually and almost unno-
ticeably transforming, until at a certain moment they metamorphose into the
latter, and as such a conscientious and far-sighted observer, and all the more so
a practitioner, must not disregard the former. There are of course forms vividly
defined and easy to recognise on both sides, but there is also a border strip
where passing from one side to the other is routine and normal. Thus in the
first half of the last century, against the rule of bourgeois liberalism describing
ever broader circles, stepped forward the Hallers and Maistres on the one hand,
and the camp of the Blancs, Cabets and Weitlings on the other. The arguments
on both sides were frequently almost identical, and economic materialism –
somebody might conjecture – was born in the minds of the Prussian Junkers.[28]
One critique served the other, no doubt about it. One should presume, through
analogy, that something of this kind is happening today in regard to economic monism. This is because economic materialism is superior to its maternal
Hegelianism in that it applies the principle of relatively and dialectically transient authenticity not only to the doctrines that preceded and prepared it, but
also to itself. Being, like any philosophy, a natural expression of a certain stage
of economic development and of the related aspirations of a certain class, it
too must vanish and transform into a new philosophy at the moment when this
developmental stage reaches its culmination, at which there is an 'exchange of
quantity for quality' and 'thesis for antithesis', when these aspirations, fulfilled,
lie in the mausoleum of history. At this moment – but no earlier. This is what
the past teaches. Until now there has been an ascending march and it is still a
long way from the end: and this is why, according to the profound observation
by that harsh critic – Croce,[29] economic materialism, despite all the onslaught
"has a life as tough as errors and sophisms do not usually have"; as such, although in its assertions imprecise and paradoxical, it seems to us and indeed

---

28   Cf. e.g. with Mehring in *Lessing – Legende* (p. 436 et seq.) very interesting comments
      regarding one of them, Lavergne – Pegvilhanie [Kelles-Krauz's footnote].
29   Croce, Benedetto, 1898, *Essai d'interprétation et de critique* ..., pp. 5, 22, 46.

it is as if charged and filled with truth – in other words, I would say that it is what is becoming and what will be in the near future the truth. This truth must gradually discharge and emerge from it – and precisely from it – and all critique can and must assist this. If economic materialism wants to remain faithful to its own principle, then throughout its scope it must most willingly expect and even outright provoke criticism. Marx, in the preface to *Capital*, gave it Dante's proud motto for the road: *Segui il tuo corso, et lascia dir le genti!*[30] – he can make it his own, modifying it somewhat in line with his scientific nature, to: *Lascia cercar!* – let everybody seek at ease! We know in advance that they will only find what economic development suggests to them, and that they are certain to find it sooner or later, even if they are walled off from this with who knows what. But in these searches as well there must be a mixture of the resistance of the past with an overstepping of the present; and in this life process the cemeteries recently abandoned become flowery meadows. The gleams of twilight and aurora merge within this entire 'crisis of Marxism', and indeed sometimes it is difficult to recognise where old-fashioned liberalism or idealism ends or begins – or what kind of critique pulls us back towards yesterday, and what kind leads us towards tomorrow.

In any case, I would hardly class Croce's criticism into the first category, and Abramowski's – not at all.

Benedetto Croce's brochure referred to above is a highly useful read, and suggests very many a thought. The author knows how to grasp and to digest Marxism. Only sometimes he does not make the effort, and then – as if on purpose, through dilettantism – he says things superficial, commonplace and weak, for example in his critique of the concept of history as a battle of the classes, at which he quite simply forgets that this concept only applies to a certain period of history, a period with a beginning and an end.[31] The four main points of his deliberations are as follows: 1. Marxist economics cannot be considered a general economic science, but is entirely justified in application for a certain detailed problem; 2. economic materialism should free itself of all apriorism and be understood only as a rule – and one highly fertile at that – of interpretation of history (see Mehring); 3. no practical programme may be called purely scientific; 4. the author, though a Kantian in ethics, denies that economic materialism was by its nature meant to be anti-ethical.

I cannot ponder here over to what extent and in what meaning Croce's conclusions are right; I shall but open a slight digression in relation to the first point, and this in order to illustrate by example what I said in the previous

---

30   From the Italian: Do what you want, and let people say what they will!

31   Croce, Benedetto, 1898, *Essai d'interprétation et de critique …*, p. 25.

paragraph, and also in order to demonstrate – and let me be allowed to do so – that, despite an assertion by one of the superficial critics of Retrospection – I am not an 'uncritical follower' of Marxism.[32]

Marx's theory of value can, as we know, be summarised in a phrase saying that labour is the gauge of value. By what path does Marx reach this conclusion? By the path of extraordinarily strict and logical understanding, as follows: only something common to all entities being compared may be a gauge. What do all commodities have in common? Not their utilitarian features, because this is where they differ, but only the fact that each one is the product of human labour, and all labour, regardless of its specific attributes, is an outlay of life force, an outlay which – with instruments in the appropriate condition – may even be precisely measured. As such, a certain amount of human labour time is contained in every commodity. And all later theories are erected upon this cornerstone.

And this understanding is logically irrefutable. By taking this point of view and applying pure deduction, one could even discard that universally ascertained and discussed inconsistency between a commodity's price on each occasion and its ideal value, and the combining of the definition of value by price with the law of supply and demand (in Marx's article: [*Wage*] *Labour and Capital*), which intrinsically violate Marx's theory of value. Because if the exchangeable value of a commodity is defined by the socially essential work contained within it, then does not the socially essential in this phrase already contain the scale of the demand? And if the amount of work socially essential for the manufacturing of a unit of a certain commodity changes, sometimes after the production of the given unit depending on change in technology, then why should it not also be a function of the incessantly changing demand for both the given commodity and for a universal equivalent? If 100 T put up for sale cost 400 labour hours, but at the moment of sale could be manufactured at a cost of 200 hours, then $V = 2$, and not 4; but likewise, if 100 T worth 400 hours appears on the market, but at the moment of sale total demand amounts to only 50 T, the cost of which would be only 200 hours, then for each unit of the commodity there would also be only $V = 200{:}100$, and not $400{:}100$ (or $200{:}50$). Definition of the socially essential labour should also be taken on the go, you could say in a liquid state. The point of view could thus be taken to its ultimate consequences.

But entirely analogical reasoning may also be conducted from a diametrically opposite starting point. Every person is not only a creator, but also a consumer, and these are the two extremes of every exchangeable commodity. All

---

32   See Bolesław Koskowski's review in 'Głos' 1898, no. 18, pp. 418–419.

commodities have in common the fact that they derive from the outlay of a person's forces; yet all commodities, despite the entire diversity of the needs they satisfy, also have in common the fact that their usage – normally – causes a certain growth in life forces (directly, or by preventing their loss), which also with the assistance of the appropriate dynamometers could, at least theoretically, be measured. Therefore, on the basis of need, a universal gauge of value could also be logically designed. And Croce happens to say something similar, striving to demonstrate that Marxist economics and the Viennese or hedonistic school could mutually complement one another. "In Marx's hypothesis commodities are presented as a crystallisation of labour; so why in another hypothesis should not all economic goods, and not only commodities, be presented as a crystallisation of needs?"[33] And he recalls that Friedrich Albert Lange announced attempts at creating a theory of value along this path. Labriola[34] admittedly responds to this (I give the general sense of his witty response) that in real terms labour precedes the existence of a commodity, while the satisfying of a need is something only imaginable, something that would rather be some kind of wizardry to 'crystallise'. But this difference does not really exist: because measuring the outlay of labour contained in a commodity is served by, just as measuring the commodity's dynamogenic capacity (there is a certain analogy here with electrical potential, for example) would be served by, social experience – based here on previous manufacturing, and there on the previous consumption of units of the said commodity.

So if the economics of Marx and his predecessors chose this and not another from two possible and logically strictly parallel viewing directions, if it perceived one aspect of things perfectly while it paid no attention to the other (or possible others), then this is because – just like any ideology – it is relative, because it too must possess its own specific kind of colour-blindness or, to put it better along with Lange, its own specific retinal structure such that certain class-related categories of understanding restrict its cognitive capacity. Its eyes – just like those of Labriola (ibidem) – are turned, not to say chained – to the 'sweat-drenched, hunchbacked cobbler' and do not look at the 'fictitious' person who is using. But that this is so is a natural necessity of a stage of history still far from running its course. Its fundamental feature is a certain economic fact – additional value – around which all theories group, to which they lead – or actually to which they return. This is stated by Engels in the foreword to the 3rd volume of *Capital*: not only Konrad Schmidt, not only Fireman, Julius

---

33   Croce, Benedetto, 1898, *Essai d'interprétation et de critique ...*, p. 16.
34   *Letters to Sorel*, French edition, p. 222 [Kelles-Krauz's footnote] See: Labriola, Antonio, 1912, *Socialism and Philosophy*.

Wolf, or even Lexis, who calls himself a 'vulgar economist', whether modifying Marx' theory or starting from totally different assumptions, always reach this real predominant fact.[35] Only one point of view to date has proved fertile; as the fact dominating an era changes, so other points of view may and must prove fertile, points of view we can really barely conjecture today. Which is why here as well – *lascia cercar!* But also why here as well, in these quests for a utilitarian or hedonistic economics – is where endeavours at stemming the consequences of the belaboured theory of value come to an end, is where endeavours at overstepping them begin – after they specifically have been taken as a sound and essential basis.

I shall leave this economic puzzle to the economists. Returning in the meantime to the sociological aspect of the doctrine we are interested in, and reiterating after Croce his sigh: "If that disintegration they foretell for us were to be a strict critical revision, how welcome it would be!" – I assert that Edward Abramowski, so it would seem, undertook just such a revision, that – judging by work do date in this area – it may prove seriously useful.

I have in mind two of his treatises published in French: *Les bases psychologiques de la sociologie* and *Le matérialisme historique et le principe du phénomène social*.[36] Mainly the latter, as the former has already been discussed in 'Przegląd Filozoficzny' by Józef Karol Potocki.[37] It also has a further connection with my topic. I made use of it above, polemicising with professor Kareev, who in the second one as well (§ 4) would find an answer to the 'question surpassing human reason': in what way can production shape all processes of collective life, which by their very nature, as ideological, 'are totally alien to it and disproportionate with it'. The solution involves the individual, the person, being considered the only social fact, but within the individual – instead of so-called 'economics' and so-called 'psychology' being divided by an iron wall – technology and culture, that is to say production capacity and life needs, interconnect, closely interpenetrate, creating a 'social-individual node' and 'an idioplastic germ of the social organism'.

Abramowski reduces every social system to this 'technological-cultural formula'. Man's technological competence is initially lower than his 'life intensity': as such association, primitive communism, is a necessity. In the warmth of its

---

35   Cf. Marx, Karl, 1894, *Capital. A Critique of Political Economics*, vol. III: *The Process of Capitalistic Production as a Whole*, pt. 1, New York: International Publishers.

36   Paris: Giard et Brière, 1897 and 1898 [Kelles-Krauz's footnote].

37   Potocki, Józef Karol, 1898, *Eduard Abramowski – Les bases psychologiques de la Sociologie. (Principe du phénomène socjale) Paris. V. Giard et Brière. 1897*, 'Przegląd Filozoficzny' 2, pp. 92–96.

maternal and blessed womb (as Bachofen would say), beneath its caring wings grows the man-child, until his productive capability becomes equal to the intensity of his needs, and his begotten individuality no longer permits him to succumb to the constraining commands of the group. The formula in which an individual's productivity (naturally defined always by society's technical resources) is equal to the sum of their consumption conditions the first of the subsequent forms of social system – slavery; because only forced cooperation in the landed estates could with such a state of affairs give surplus value, needed by a developing individual, but which could not be given to this individual by an isolated family household. When later the individual becomes capable of producing by himself more than he requires for consumption, this enables a change from the slavish landed estates to liberal craftsmanship and rental servitude, and this new form is instituted by the demand within the ruling class for enhanced products, demand established against a background of the work of slaves. The self-sufficiency of every feudal lord's group and his lieges atomises mediaeval society, yet it is this atomisation that produces within it the mysticism that, in turn, welds them in a gigantic onrush towards the Holy Land. Feudalism thus signs the death warrant for its natural economy. Heightened needs arrive with merchants from the East, and they can only be satisfied by monetary trade: the feudal surplus value adopts a monetary form, which already – although it maintains still its consumptive goal – makes it unlimited in its possibilities. The aspiration to increase surplus value, and production not for direct requirement, push towards new cooperation in large villein farms and mercantile craft guilds, and from this new form of surplus value emerges capitalism. The further dialectic of history, based on the technical-cultural formula by which the minimum work provides the maximum usage, we must leave aside.

This is, as we can see, a construct flowing from the thorough digesting of the principles of economic materialism, embracing the entirety of history with a broad sweep – and indeed the form itself of this lecture is alluring, and sometimes impressive – a construct capable of naturally spinning the future out of the past, and that strictly – even aesthetically – monistic. The straight and constant growing of one factor relative to the other in a basic algebraic formula, straight quantitative changes proceeding constantly in a single direction and entailing an entire and extraordinarily colourfully presented diversity of social transformations; and even that 'impetuous agility of economic relations' of which Abramowski speaks in his critique of the *Law of Revolutionary Retrospection* so full of understanding.[38] Clio's sacred parchment scroll, *gesta*

38   Abramowski, Edward, *Kazimierz Krauz. Socjologiczne prawo retrospekcji (ocena)*, "Przegląd Filozoficzny" 2, pp. 80–92.

canentis, grasped at one corner by a skilful hand, unfurls automatically under its own weight, disclosing before us a never-ending ribbon of ever new images shimmering in thousandths of rainbows. I say again: to read it constitutes an immense aesthetic pleasure.

Except ... except that it is always only a construct. In the womb – no! Rather I shall say: on the borderland of the mono-economistic school there already existed one similar, built by – who would have expected such a comparison! – by Achille Loria. With him as well everything boils down to a quantitative process, proceeding from an even more inflexible impetuousness: to the gradual taking over of the earth, as the entire fundamental social relationship changes – the relationship of the two classes: those 'having a choice', and those 'denied a choice', while there are periodic processes of the disintegration and rebuilding of the entirety of ethics and the law, of the entirety of religion and philosophy. It was undoubtedly he whom Labriola had in mind when (in *Le matérialisme historique*, Chapter v[39]) on behalf of the entire school he so firmly renounces any 'evolutionary apocalypse', any *histoire démontrée, démonstrative et déduite*. One understands that Abramowski is a very long way from such despotic treatment of the facts as shown by Loria; nevertheless, one must notice that – unlike the latter – he does not execute his construct in the details. Yet ever am I afraid that Abramowski too, overly preoccupied with hacking an even perspective through the thicket of history, has created a view that one could use to illustrate the rather subtle shade of difference taking place between our science, sociology, and philosophy of history ... But to know through Abramowski such a breath of German idealism, and perhaps mainly that of Schelling! Behold a few examples, so as not to be accused of lip service:

> It is probably understood that the most primitive communism, that which constituted the proper cradle of the human family, that in which there was not yet any difference between family and society, and which had barely the germs not of law but of custom – was not a result of people being convinced that they were unable as individuals to fight with nature, but simply – and we shall quote Haller senior – the natural social state of man. One can scrutinise, for example with Lippert, how children and the children of their children group naturally around the mother, gathering nourishment (though not yet producing it) and helping each other in danger. Neither am I attributing Abramowski a rationalistic view, which I deny here. But in such a case it is clear that the individual economic formula, of $P < T$ (production capacity is less than 'life intensity'), is not a genetic formula of proto-communism. The transition stages from

---

39   Labriola, Antonio, 1908, *Essays on the materialistic conception of history*, pp. 124–139.

that lowest state of savagery to that Morgan-Engels communism, to Lippert's so-called 'second matriarch', are still very dark and almost totally not yet 'constructed', but barely hypothetical; if one were to adopt Engels' hypothesis,[40] that the proto-primitive human groups, already with males in charge, despite these males' antisocial jealousy (as among many animals), merged into hordes in the face of the impossibility of fighting alone with nature, hence the hypothetical unlimited community of women, then things may have been slightly different with that formula, although here as well – what a role must have been played above all by the discovery of fire, and not a new type of social contract! Further, in regard to the disintegration of that communism, then both in regard to the lowly horde[41] and the relatively high stage of the matriarchal 'phalanstery' of the red-skins,[42] researchers attributed great import to the fact of a particular multitude splintering into a few groups and their dispersal, a fact caused simply by the difficulty of feeding enlarged human population in a single place; this fact pushes the man into the foreground, leads to war and the abduction of women, while the spoils of war (later on the Roman *peculium castrense*) and the abducted woman frequently constitutes the first private property on the same principle by which as the division of work between the sexes advances the fruit of the hunting and their tools are considered the property of man, while the household and the related beginnings of agriculture – the belongings of woman. Thus we have here – on the one hand – the consequences of man's still direct dependence on the natural environment, due to the lack of sufficiently advanced tools – while it is not P = T, but really P < T, that instead of bringing together splits apart! – and on the other hand is the impact of the type of production, its qualitative aspect rather than the quantitative. But Abramowski does not really delve back into those times; the action of his historical drama begins only on the eve of Greek statehood, and with him too slavery is classic. In the meantime, in the transition from the slaughtering of captives (sometimes their devouring) or their incorporation into the

---

40   In the latest edition of *The origin of the family, private property and the state*, in French, 1893, pp. 25–26. This is even less than a hypothesis – an allusion [Kelles-Krauz's footnote]. See: Engels, Friedrich, 1902, *The Origin of the Family, Private Property, and the State*, Chicago, IL: C.H. Kerr.

41   Kovalevsky, Maxim, 1890, *Tableau des origines et de l'évolution de la famille et de la propriété*, Stockholm: Samson et Wallin – Ch. 3 [Kelles-Krauz's footnote].

42   Lafargue, Paul, 1895, *La propriété, origine et évolution: thèse communiste*, Paris: Ch. Delagrave – Ch. II [Kelles-Krauz's footnote].

victorious tribe on the rights of equality, to slavery, did not the taming of animals, the shepherding, that form of production resulting logically from hunting, play a decisive role and thus also give to the man – together with ownership of the most important riches – patriarchal power? Did not the breeding of cattle evoke at the same time demand for a serf labour force more numerous than the members of the dynasty, while also enabling a surplus of the fruit of this labour over the consumption, thereby for the first time rendering P > T? Henceforth the formula can, for that matter, better serve; however, at the transition from the Roman to the feudal system, Abramowski takes no account whatsoever of the interference of invaders, bringing with them – if not a matriarchal, kinship form of communism – then powerful traces of it and a derivative, third form – the 'family community' of Kovalevsky or Lafargue's 'kindred collectivism'. These traces of communism of the invaders were the first putty cementing the smashed mediaeval societies into nations; the second, stronger – the need for care and defence in that terrifying turmoil felt by the producers, 'recommendation', the action of the king as the guardian of peace and justice, in other words a certain type of organisation of agricultural production by appointing knights to guard it against enemies. The path via mysticism also leads, granted, to integration, but it cannot be the only one, because in addition it will have to be circled. Finally, in the transition from 'feudal surplus value' to 'capitalistic surplus value', the inventions of new tools and machines also play a decisive role, enabling the multiplication practically to infinity of operations ending in added value.

From the above remarks, overly constricted and hurried, the conclusions are thus:

The formula P – T holds great scientific value as the quintessence of every social form, as its characterisation, precisely as a formula of a given system's static, its equilibrium.[43] However, it seems to me unsuitable as a key to the mechanism of social development. This development is not symmetrical; and the edifice it erects – by no means stylish, but full of extensions, bizarre crossings and connections, corridors and pits with no way out – a veritable labyrinth. Ariadne's thread is in this maze, but it comprises the development of forms of production, or to be more

---

43   "De cette formule peuvent être déduites toute l'économie, la politique et l'idéologie" ... [Kelles-Krauz's footnote]. See: Abramowski, Edward, 1898, *Le matérialisme historique et le principe du phénomène social*, p. 24.

exact – the after-effect of the ways of acquiring nutrition, while at the
moment when tools appear (the artificial environment) – it is the turn
of the transformation of tools, which Abramowski barely paid any attention to (a trait he also has in common with Loria). This turn is not,
of course, accidental. It is initially squeezed out by the relationship of
two elements: the organism – above all the external organs of the human
animal, to the surrounding nature: hunter-mechanics (Reuleaux) strive
to grasp it within a logically unfolding series; one could even imagine
(only imagine) a formula analogical to the universal formula of Du Bois-
Reymond, but limited to sociology, which would embrace within it the
entire development of tools together with the entirety of social development obedient to it.[44] Mankind's universal trait, the desire to live life
along the line of least resistance, to aspire for ever greater productivity of
labour, is the spur that incessantly pushes and will push the former kind
of development, and behind it the latter kind. This is probably how one
could understand Abramowski's development of the 'technical-cultural
formula'.

With such an understanding of economic monism, what will be the role of the
'superstructure category'? Will 'idea' fall to the level of an 'epiphenomenon'?
Futile fear: perhaps when popularisers in their polemic zeal denied the 'idea'
creative force, but the proper science of economic materialism never presented the relationship of 'economics' to 'ideology', as if a river flowed beneath a
mirror. What always remains irrefutable truth is that "Arkwright's invention
contained within the entire preceding ideology", that "culture and technology

---

44   At this opportunity a word about an article by one of our young critics of economic ma-
      terialism, which at the time drew my attention and is also linked to the "crisis". In this
      article, entitled *Prawa przyrody i ich wartość dla historii* ('Głos' 1894, nos. 11–13), in order
      to prove the schematic nature of historical materialism Mr J. Stecki criticises in general
      the value of sociological laws, and even all scientific laws. But even if in astronomy one
      cannot anticipate various deviations, yet despite that its "dynamic" laws have a value that
      is even anticipatory, can one demand more of sociology and of the materialistic under-
      standing of history? Every law is an abstraction, but that it by no means loses in value as
      a result is proved perfectly nearby (in no. 12) by Józef Karol Potocki in one of the chapters
      of his excellent study, *Ginekologia i socjologia* [Gynaecology and Sociology]. In general, if
      many critics of economic materialism head to war recklessly against him, then Mr Stecki,
      on the contrary, has resolutely donned armour disproportionate to the dimensions of his
      opponent: by no means do the claims of economic materialism reach the numenality of
      the laws it has formulated! It is also as if somebody had fired a cannon at a fly – where
      after the shot the fly is sitting on the cannon's barrel ... [Kelles-Krauz's footnote].

mutually create each other".[45] Abramowski also recalls, and perfectly rightly so (§ 12, 13), that no aspect of social life may be separate from others,[46] that they all mutually condition and define one another, that every economic fact has its equivalent in every other category and vice versa, that any one may be reduced to the others, and finally that there is no independent economic evolution, or of any other kind. We read literally the same in the brilliant *The Poverty of Philosophy*, in 'note three' to the chapter 'The Method', which – were I able – I would quote in full here. The social organism must not be drawn and quartered, its parts cannot be dialectically constructed without the whole: "[I]n society ... all relations coexist simultaneously and support one other".[47] Antonio Labriola devotes an entire and beautiful chapter[48] to the critique of the theory of 'independent factors', from Herder to Rogers – but at the same time explaining the necessity of this abstraction when writing history. Which is why I ask: does it really result from Abramowski's premises above that no category of facts may be granted 'precedence'? That by reducing one to another we are caught in a vicious circle?[49] To what I have said above in my polemic with professor Kareev, I would add only one remark: that indeed Abramowski as well, grasping the historical process within certain borders, from a certain point to a certain point, acknowledges the fundamental significance of his 'technical-cultural formula' and takes it as a criterion when comparing periods.

Much still could be said about Abramowski's understanding of the social dialectic, about the role of ideas in revolutions, etc., but this article cannot be lengthened any further. Besides, in a separate work on the law of revolutionary retrospection I shall accommodate it all, as well as the critiques of other reviewers. I declare in advance that in Part 2 of Abramowski's brochure there are, in this respect, some very valuable suggestions. Here I would like but to add a

---

45   Abramowski, Edward, 1898, *Le matérialisme historique et le principe du phénomène social*, p. 3.

46   Although at the beginning, in § 3, Abramowski seems to be saying something different, he considers form of production inseparably interwoven with the entire formal side of social life, and alongside it he sees the "shaping matter" of the form of production; but this matter is precisely that "technical-cultural formula", the development of which, as we shall see further on, is also totally interlaced in the social dialectic. However, the difference outlined here exists: the form of production, even if as the very first legal form (Stammler), is connected to the entire social form in a different manner than the quality and size of the tool of production [Kelles-Krauz's footnote].

47   Marx, Karl, 1955, *The Poverty of Philosophy. Answer to the Philosophy of Poverty by M. Proudhon*, Moscow: Progress Publishers, p. 120.

48   Labriola, Antonio, 1908, *Essays on the Materialistic Conception of History*, pp. 9–91.

49   Ibidem, p. 15, 36.

couple of comments regarding the social differential – and I am sticking to this term received favourably by both Krzywicki and Abramowski.

In his brochure, Abramowski formulates a totally analogical notion under the name "the smallest element of social life, the genuine sociological atom",[50] which by constantly evolving ensures continuity in history. It is the relationship of technical capacity to the intensity of needs within a human individual. In his review of *Retrospection*, Abramowski points out that by defining the differential as an 'infinitely small change in need' I gave an incomplete notion, only taking into account as if one pole of the vibrations, but neglecting creative aptitude, which only socialises the need. The need for breathing, very significant for the individual, does not come under the scope of sociology at all, for example. But I specially made no mention the social character of the needs in question, considering this as understood. As for the opposite need-pole in the differential – I say of it: "In social development, infinitely small and unnoticeable changes taking place in the ways of satisfying all sorts of needs integrate".[51] In general, in line with Marx,[52] I opine that a need can only change through its satisfaction (which also contains the processes resulting from its satisfaction). This is why I believe Abramowski is right in his thought that at any moment within a human being, two great opposing currents of social electricity meet, as a result of which a spark of novelty gushes forth; breaking down the historical processes into such elements is only capable of explaining the way in which progress in productiveness and transformations in tools affect social forms and each other. Once again: economic monism equates with social phenomenalism.

I shall end with this conclusion, having of course not exhausted the entire scope or all aspects of the phenomenon of the 'crisis of Marxism' – because even three times as much space would not suffice for that – while having shown to the reader but a few of its most characteristic and latest manifestations.

---

50   Abramowski, Edward, 1898, *Le matérialisme historique et le principe du phénomène social*, p. 23.

51   *The Sociological Law of Retrospection*, in this volume.

52   "By thus acting on the external world and changing it, he at the same time changes his own nature". [Kelles-Krauz's footnote]. See: Marx, Karl, 1906, *Capital. A Critique of Political Economics*, vol. i The Process of Production of Capital, Chicago, il: C.H. Kerr & Company, p. 198.

CHAPTER 6

What is Economic Materialism?[1]

The answer to the above question may at first glance seem superfluous. There have been numerous, vivid dissertations regarding economic materialism published over the last dozen years or so in the German, Polish, Russian and recently also the Italian and French press; one should presume that the reading public knows what kind of views as a whole they should understand by this term. Besides, back in 1859 Karl Marx, in his brilliant preface to *A Contribution to the Critique of Political Economy*, had already given succinct wording to his social philosophy; this formula, repeatedly cited and reprinted, has on many an occasion served as a basis for the doctrine's further development and as a target to its numerous critics.

However, no matter how deep and accurate this first formulation of Marxism, today it no longer reflects the state of this doctrine.

Marx, as is known, emerged from the womb of German idealism. Seeing that this philosophy, together with its most outstanding representative, Hegel, was 'walking on its head', he resolved to 'put it on its feet', on the firm ground of 'earthly reality', yet maintaining the attributes constituting its truth and glory: monism and the dialecticism of the revolutionary spirit. Hence in formulating his views, he always bears in mind German idealism, with which he compares them and against which he sets them; thus at times the conventional character of his terminology, leading to misunderstandings, such as, for example, the opposition of the notions of 'consciousness' and 'existence'. Apart from this, Marx does not embrace the entirety of views constituting economic materialism today within his preface. His friend and heir, Engels, admittedly using his guidelines and notes, added an entire new chapter regarding primitive man, and again in the preface to his well-known *The Origin of the Family* provided a new 'text' – sought-after plunder for that category of critics wittingly termed by professor Labriola the 'philologues'. There was then a long period during which the materialistic understanding of history gained numerous proponents and was applied in monographs and programmes to various theoretical and practical issues, until ultimately Karl Kautsky, the most brilliant of Marx's disciples in a scientific sense, considered it essential in the face of critiques based on misunderstandings to perpetuate the fundamental traits of the doctrine in an

---

1 Source: Czym jest materializm ekonomiczny?, "Prawda" 1901, no. 37, pp. 450–451; no. 38, pp. 462–463; no. 39, pp. 475–476.

accurate definition. He did this in 1896 in his journal, availing himself of the opportunity presented by the polemic with Belfort Bax, with his characteristic writing talent and clarity, thanks to which his articles became one of the essential sources for all those dealing with this matter. However, this work is a polemic and circumstantial piece, simultaneously an apologia and an indictment, and as a consequence is naturally uneven and incomplete. One could say the same regarding other expositions of economic materialism written by this theory's proponents, e.g. Mehring or Lafargue; others – by Labriola and Beltov – are entire books, not devoid of the same faults either, but with other significant strengths. We see therefore that a concise, though as far as possible complete and systematic exposition of the materialistic, or – as I would prefer to express it – the mono-economistic understanding of sociology is desirable; an exposition not polemic, yet in a manner of speaking scholastic, constituting a goal in itself. There has, as of yet, been no such exposition; therefore, the reader shall find it in this work.

A difficulty or two arise here, the chief one of which derives from the fact that our school's sociological conception has spread so widely in recent times. The picture of economic materialism, if only sketched in the most general of outlines, but complete, must embrace today not only the works of Marx and Engels, and not only must we add to this foundation the works of their most brilliant disciples in this area, of which there are three or four; we also have to take into account thoughts scattered throughout works by numerous less outstanding Marxists; and not neglect – as that would be a grave error – the contributions by those sociologists who, though not belonging directly to the said school, succumbed to its decisive influence, such as De Greef and Loria; those who came to recognise the same main principle along different paths, such as Rogers, Lacombe and Lippert; and finally even those who work for the development and perpetuation of the said theory, frequently against one's will and ineffectual reservations, which in my opinion applies to the entire school of historical economics and economic history.

All these elements constitute a homogeneous whole in their most general attributes, and this is because all emerged from a single, great foundation: society of the 19th century, which is to say of an era whose characteristic historical feature is the gradual effectuation of a great economic revolution via the growing awareness of the broad masses; yet this homogeneity is ceasing to exist, since we are passing over to the details; here there are differences between groups even in still very important issues, even between particular writers. This is quite natural; after all, any imitation is at the same time transformation; therefore just the very dissemination of a theory in various circles must destroy this homogeneity – at least that as narrowly understood, allowing it to be found in its entirety and everlasting changelessness in every cited 'text'.

From the above one may also deduce that we, too, despite attempts at remaining within the role of a simple clerk, will not avoid giving our exposition a certain personal tint. Because when somebody belonging to a certain scientific direction, and wishing to contribute as capable to its development, sets himself – as we in this case – the task of highlighting its fundamental attributes and separating them from those of a secondary nature, then he will quite naturally consider as the most fundamental in the entire theory that which serves as a premise for his own conclusions and ideas.

Now that we have this justification and reservation behind us, we may proceed to the task itself.

I

Human life is a result of three factors to which it may also be fully reduced; these factors are the actual person, nature and society, or – less succinctly but for that more accurately – the biological attributes comprising the genus *Homo*, the natural environment in which a specific group of humans lives (the cosmic, geological and topographical conditions, the flora and fauna), and finally the lasting relationships between people. Man is subject to the necessity of acquiring the means for living and for protecting life; his attitude towards nature is what mainly depends on this necessity, and man's association with other people is also based upon it: because either this bond, having arisen autogenously between mother and children, becomes for man the sole deliverance from doom in childhood and then imposes itself upon his consciousness as an imperative, which entitles him to believe that the 'social state is the natural state of man', or – influenced by attempts towards ever more efficient defence and ever more abundant and diverse productivity – there is a joining, to some degree or other voluntary or coerced, between the father and the mother with her children, between families, tribes and nations, with one another, where we have real examples of 'social contracts', or finally the action of the factor of existential necessity is manifested in the instinctive and deep conviction among members of highly-developed societies of the absolute impossibility of breaking social bonds, of the irrationality of non-social life. The very fact of a community fundamentally alters the attitude of a being, of a living creature, both animal and man, to nature; community is an artificial environment that stands between its members and the natural environment, and changes the latter's impact to the benefit of these members. But not only does society itself result from the attempts at defence and productivity; they also lead to the discovery of tools, which are only natural organs of the human, artificially strengthened and tailored to their tasks using means provided by the surrounding nature. Yet because a solitary person cannot exceed a certain very low degree in the perfection of tools, society and technology become inseparable very early on, mutually conditioning each other and together constituting the general artificial environment that separates man from the natural environment.

Animals also sometimes have tools and frequently live socially; but only to man (at least among the higher species) does the lasting socialisation of technology apply, a consequence of which is a kind of intensifying of the isolating and protective forces of the artificial environment, such that it places man in an entirely different position, above all other living beings.

The first and extremely important manifestation of this force is the change to the nature of adaptation: when adaptation to natural conditions among all living beings takes place with the assistance of changes in organs and in the organism in general, without which the being either cannot cross the borders of its natural environment or dies if it has to live in a different environment, man in the meantime adapts through changes in his tools, thanks to which he can – within certain ever wider limits – freely select a natural environment, and his body remains almost unchanged in different places, times and conditions. Instead of the organism, it is the tools that transform beneath the incessant push towards ever greater productivity. But they change quickly and visibly only from the moment when they cross the threshold of socialisation (that is, the making of a group with their shared energies). Beforehand man lived on the world for many a century among a variety of geological and climatic changes, bearing their consequences, but – just like all animal species in their main established traits – as long as he was able to live, he always lived in the same way, without any major mental changes, without history. Human history, as rapid and rich as it is, only begins from the moment when the tools of production and defence are manufactured socially; since that time, both the natural environment of mankind, and the physical organism of the human being, have barely changed; only society itself has changed, and so its changes, its history, derive entirely from changes in productive technology (since defensive technology constitutes only a branch of the productive, and at that a branch whose relative importance is continuously diminishing).

The tools of production, and technology – in the broad sense of this word – juxtaposed with the natural environment, define the method of production. Yet the very first 'method of production', if one may say so, the gathering of vegetable produce and animal prey, precedes all tools and is based solely on the natural organs of grasping and crushing, those direct antecedents of the most primitive tools. The later hunting, fishing, shepherding (necessarily preceded by hunting) and agriculture are sometimes conditioned by the technology of which society is in possession, in its application for the type of resources appropriate for a specific natural environment; and when talking about technology, one cannot forget about fire, the artificial generating of which depends on having the right tools, but which even if it is not yet actually generated, but only sustained by people, it comes under the general concept of technology as embracing everything that, under the management of man, substitutes or supports an action performed by his natural organs. The frontline role played by fire in the creation and shaping of primitive societies is known to all.

Later methods of production, right up to the great universal machinism of our times, supersede each other together with the development of social technology, which under an incessant push towards greater productivity expands, differentiates and becomes more complicated. Simultaneously there is a constant decrease in the natural environment's influence on the type of production itself, and all the more so on the rest of social life: because technology allows human society to affect nature and evoke changes within it, frequently greater than changes self-generated. The method of production and the social relations defined by it also affect the physiological life of man, sharpening or dulling one sense or another, developing or retarding a particular organ or another, generally causing what we call the degeneration or improvement of the race; perhaps one day they will influence – should Dr Schenk's attempt succeed – the sex of future generations; not to mention the physiological changes that, in the human mind, must accompany a train of thought constituting a product of society. Therefore even changes in nature and in the human organism, since when history has been running its course, depend on technology and the method of production. At the moment when social productive technology has allowed man to master nature, since it has spanned – like a bridge – between human desire and the wealth of nature, it defines every relationship or at least every change in the relationship between man and nature – because above all it defines all relationships between people, the entirety of social life.

II

The manner of production defines social life in its entirety. Essentially: at the beginning, any activity of the mind and will of people in a society, not excluding displays of so-called primitive 'art', 'philosophy' or 'religion', has as its sole purpose and object the preservation of life and satisfaction of the fundamental material needs; later, though, as ever newer and more diverse countless material and spiritual needs emerge, then – on the one hand (negative conditioning) – each of these needs may only surface when the material wealth of society allows, and – on the other – the very character of every need depends on how it is satisfied and on the type of capacity or incapacity for satisfying it.

And so what the positive and far more important conditioning involves is that each of these secondary needs may be satisfied by no way other than with the means provided by a specific manner of production, and only in such a manner that it not result in any major, even indirect, detriment to the matter of fulfilling the fundamental material needs (and at least the needs of that part of society which, in a specific case, it concerns), but on the contrary, that in the majority of cases, and in all important cases, the satisfying of secondary needs further the fulfilling of those that are fundamental.

We may summarise this all in a brief and accessible formula, but vague and ambiguous, which we shall use only because the above sentence lends it the appropriate meaning. And so, wording it differently: ethics, law, politics, religion, art, science and philosophy – they all have a 'utilitarian' source and existence, due to which they cannot negate the manner of production, but must adapt to it.

Therefore above all the division (or indivisibility) of work, together with the manner of management, which define the method of division and circulation of riches, adapts directly to the manner of production; then the manner in which the riches are consumed adapts; and this entire economic organisation is connected so very closely to ethics and economic law, and simultaneously the familial and political system together with the familial and political ethics and law. In every area, ethics and the law bring the recognition of opinion and the sanction of force to the social system that forms by itself, which is to say that it adapts blindly to the needs of generating riches. Knowledge, as long as it is not just the systematisation of ethics, law and self-generated social organisation in general, is not really anything other than the totality of the information required for producing the riches, and it ever aims towards this goal, no matter what degree of specialisation, accumulation and sublimity it achieves over time. Speech, that essential tool of socialised production, should be considered a part of knowledge, before over time it becomes one of the areas of art. Art, in one meaning, constitutes part of the material production and depends closely on the state of its technology; in another, more general meaning, free of considering the tangible side of things, it is – one could say – a certain type of ethics of instincts, which is to say a system of actions or thoughts and feelings favouring people's execution of the edicts of social ethics, precisely thanks to what constitutes the character of art, and namely that any trace of a primeval, utilitarian basis of these deeds and things perished, ceased to be conscious. Religion and philosophy, having one and the same task – a general explanation of phenomena – and on the whole constituting synonyms, form a combination of science and art, both types of science and art as we have distinguished above – a systematisation of all the beliefs and all the edicts of society.

III

It is precisely the above totality of views that is expressed by the correlatives of basis – superstructure, and content – form. These are illustrative, allegorical terms – as are the greater portion of those used in the higher sciences. By following the architectural allegory appropriate for equilibrium, or the geological and plastic allegory containing a certain dynamic element, we may present society schematically, either as a structure of a few storeys resting one upon the other, or as a body comprising a certain number of layers arranged around a core, adapted to it and to one another, that is the external layers to the internal ones. The economic category of social phenomena comprises the base of the entire superstructure, the inner content of the entire social form; but also within the limits of this formal entirety then ethics is, for example, the foundation of law, while politics, science and art serve as the basis of philosophy; on the other hand, and within the limits of the overall economic category, the division is based on a foundation of production, while the actual manner of production – is based on technology. Each layer of social facts is therefore fundamental in relation to the formal class of phenomena that lies upon it; and all social phenomena may be unfolded in a series according to their degree of formality (secondary, tertiary, etc.) in relation to the social technology of production. This series was arranged differently by Engels, De Greef, Lacombe and Labriola; much still remains to be done for one to be able to define it as adequately investigated. As for myself, I believe that it contains three main grades: 1. economy; 2. ethics and law – related to property, family and politics – or in other words the norms of social action in general (Tarde would say: 'social teleology'); and 3. knowledge; art; religion and philosophy – 'social logic', norms of thinking, of understanding (and reproducing) the world. As we see, each of these three main grades is split into a few parts. A given formal category of phenomena adapts directly to the one that constitutes its closest foundation, and indirectly, only via the form of the latter – to the lower fundamental categories. Yet here we have to draw attention to the floundering of the series: because after all systematic law, both as a systematic philosophy or religion, are later social constructs, formal both in relation to ethics, and – on the other hand – to science and art; the germs of science and art, conditioned by primitive material production and by the germs of ethics, already existed at the beginnings of society, before the appearance of systematised law. In general two formal classes of phenomena unequal in relation to the economy, the 'theological' and 'logical', may – though beneath a shared impulse of economic development – develop to a certain degree one independent of the other, as a result of which the relationship between formality and dependence, between for example law and science, art or even philosophy – may in certain eras really be reversed. Nonetheless, in societies that are strongly – or I should say defensively – organised, such as contemporary ones, the order of the series laid out above (one would like to say the 'normal' order) seems usual, meaning that philosophy and religion, art, and even proper science remain at the service of the given social order, eschewing its undermining, and on the contrary, reinforcing it with the assistance of the appropriately discovered circumstances necessary precisely for it.

IV

Indeed, what is the real and no longer allegorical role of the 'social form' in relation to 'social content'? It is, by its very principle, the relationship of the means to the goal. Satisfying biological needs is the goal of economic activity; yet the latter becomes and remains the goal, and at the same time the fundamental condition for social life and its most important need. Ethics in turn is a means ensuring the appropriate functioning and enduringness of the economic system, preventing disturbance in the processes of manufacturing, division, and consumption. Law is the means for consolidating and strengthening ethics. Political power – the means guaranteeing that the law is executed. And so on: science, for example, directly provides the means for production, but it also provides such premises that the precepts of ethics adapted to the existing manner of production could always be the conclusions drawn from them.

Yet thanks to the general quality of man's psychological nature, which itself is perhaps considered a symptom of universal inertia, a means originally subordinate to the goal but which, as it is performed, finally supplants it, removes it from the field of awareness and itself becomes a conscious and conclusive goal,[2] in the face of which the true, fundamental goal seems now but

---

2 Tarde, who often despite himself provides arguments for economic materialism, expresses this thought in a sentence proclaiming that *les simples désirs se transforment en volitions par des syllogismes subconscients (L'opposition universelle)* [simple desires change into will through the syllogisms of the sub-conscious] [Kelles-Krauz's footnote].

a subordinate means. This phenomenon sharpens further under the influence of the division of labour and the division of society into classes, since thanks to these facts science in general and each science specifically, politics, and art, etc., become – for specialists and in general those showing a keener interest – goals in themselves, and to a certain degree adhere in their development to the laws of the so-called 'appropriate logic'. Thanks to these factors, science and art become 'selfless', and in general – the social form, having formed, assumes in the same way a certain independence of its content, which is to say its basis. This independence is manifested above all – and mainly – in its resistance displayed towards the evolutionary and transforming drive of social content. In a manner of speaking the social form here plays the role of a caring, preserving bark or shell: it delays the transformation of the content, of the inner, deeper layer, just as something freezing over delays further cooling, as simmering stops further heating, and as in general the accumulation of the products of a particular process put a burden on further progress by the same process.

However, on the basis of another fundamental attribute of human nature, the constant aspiration to achieve as great a result as possible with as little effort as possible, and thereby ever greater labour productivity, that most internal content of social life – technology – transforms incessantly and constantly advances. Naturally this holds true within one and the same society; regress in technology occurs in reality only when some less-developed society conquers or destroys another, one more highly developed. This refers of course only to cases of absolute regression; because if technology worsens or stands still as a result, for example, of excessive protectionism or for political reasons, perpetuating a low level of wages, then the regression is only relative, while in actual fact the production managers remain obedient to the general law of lowest possible effort, except that this law's action, thanks to the specific social environment, is bizarrely reversed. Whatever the case, these are exceptions. Generally speaking, under pressure to increase productivity, society's technological foundation is constantly transforming, despite resistance by the form. Thus the moment arrives when the social form lags behind the content. This is a state we may call normal, usual. At any given moment, every social superstructure, the entire 'ideology', is by its very nature at least a little behind technology; this delay becomes ever greater as one rises towards the higher storeys of the social structure, towards phenomena of a higher degree of formality. Ethics is delayed; science is also left behind; civil, familial and state law; art, philosophy and religion – they contain ever more anachronisms, forms suited not to contemporary but to extinct foundations.

However, the transformation of the technological base proceeds until, finally, the bark gives way or breaks; the clash between content and form ends always with the victory of content; form adjusts to the new content, either by itself, gradually, or – if it lacks the flexibility for that – by being torn violently asunder. This adaptation begins naturally from the category of phenomena constituting the nearest superstructure; this is followed under duress by the phenomena of more distant formality, which therefore have more indepen-dence, as less connected to satisfying the fundamental needs. Phenomena of a higher degree of formality succumb to a defining and moulding influence only via layers of facts of lower formality, which even play a role in regard to them – and thus, for example, the general principles of law in regard to using power – as if new artificial environments: for example the rays of the base's influence – economic or ethical impulses – only get through them specially refracted.

Anachronisms, in the ordinary, folkloric meaning of the word – the anach-ronisms with the longest duration – are forms that used to be suited, but which for their harmlessness and indifference were abandoned at the side and oft for-gotten by the forces of the new adjustment, forces directing their full empha-sis onto more important and more dangerous obstacles. Such anachronisms are most common in the areas of aesthetics and religion; however, there is no shortage of them on any of the storeys of the social structure. This results from the fact that the process of adjusting the superstructure to the transforming foundation bears no similarity to the even, planned and systematic occupation of a conquered country by armed forces. No change in the manner of produc-tion is reflected in the social superstructure along a normal line of ascent; the path taken by this current of successive self-conditioning consequences is of-ten very complicated, full of deviations and leaps across storeys and layers that support one another in the most diverse and immeasurably numerous touch-points; this line may perfectly bypass this or that fragment of the edifice. It will return to it in time, perhaps after whole centuries have passed. There always comes the moment when the entire superstructure of the atrophic base also ultimately vanishes from practical life; of course we are not talking here about archives. But by then the development of the foundation has once again, and since long ago, managed already to run ahead.

V

One can already clearly see from what has been said up to this point that eco-nomic materialism does not consider the social form, the 'ideology', a simple epiphenomenon, and it does not portray its role in regard to the economic foundation as if a river flowing beneath a mirror. On the contrary, alongside the relative independence and power it attributes the form with influencing the very foundation. In the preceding chapter we saw the preserving, delaying action of this force; yet this is by no means its sole action.

After all, if the state of the form's maladjustment to the content delays the development of the latter, then the fact of adjusting must, of course, accelerate this development. This can be ascertained directly at moments of upheaval. For example the development of modern manufacturing forces destroys guild law and altogether feudal law; establishing new law also literally unleashes productive forces. Yet this phenomenon occurs not only on a grand scale, periodically, but also on a small scale, gradually, at every moment. At every moment a change taking place in social content clashes against a waning form and exerts upon it a partially effective adjusting pressure; but before the new form thus created becomes a new obstacle to further change, the very fact of its occurrence shifts the process of the basis's transformation forward by a step. These two processes mutually condition one another, and virtually constitute just one process: just like when a candle burns, the melting of the fat determines the flame, while the flame in turn melts the next piece of fat. In the social process, the cause is constantly becoming the consequence, and vice versa; such is the most general meaning of the famous and, according to some, mysterious Hegelian-Marxist dialectic. It seems to me that when we thus break down the social process into moments, into infinitely small ones, then the 'manner of joining' (Sorel's *mode de jonction*) of the defining base with the defined superstructure, the relationship between this variable and this function, ceases to be so very mysterious. One can then easily understand that social life constitutes a unity, that there exists a relationship and mutual dependence between all of its manifestations, that economic development cannot be understood without legal and philosophical development, and vice versa, and that altogether any phenomenal category may only be isolated from the others in pure abstraction; yet at the same time one has to agree that scientific research necessarily requires the integration of these infinitely small moments within certain limits, whether broader or tighter, that the abstraction and classification of phenomena when investigating a certain momentary period are an essential condition for exiting the enchanted circle of mutual dependence, and are as such totally justified, while then it is obvious that all other social actions are based on an economic action, and that the spring behind all social movement is the incessant drive towards greater productivity and reduced economic effort. This drive defines a number of technological inventions, although the pre-existing and inherited social form always interacts with it. As for all those changes and imitations, the web of which constitutes social life, then we shall formulate the following law: newness appearing within a fundamental area of phenomena always evokes, sooner or later, appropriately suited newness (change) in the superstructure; and although – on the principle of a certain independence of form – certain changes not having any direct causative connection with the fundamental process may assert themselves within it, the newness of the formal aspect may only be consolidated if it reflects the condition of the social base. On the same principle, the imitation of one country's social forms by another is only possible when the social base in the imitating country is already prepared for this to a certain degree, and then such imitation accelerates the development in the imitating country in the direction of the country imitated.

Apart from the most general meaning stated above, this dialectic also has a certain more precise significance. The social form solidifies, crystallises within the prevailing rules, institutions and dogmas. It is not in a hurry to follow the development of the economic, customary or scientific foundation, etc. This development proceeds gradually, in small steps, for now unnoticed by human consciousness. It is only after some time that suddenly these tiny advancements add up to a single whole – and it turns out that the social form previously well-suited is currently in contradiction with social content. Therefore it changes, as it were, its sign, its direction: "reason – nonsense, good – evil becomes", as Goethe says. A well-known example: the same institutions that guarantee the freedom of competition at a time when enterprises are roughly equal become the buttresses of monopoly and the destroyers of freedom at the moment when this very game of free competition makes enterprises highly unequal. Yet when we consider that the social form at the time of its adaptation itself contributes, as we already know, to progress in the foundation, to the dislodging of the foundation from beneath the superstructure, then we shall understand the deep and real legitimacy of the statement that every social form carries within itself and through its own normal action sets into motion that fatal spring of transformation into one's opposite. Each one, at the moment when it corresponds to the foundation and contributes to its development, is good and genuine: without that, it would not have been created; yet each one too, without exception, becomes bad and false. It is not then discarded immediately and in full, but adjusts to the new content with the help of the slow and gradual substitution of new meanings, concessions, ostensible illogicalities and contradictions, until ultimately 'quantity passes into quality', at a certain moment of violent revision of everything – the gradually substituted new meanings of terms sum up, and the contradictions are reconciled within the new system. But uninterrupted social development commences Penelope's work all over again, the social form once again yields to contradiction from the foundation, and because it itself was already the contradiction of the previous form, so out of necessity the new one reproduces the last but one. Thus, for example, for a certain degree of development in manufacturing tools it is right for these tools to be in the possession of the manufacturer; higher development of the tools cuts the manufacturer off from the tools; an even higher level must again connect the manufacturer and tool, but instead of in an individual form, in collective form; and each of these three economic-legal forms is unconditionally essential for evoking the greatest level of labour productivity with this particular state of technology. This example – and one could cite plenty of others – demonstrates sufficiently that the 'negation of negation' never identically reproduces forms of the past, but is in reality a merging, a 'synthesis' of two contradictory forms, each of which taken separately is thereby irrevocably ousted by it.

VI

Everything that we have said applies in general to all human societies. However, there is a certain very important category of societies that possesses certain specific qualities: they are class societies. The ones we call class societies are those in which the division of labour is such that one part of society specialises in the management of production as a whole, and is in permanent command of it, while the remaining part has no access; management of production entails the handling of the means of production, and further – the ownership of these means: the tools and forces of nature.

The division into classes appears in full clarity at that moment in history when the people emerge from the so-called primitive farming community. In this system the ownership of means of production is shared, and the management of labour, at least at the beginning, is not specialised. But the farming community was preceded by social systems based on such methods of production as gathering, fishing and hunting (a variety of which is war), systems in which there existed a division into two classes, also largely determined by biological factors: we are talking here of the male and female classes – and a division into rich and poor, into lords and slaves, was already taking shape. The individual aspiration for maximum usage, though significantly dampened, was never actually totally rooted out of the human spirit in the age of the farming community. This aspiration, expanded by exchange and war – those two auxiliary means of manufacturing – shattered the community at the moment when from a means for saving the weak person, as it was at the beginning, it became an obstacle to increasing productivity which it itself enabled. With the state of technology as it was then, an increase in productivity could only occur to the benefit of a small portion of society, and with the aid of exploitation of labour from the rest. As a result institutions of coercion are established, essential for ensuring the lastingness of such organisation. As time passes the system becomes more complicated: society is still split into two main factions – the haves and the have-nots, while each of these factions is also split into a few parts, and society contains not two but a few classes, each of which is characterised and defined by a certain special role – whether direct or indirect – in the economic process. When law itself establishes (or rather validates) the classes, then we call them strata or castes; yet this is only a particular form of the overall phenomenon. All societies, since the disappearance of the primitive community, have been and are class societies.

The fact of division into classes derives directly from the method of production, from the division and management of labour, and it is so fundamentally important that it takes the position of the base in relation to the entire further social superstructure, starting from the division of wealth, from economic ethics and law. It is like a new artificial environment that has a profound influence on the very course of production itself, while the rest of the superstructure must adapt to the production, precisely through the forms of this new shell. The class constituting the main owner of the means of production shapes the whole of society in such a manner as to ensure itself the uninterrupted lasting of this state of things; with this goal, it takes control above all of state authority by all possible means. But economic development in the direction of ever greater productivity continues to advance, and slowly but surely it undermines the existing dominion, and increases the strength of another class which, having been restrained and oppressed, becomes antagonistic. It fights for power as a means for ensuring it with the management of production and a favourable portion in the division of wealth. Its pressure affects the entire space of the social form, and forces the ruling class to make concessions, it drives it into contradictions in every field. Finally the new class, borne on the wave of the new means of production and supported by the new progress in technology, achieves ultimate victory and then it in turn shapes the entire social form according to the requirements of its dominion, and strives to root out the traces of the previous dominion. Following which – history begins anew.

The division into classes impresses a deep and distinctive stamp on the whole of social life. It necessarily entails a battle of the classes, a battle namely for power. The entire superstructure rises above this volcanic and constantly quaking base. Each class produces for itself an entire understanding of ethics, law, science, art and philosophy; in a word – of society and the world, an understanding such that all of its components head (though some from a great distance and by the most winding of roads) towards justifying and consolidating the means of production and a state political system – of the present, past or future – useful to the class in question. Every social fact is permeated with some kind of class spirit: the entire society is, we would say, class-ridden; at any given moment, in any of its movements or manifestations, it is as if a resultant of varied class aspirations acting upon one another at different angles. As for the manner of the form adapting to the content in class societies, there is something else that is remarkable.

Namely, one has to distinguish two ways in which form adapts to the social content: unaware, or at least – to put it more accurately – independent, self-generated, and the other – aware, artificial, intentional. The former is in a manner of speaking a sluggish, gradual and anomalous cast of all types of dictate and creed around a centre of basic needs and actions. After some time a layer of such a cast covers the core content and now its forms have a moulding action. From here a social apperception as it were forms: human consciousness aims *a priori* in a certain direction (positive influence), while at the same time a sifting of some kind (negative) shuts before it certain other paths of thought and action, makes them invisible to it. This social apperception, this sifting of thoughts and drives, is precisely what causes the members of a particular society or a certain class, even though they always have their own vital collective interest in plain sight, to consider themselves completely selfless and to really feel this way; it is precisely beneath this form of the selfless ideal that the social or class interest takes root in people's souls the most deeply; therefore only desperate boorishness can explain all the actions and thoughts of the members of a given society or class in the direct interest or that taken consciously as their goal. Nevertheless, one has to admit that such a phenomenon is more common in class societies. In general, classless societies have a more self-generated development; in them the form stratifies gradually on the base, without quakes, crystallising and breaking apart again, beyond – we could say – the consciousness and will of society. In the meantime, with a battle of the classes – each of which defends their own interests against the rest – then out of necessity a conscious and intentional, so-called 'rational' organising of society prevails: every system develops and manages its affairs strategically, in a fortification-like way so to say. The apperception hardens in the battle; the sieve tightens; therefore the form resists more the transformations of the base; its delay, when finally ascertained, takes on the dimensions of an abyss that requires a revolution to even out, and this in turn violently oppresses the needs and instincts prevailing before it. Which is why development in contradictions is more bruising than in societies not divided into classes; the disintegration and renewed integration of social dictates and creeds, so accurately discerned though arbitrarily explained by Loria, create highly opposed subsequent phases.

But the entire period of class societies is one great antithesis of the primitive community. The development of technology to a degree making it possible for all to make use of the highest material and spiritual goods, and the accompanying development in the proletariat's consciousness, is bringing closer the moment of 'synthesis', and together with it – closure of the dialectic cycle of history, of that history – we should understand – that our cognition has managed to embrace so far in the past, and anticipate in the future.

• • •

The above lecture should, logically speaking, be supplemented by two further chapters: an outline of the genesis and development of economic materialism against modern class psychology, and a glance at the 'crisis' of this theory and the probable direction of its further development. We shall do this at another opportunity – and probably, out of necessity, elsewhere.

VII

The bourgeoisie of the 18th century was both materialistic and rationalistic. Materialism and rationalism were, in their hands, a mighty weapon, a dangerous means breaking down all the intellectual and emotional norms that stood guarding the feudal manner of production and feudal state institutions. Professor Alfred Weber also says pertinently: "Equality before the law of nature, identical determinism for all, not ruling out the Highest Being: such was the shared motto of the materialistic philosophers before the year 1789 turned their motto into the Revolution". The close relationship between the social aspirations of the bourgeoisie and their philosophical views is disclosed no less emphatically by the following words of Holbach: "The universe is not an absolute monarchy as Duns Scotus would like, neither a constitutional one as Leibniz imagines, but a republic". But the bourgeoisie imagined that his revolution would be the only and the last, that it was equipped with the absolute truth, and above all – the real definition of unchanging human nature; and because of this they considered their entire past one gigantic error, a senseless violation of this nature. Hence the inability of materialism to understand and explain history: at the most it knew how to accuse the clergy and the princes, constantly revolving within the following vicious circle: "Public opinion governs society; and upbringing (in other words society itself again) creates public opinion".

The counterrevolutionary school, given the task of defining the existing state of affairs, strived to justify this system with the consideration of social usefulness, but because it was a system in which local and state qualities and differences, specific attributes and phenomena were granted particular care and respect, thus it was natural that this school withstood the revolutionaries with its historical and realistic senses. On such principles, Haller, Maistre and others – right up to Hegel – 'rebuilt' social science while at the same time 're-storing' the pre-revolutionary system. "Everything that is, is reasonable". Such was their memorable slogan – and everything changes only gradually, as the shifting social usefulness takes the ground from beneath its feet. This is why one can find views quite close to historical materialism, for explaining social phenomena with the aid of the class battle for material interests, among them and in general among all those who participated in the reaction against futile rationalism, against absolute faith in political or rather in any purely formal revolutions.

But the centre of gravity of such views here is also sometimes feudal farming, attributing this economic form together with its expressions – political (kingdom of divine grace), and religious (the hierarchical church) – with the highest level of economic and social usefulness. As such the subscribers to these views cannot leave society – or the universe – to the mercy of the elemental forces: those impulses from below must be taken by the reins, must yield to management from above; in other words – the Absolute and idealism. Therefore, if Hegel presents the development of mankind as a dialectic process, meaning natural and essential; if he deduces the philosophy of history from the vicious circle of the materialists, reducing both expressions of this relationship to a common cause that lies even deeper that the legal concepts of Guizot: *état des personnes société civile*; and if besides all this he knows how to avoid the fiction of eternal, unchanging human nature – it is only because in the march of mankind he sees only a subordinate and inevitable reflection of the absolute idea in its continuous becoming, an idea which after all is ultimately nothing other than but a projection into the beyond of man's mental nature, of the action of his mind.[3]

Within the battle of these two classes – bourgeoisie and feudal – a third grows unstoppably, its distinctive feature from the very beginning being that it does not identify with either of the two preceding ones, yet intends to inherit from both. The mutual assaults by the two old classes are, in practical life and in theory, only of benefit for the rise of the new one. Just as its ideal of the future harmoniously combining perfect freedom with organisation of society,

---

3   Plekhanov, Georgi, 1897, *Beiträge zur Geschichte des Materialismus*, Stuttgart: Dietz [Kelles-Krauz's footnote]. See: Plekhanov, Georgi, 1976, *Selected Philosophical Works,* vol. II, Moscow: Progress Publishers, pp. 31–182.

and universal prosperity with the highest degree of productivity, so too the social conception of this new class exceeds the conceptions of both the previous
with the help of such perfect synthesis that one really could compare it with
how Kant, reconciling the views of Locke and Leibniz, thereby displaced them
forever from scientific thinking. The class in question is namely above all not
a tributary of rationalism: you could say that it has realised through its own
experiences that the highest form of bourgeois reason very easily transmutes
into ignorance; that with all of its claims for toughness, it is but an expression
of very fleeting interests and economic relations; apart from that, it senses sufficient strength within to prove by action the relative value of every constituted social form, to twist the circle of the social dialectic. Yet this is precisely
why this young class knows that the motor to all existence and development of
society lies not beyond or above it, but is rooted deep inside itself: in the incessant drive for ever greater productivity, under the thrust of which the entire in-
terminable succession of technological inventions unfolds. Of course, in these
inventions, in the productive technology, nothing other than the human spirit,
human nature, is manifested; yet this nature has nothing everlasting about it,
and is by its own very essence constantly volatile, and this not thanks to the
effect of some superhuman cause, but simply because the needs that 'human
nature' specifically comprises change under the influence of their fulfilment
and as this happens. The endless formation of the fundamental factor is therefore transferred here deep into the middle of society itself. And in order for
this formation, for this endless transformation not to cease at a certain point,
as Hegel wanted, and in order even for that moment – at which that which still
is ceases to be rational and should give way – not to be delayed; with this goal
the new philosophy merges into one the Hegelian dialectic and materialistic
tradition, that means of revolutionary disintegration so effective in the hands
of the French bourgeoisie.

The German bourgeoisie in the 18th century was still much too weak to be
able to borrow that sharp weapon of materialism from the French. Their philosophers, with Kant at the forefront, would have had to be satisfied with the kind
of adaptation of Rousseau's rationalism to the situation of their class, which at
that time could only and barely in the name of individual ethics and dignity
protest against the 'enlightened' Voltairean but rotten despotism, that rationalism had changed into idealism and metaphysics, and later, by then with total
ease, into the idealistic philosophy of the social Bourbon Restoration. But by
the mid-19th century the German bourgeoisie had gained sufficient strength
to be able to wage a more resolute battle with feudalism, and then it turned
towards materialism. This transition is achieved gradually by the Hegelian left,
mainly Feuerbach; and it is precisely that moment of materialism and idealism

combining that is the moment of the birth of Marxism, of the social philoso-phy of the new class.

This philosophy was born in Germany; the labour movement there was much more of a possibility than a reality, which was conducive to the emer-gence of sweeping generalisations. In France, on the other hand, social philos-ophy always was more permeated with the real needs of the moment, and the thinking of the proletariat turned rather towards specific tasks as well as eco-nomic and political issues. However, the utopians – as we know – contributed to the emergence of Marxism, and among them mainly Saint-Simon, who came very close to seeking a way out of the interaction between social factors in the fundamental factor of the development of technology. And in my opinion, this also explains why August Comte's positivism based on Marxism had no impact and why Marxists today are still almost deliberately ignoring and not appreciating him, even though if investigated for itself, its content, Comtism could – just as well, it must be said, as Hegelianism, if not with greater reason – be a source and preparative step for Marxism. Comte's role in France may be compared overall, *mutatis mutandis*, with Hegel's role in Germany. Both were great 'restorers' of social science following the revolutionary-rationalistic dev-astation; but while Hegel openly defended Prussian feudalism, Comte went no further than a deep adoration for the Middle Ages, although by doing so he united many intellectual acquirements of the progressive bourgeoisie. But Marxism, 'drawing from the spring of Saint-Simonianism', for that very reason did not need Comte's help to produce a higher synthesis from the thesis of feudalism and antithesis of the bourgeoisie; its synthesis was even much more consistent in its revolutionariness.

We have no intention here of drawing an entire parallel between Marxism and positivism. We shall try on another occasion to demonstrate that positiv-ism brought boldly to its consequences must agree with Marxism,[4] a vivid ex-ample of which we have in the Belgian sociologist De Greef. But Comte, having reached a certain point in these consequences, withdrew. Like Hegel (to such a degree did these opponents of rationalism still bear his stamp!), Comte consid-ered his own system the crowning of the entire, eternal development of human thought, and viewed it as some kind of untouchable revelation. In his aversion to communist utopias, he also changed his own social stasis into a certain de-gree of conservative utopia, the cornerstone of which is the inviolability and immutability of the bourgeois form of the family; and in order to justify this immutability, then entirely like the rationalists and Utopians he fought, he had do devise a concept of 'human nature' that – in certain respects at least – was

---

4   See *Comtism and Marxism* in this volume.

unchanging. As such he was unable to abide fully by one of his fundamental ideas, according to which the higher manifestations of spiritual life depended on the simple 'desire to avoid pain and death' (a concept anticipating Lippert's *Lebensfürsorge*), because it would mean giving the social form so carefully constructed by thought as prey to the 'vitriolic action' of the economic content constantly moving forward. Hence his striking contradictions; hence the antagonism between his teaching, grasped as a dogmatic system, and Marxism. Despite this, we owe him for that atmosphere of positive research that he gave the social sciences, and which today has become a general property and in which Marxism feels perfectly at home, since it can only favour its expansion.

This is because Marxism, in spite of those who do not know it, is not a dogma at all; even the word 'system' is inappropriate for it. It is a method of research, or rather, because every method must entail a certain core of premises and conclusions, it is a means of grasping social life in order to explain it; and as such Marxism considers the contemporary positivistic atmosphere in science its best element, it breathes it deep into its lungs, and without it would be unable to exist. We thereby see that Marxism conforms here with the positive school – in the broadest sense of the word. But Marxism rises above this school's eclecticism; it does not make do with the ascertaining of the interaction and co-dependency of all manifestations of social life, but digs deeper – and believes that it has found the fundamental process from which all these manifestations derive, and which governs them all. In practice this difference is not, to be honest, that very significant: after all, no Marxist will claim that all social phenomena in a particular country and era can simply be explained through the economic relations of this country and era, and none will deny the momentousness of allotopic and allochronic causes, or that the political, legal and religious forms experiencing the former, displaced base may play an almost independent role. And yet the fundamental difference indicated above does not cease to exist; because the economic monism of Marxist sociology means that the social form once deprived of its economic content and base – after a sufficient stretch of time – must always disappear without trace; that the social nature of man may, together with the conditions, change entirely; that, for example, even innate criminal tendencies are essentially only a social product and as such disappear they must, since their bearers will enter a social environment not conducive to the materialisation of these tendencies; that therefore, in the ultimate conclusion, nothing (apart perhaps from entirely unanticipated things, and as such not a part of today's sum of knowledge) can block the materialisation of the ideal of freedom and equality, with which the new class is proudly negating the immemorial class system.

VIII

Economic materialism means understanding the social past via a certain defined class, and therefore is of course strictly connected to its programmatic aspirations, its understanding of the future. Even so, these two theories may be considered independently of one another, and indeed each of them has its own separate supporters. There are many scholars who explain history and social life economistically, while at the same time they are opponents of the practical programme in question; then again there are some scholars favourably disposed towards the programme, and even many of its immediate supports, who either partially or entirely reject economic materialism. This derives from the fact that the respective class borders on and is in contact with other classes, that its intellectual environment at these borders merges with other intellectual worlds: on the one hand – with the relativistic historical-economic school, created by the elements of the *ancien régime*, the agrarians and the petite bourgeoisie stung by the revolutionary rationalism, and on the other hand – with the modern petite bourgeoisie and the intelligentsia.

When the new class consciousness formed, the first to go there took a highly negational stance regarding the entire capitalistic society, and drew up a theory totally unacceptable to any of the classes participating to any degree in the hitherto dominion. However, as the strength of the new element grows and the social form begins to give way in various places beneath its pressure, this element re-enters society to take possession of it, and other classes gradually begin moving closer, taking its path, striving at the same time to halt its march, to slow its pace. Sometimes it recognises by itself that slowing down is necessary so that others can keep up ... And behold, this is a significant substrate for the triumphantly proclaimed 'crisis' in the political sense; and its resonance in the scientific sense – is that 'crisis of Marxism' as a sociological doctrine so exploited in the last few years by specialists in scholarly topicality ... From this point of view as well one cannot be surprised if the arguments and charges of the harbingers of 'crisis' are neither particularly new nor characterised by a thorough understanding and digesting of the guiding ideas of Marxism. Their main action is seeking out contradictions in the writings of individual scholars and employees in the realm of our theory; the investigation of 'texts' and deliberations over the meaning of every word reaches the scales of some kind of genuine exegesis. Perhaps some future historians of literature will get something useful from this; but in the meantime, then by no means is it always he who searched out the most 'texts' and quotes in all different languages who achieved the best grasp and who reasons the most pertinently...

How often, for example, do we hear regret over the fate of the 'idea' maltreated by 'materialism', of the individual pressured by the 'fatalism' of the Marxists. Apparently, the latter have the gall to derive the 'idea' from the 'fact': an absurdity, a transgression against cognition theory, which has to be countered with the 'psychological' conception! All of this is quite simply a misunderstanding. Marxist sociology is equally as psychological as any other sociology, but the 'idea' and 'fact' are not two alien elements for it. Just like contemporary sociology as a whole, Marxism too perfectly realises that society comprises individuals, and that everything that happens in society happens in individual souls. After all, the fundamental 'fact' of Marxist sociology, the economic fact – the usage of and even the existence of work tools – is just as psychological as the philosophical or aesthetic 'idea'. But in this manner, we are only shifting the issue to other ground; because in this case we must put man's various mental functions in order according to their degree of importance, and then the economic function obviously takes the main position. The complex issue of the theory of cognition, as set against philosophical materialism, does not really exist at all for 'economic materialism'. And this is because this sociology is phenomenalistic: it does not deal at all with the relation between human consciousness and the external world taken as a thing in itself. Yet this does not mean at all that that it does not deal with the process of continuous exchange between human consciousness, taken as a phenomenon, and the external world also treated as a phenomenon; quite the opposite, as after all it is for us the process of this consciousness forming. But this suggests that Marxist epistemology cannot be purely logical, but in a way historical; Labriola explains this in his letters to Sorel,[5] in a manner – interesting to note – entirely resembling the explanation of Comte's apparent lack of an epistemology recently given by Lévy-Bruhl.[6]

As for us, we do not expect great things for the development of Marxism following the 'return to Kant' recently so proclaimed. We would, in any case, understand this return somewhat differently: we would like to socialise the critical stance. We would like to reiterate that society, any group, and – of special importance to us – the class an individual belongs to, puts a certain stamp on its consciousness, imposes *a priori* a certain understanding of society and the world, from which a person cannot be free just the same as from the

5 *Socialisme ét philosophie*, Paris 1900 [Kelles-Krauz's footnote]. See: Labriola, Antonio, 1912, *Socialism and Philosophy*, pp. 5–181.

6 Lévy-Bruhl, Lucien, 1900, *Philosophie d'Auguste Comte*, Paris: Félix Alcan [Kelles-Krauz's footnote]. See: Lévy-Bruhl, Lucien, 1903, *The Philosophy of Auguste Comte*, New York: G.P. Putnam's Sons.

necessity of looking through their retina. This also means that the appropriate class apperception must be unconditionally suitable for the proletariat, and that their philosophical system, just like the systems of all previous classes, is in its essence relative and transitional, and so that it too will cease to be, to seem, real – at the moment (but not earlier) when the new social apperception generated by the future classless society replaces today's, born of the battle of the classes. The philosophy of this society of the future, emerging from Marxism, will by its very nature be something different, and in certain respects at least the opposite to Marxism; but what exactly – that we cannot know today, we cannot conclude from anything that was or is, we cannot even anticipate with at least some prospect of accuracy, because no such predictions today can be free of today's class apriorism – of one kind or another.

In this meaning, I will happily admit that there may be, and even that there must be a crisis in Marxism; however, if one has to go through such a crisis without regression, back to outdated ideas, then there is only one road open for that: applying the principles of economic materialism itself all the way to their ultimate consequences, in other words until they are totally exhausted.

Yet I have in mind one point with which economic materialism to date has been coping but not without difficulty: a point of an ethical nature, which is also the focus of the entire 'return to Kant'. Because Kant, that member of the bourgeoisie who was already very displeased with society around him, but who felt insufficiently strong to be able to attack it and transform it, created precisely because of that one of the most beautiful ideals of human dignity, individual purity, and morality. With Fichte, the mouthpiece of the rise of the German bourgeoisie, this ideal became actively revolutionary. French rationalism, inherited from the Revolution and practised by strata of the bourgeoisie not yet sitting at the laid table, in a political sense still in the ascending stage, was less poetical and more practical but it created a new concept of 'human nature': a concept identifying this nature with eternal justice and never-fading right, a concept that has served these strata more than once and is serving them again today – as a bridge leading to views and aspirations appropriate in the new class. In their difficult situation, among the illusions, disappointments and temptations, the petite and moyenne bourgeoisie possess in this concept a beautiful individual basis of social idealism, and are instinctively afraid of acknowledging the dependence of critique and philosophy on a real economic foundation, of the individual ethical principle vanishing like a spirit when encountering this basis.... Which is also why Friedrich Albert Lange wishes to guard the 'order established in human nature'. Just as Jaurès, more revolutionary than Lange, defends his belief that since the dawn of mankind there has been a protest 'against the inhuman exploitation of man'. And the 'social idealism' of Fournière – of them all – feels offended by the 'amorality' of economic materialism.

I do not know, admittedly, whether one should defend against such an allegation a doctrine that proclaims, after all, that social tasks stand before the human consciousness, when – at least in a hidden state – the means for their resolving and fulfilling have already been given, while the same also excludes any hesitation, any scepticism, and gives unflappable trust, self-confidence in carrying out the most dangerous of social duties; a doctrine that, proclaiming on the other hand that all social movement is achieved in people and by people – all people – deprives even the weakest and smallest of them of any right to inactivity, to fatalistic quietism. Of these two main principles, each cornerstones of Marxist ethics, which – as we can see – exists no matter what Croce declares, the first resembles Comte's ethics, but the second stands above its intellectual-aristocratic spirit. Economic materialism takes the idealistic and ethical feelings of the individual very seriously. For example it cannot and it does not want to deny that, if not for the consciousness of the proletarian, which after all is based above all on their own sense of dignity, then the concentration of capital could lead not to an equalitarian society, but to a new type of feudalism, to the rule of some kind of 'super-humans, beasts'. And so if idealists are now charging us – and quite rightly in my opinion – that such feelings of justice, of the love of the whole, of sacrifice could not in any way have come to be in a society where everything has for centuries been hostile towards them; that the ideal of the communist system guiding the steps today of the new class is outstripping today's economic status, and as such can no longer be a product of this state – then what are we supposed to say in reply? Should we thus renounce explanation of the entirety of the social form by social content, reducing the superstructure to the economic basis? Do we therefore have to acknowledge the dualism of human nature?

By no means. This issue of the emergence of a revolutionary ideal preceding economic development, an issue that is, perhaps, a concealed axis of the entire 'crisis of Marxism', and which – as far as I know – of the Marxists, Kautsky alone has tackled cursorily (in his polemic with Belfort Bax in 1896), finds – so it would seem to me – a solution entirely consistent with the principles of economic materialism in my law of revolutionary retrospection, articulated at the first two conventions of the International Institute of Sociology in 1894 and 1895, a law which on the other hand is a modern form, consistent with the requirements of scientific realism, of the Hegelian 'negation', of Rousseau's 'return to nature', and of Vico's *ricorso*. The source of the ideal of the future, and so too of any idea, must namely reside in the past – in some waning social form – and in our case primeval communism is the source of the proletarian ideal. When this communism yielded but slightly to the first class society, bitter regret emerged in human hearts; and just as the snail's tear transforms into an iridescent pearl, this regret and yearning too was soon to transform into an idealised picture of a past lost. Various forms of economic communism, which after all have never entirely vanished from the lives of societies, and have been constantly experiencing that same process of disintegration at different times, have continuously aroused and nurtured in people that inherited regret, have renewed the ideal picture, which by constantly absorbing factors of contemporary society, was soon to become the basis of modern utopias, those predecessors of scientific socialism. At the same time and in parallel moral communist instincts, persecuted, oppressed by the social system with all possible means, only rooted themselves deeper inside the soul of the people, and becoming more subtle in the constant battle they transformed into a great and exalted feeling of personal independence, of free intellect and 'inborn justice', which today is the main foundation of aspirations for the future system.

This economic genealogy of the social ideal and ethical feeling denies them the right to feign 'ruthless' and disproves the final argument of idealistic dualism. At the same time it provides proof of the rightness of the fundamental thought of Marxism: of the experiencing and readjusting of the social form; in a specific case, this experiencing and readjusting are set apart by a sequence of centuries – or rather they fill themselves with this sequence. Further on we have the realistic application of the historical dialectic, and at the same time the highest rung of dialecticism: because the social form, which by its nature is retrograde and lags behind, here becomes progressive, overtakes the base, and functions in a revolutionary manner, simply thanks to its greater remoteness. The inanimate here overcomes the animate – only so as to lead it forwards ... And believe, this genealogy materialises in a manner that I dare say is almost aesthetic, the unity of social life, from the foundations to the very peak, from the origins to the ultimate end. Such it is: one and the same breath invigorates an entire range of human history, tuning into a hurricane at its peaks, where the exclamations of hopes close to fruition resound. Yet this breeze and all of its tonalities come towards us from the depths of life!

A Few Main Principles in the Development of Art[1]

What outcome has a review of the facts regarding the beginnings and the history of various fine arts led us to? How may the direction of the development of art to date be described on this basis? This we almost expressed in the last-but-one sentence of the previous chapter.

In its beginnings, art is simply one of the parties of man's biological activity, the activity of acquiring food and multiplying. Theoretically speaking, it is most probably the least important part of this activity, in the sense that if we were to imagine the retrograde development of man, then probably those activities that are not actually essential for existence, ones we call artistic and which involve doing things for one's pleasure, and not satisfying inescapable needs, would disappear. Theoretically, between the satisfying of these needs and additional pleasure, which is not an essential condition for satisfying elementary need, there is an entire distance, a whole ladder, on the lowest mundane rung of which stands life, and on the highest – art. But this ladder does not yet have the intermediate rungs. In a specific reality, artistic actions are strictly connected to those related to life, they interlace with them, flow from them, and as such are dependent on them – yet they also further them, due to which they are of major importance in the life of every individual. Besides, every individual performs artistic activity according to their own preferences and inclinations, yielding only to their own urges, seeking only a repetition – in the fulfilling of life functions – of their discovered and proven pleasure. If not so premature for applying to this state of things, one could therefore say that art – in its beginnings – is of life importance, is direct, and is individual.

We know well that the social state is the natural state of man, that man did not live solitarily before he began to live socially, but that as far as we are able to imagine his life, we must imagine him living in a group. But we know too that this group, that this original horde – purely hypothetical – may only be called a society by stretching this notion as far as possible. It is still almost totally devoid of what is the most important in the social life of people, of what constitutes the strongest cement in society, and namely: first of all, technology

---

1   Source: Kilka głównych zasad rozwoju sztuki, "Poradnik dla samouków", Warsaw 1905, Part 5, vol. 2, pp. 887–1013. The chapter below is a fragment of a longer essay.

based on performing together – because the economy of such a primeval horde boils down to gathering food, and even when hunting begins, the production and usage of stick and stone requires almost no social interaction; and secondly, social organisation – because the entire primitive organisation boils down hypothetically to a certain gravity of the mother, or more generally – of the elders. The development of social technology, meaning collective hunting and fishing, joining forces in the production of boats and shelters, and perhaps above all the discovery of fire, which a part of the horde – the women and children – must guard while others run around for food – then the development of social technology, essentially entailing the organisation of work and as such defining its management, thereby gives the start to the development of lasting and more complex social organisation, and only these two factors – social technology and social organisation – create society proper, meaning the vital interdependence of people and all the actions of these people. We have seen in a whole series of examples that it was the social environment that slid between the elementary actions of man and his artistic actions; his actions occupied the hitherto empty rungs of the ladder between life and art. Because man's vital actions in society and the satisfying of his elementary needs were dependent on social-technical action, and even – putting it more broadly – on social-economic action, such that from a sociological point of view economic actions should really be acknowledged as vital actions, and as we have also seen that in the beginnings artistic actions autogenously result from and favour them, then we should formulate the above assertion differently still: that as society develops an ever greater number of intermediate links squeeze in between economy and art, and also increase ever further the distance of art from economy, from the fundamental social actions, or – as one would say colloquially – from 'life'.

Such is the most general formula of the development of art to date. Let us take a closer look at the three elements contained within.

The organisation of work and its management that derives from technology passes to a certain degree into the organisation of government, and all these organisations have their morality, which is to say an entirety of ways of conduct required by them and their law, meaning a system of more precise regulations that is watched over by force. All these things are socially essential; and more important than artistic actions, because without them the economy – as in the social satisfying of elementary vital needs – could not exist. Besides, the performing of each of these social organisation functions, because they are after all a result of people's adaptation, is also sometimes connected to pleasure, to being emotionally moved, and therefore also gives birth to art, and it turns out that this art is conducive to the performing of these essential actions.

Therefore art, in all of its branches and its manifestations, must adjust to this social content and is the fruit of this entire substrate. This is not all; before a more significant development of technology and social organisation, primitive man already could and had to have certain views regarding the world's phenomena surrounding him, their relations and their causes, because such views must emerge by themselves in life itself, in active and passive contact with nature, when taking nourishment and when reproducing. Alongside the germs of art that we have investigated, they are the germs of science, of philosophy and religion, which here do not belong to the masses. Yet this much about them we have to say, that when the notion of 'life' in society really does expand to embrace the entire organisation of work and government, together with the appropriate ethics and law, then philosophy (a term with which we embrace all three – later to be differentiated – parts of worldview: science, philosophy and religion) also becomes dependent on this entire social organisation, it shapes, develops and takes form such as not to harm it, but to support it. The significance of the system of beliefs and experiences as the logical basis of the system of dictates is so great, that as time passes it too acquires precedence before art and superiority over it, all the more so that by the very fact of adjusting it gives birth to pleasure and emotion, to artistic manifestations. Therefore, as we were saying at the close of the previous chapter, in a developed society art stands at the very summit of the social pyramid, and beneath it – between it and 'life', meaning the economy – lie entire strata of ethics, law, statehood and religion; it grows from and draws sustenance from every one of these layers, so if we say that art in a developed society is through-and-through social, that means that in the soul of every individual, artistic drives and actions are full of social content, and also that satisfying and performing them is related to society, is dependent on a great many considerations for the immediate and more distant environment, and its beliefs and dictates. In other words art, created socially, is also socially constrained.

That is one thing. On the other hand art's distance from the economic base also means that art has become less important in life. We have seen how very important art is at the beginnings of mankind, for the life and development of humanity, how it encourages and ties primitive man to productive work, whose exacting demands he might not be equal to without art. Yet there is still another factor beginning to fulfil that action of tying people to steadfast and purposeful work: the organisation of work and government, together with the entire relevant ethics, law and worldview. The kind of ethics, right down to the minutest of details, and the kind of law, is of primary, decisive importance for the course of the fundamental economic actions, for the functioning of a specific social system; in these fields, any deviations from the socially necessary norm are the least admissible. From the point of view of the fundamental functions they are also not very desirable in regard to worldview; however, in the course of development and growing complexity, greater freedom appears in this respect, because not every detail of worldview must necessarily affect ethics and law, and therefore the economy and the political system, right away. At the moment when art ceased to be a direct assistant of vital-productive matters, and when the organisation of work and government, of both state and church, became together with ethics and law and with the help of world-view strong and certain, frequently stupendously powerful means for keeping people within the notches of each particular society and for driving them to all sorts of production and activity, then art became an activity that in a way really was auxiliary, sumptuous, on which ultimately nothing of importance depended. First of all everything that is necessary is fulfilled, then certain people practise art separately. Such a contradiction has formed over time between all these important, vital, and obligatory actions that constitute man, and art, that the philosopher sees in art even the borders of human nature being cast aside by man, while another states that every civilisation comes to an end – only comes to an end! – with the blossoming of art. Being so unimportant, standing as if beyond the confines of normal social affairs, art does not necessarily have to be totally adapted to the basic functions. The drive and adaptive force of these basic functions is probably so great, that art, you could say as an 'ethics of instincts', retains such contact with them that they reach it in their might, but they only reach it indirectly – only via all of those links that have squeezed in between these basic functions and art. Art does not cease to depend on technology, which we are less concerned about here, but in regard to dependence on the system, then ethics, law and ideology adjust to it directly, while art must be adapted to it, and is their raising to the state of selfless pleasure and emotion. If, therefore, in a developed and complex society, with a rich past and reserves of imitation from outside, while in the present numerous and diverse social slogans cross one another, then in ethics and law there are diverse deviations and independent combinations of elements, if they are still more numerous in the worldview – and in this respect art has the greatest level of relative independence and diversity. This is due to both its reduced social importance in life and also its indirectness.

The above suggests that the hitherto direction in the development of art in humanity contains a double contradiction: from the originally individual (in the sense defined above) it became social, yet simultaneously from a vitally important function it became an amusement almost detached from social tasks, from action adjusted to and strictly defined by the needs of life – to a field of relatively the greatest discretion.

That latest aspect in particular draws attention in today's times; this feature of art is the one most valued and highlighted currently by artists themselves, since for quite natural reasons it is identified with individualism.

The theories of art prevalent today, and particularly among artists themselves, differ – at least at first glance – from the above results of our sociological investigation in the fact that we cannot just pass them by with indifference. Besides, examining them will be the final completion of the investigation itself; because in today's thoroughly conscious era, or at least an era caring about consciousness, artistic creativity undoubtedly depends very significantly on the artist's notion of the task and essence of art. This is one more proof and manifestation of that indirectness of art, which unfortunately frequently shrivels it dry.

For centuries now human society has had no system other than class-based. Since the time when the primitive community ultimately vanished, the productive forces have been appropriated by only a part of society, and to date only the forms of this class appropriation are what have changed in all revolutions, even the deepest of them. A thing about class societies is that they have to organise themselves as if defensively.[2] The possessing class has a direct interest in there being no change to the existing state of affairs, the existing form of production, the division of work and management, this form entailing mastery of the means of work; which is why, with the help of various deliberate and nondeliberate, automatic influences it adapts to this state of things ethics and law, the form of the government such that the government belonged to them, as well as the 'selfless' ideology. This is not all: aversion and distrust is generated towards everything that breathes of variation. Particularly when society already has certain experience behind it, a certain history of struggle and social revolutions, and when it is aware of them to some degree, then the possessing class knows, in its more outstanding thinkers – and on the whole this class feels good – that in social life everything is tied by invisible threads of some kind, that every dissimilarity and every aspiration for such in whatever field is dangerous and may entail deep changes, and is therefore comprehensively conservative and requires class-related and ideological discipline. On the other hand this rebounds off of the non-possessing class – not possessing in the system in question either the means of production or the appropriate political authority – which, as a result of this, is fighting with the system and the ruling class. It aspires for change and favourably welcomes changes and varying trends manifested in the ruling class, but in the struggle it also needs

---

2 See my *What is Economic Materialism?*, § 6 [Kelles-Krauz's footnote]. See also *What is Economic Materialism?* in this volume.

discipline and solidarity itself, it needs a certain class ideology acknowledged by the entire fighting class, and therefore does not look favourably upon diverse aspirations within its own womb. In this manner a certain obligatory uniformity forms throughout society, both within the possessing classes and among those not possessing, although not to the same degree; and this uniformity involves everybody fulfilling their duties, and mainly fulfilling them quite consciously, namely realising that they should be fulfilled, even that they must be, because doing so is advantageous. The idea and mood of purposefulness and usefulness prevails almightily.

In the meantime, what is the essence of art? The essence of the artistic mood, of the artist's psychology? We have seen that art always derives from actions that are biologically or socially useful, that it itself favours the latter and is useful for them, that it may be created and experienced only when all awareness of benefit has escaped a given action, and all that is left is selfless pleasure, or to put it more generally – selfless emotion. Any action that leads directly towards a useful goal may easily be grasped in regulations, in norms, in an entire conservative system; but its additional layers or aspects that only give rise to pleasure or emotion, without being so fundamentally important for elementary success, manifest from their vital functions, by their very nature, a greater varying tendency, particularly at a later time when art becomes distinct and when intermediate links slip between it and the elementary functions. We have seen that art is then even that area of social life that succumbs the least to standardisation, that area in which all, even the most defensively organised society, is relatively the most tolerant of certain deviations from the norm. It tolerates – but this does not mean that it has to favour them. On the contrary, precisely because art – on the strength of its deepest, most elementary nature – possesses the greatest varying tendency, precisely for this reason all art is, for the entirety of such classes and such societies, treated in advance as suspect. All art – and every artist. Probably in every person lies dormant an artist to some degree or other, because every person possesses that inclination for pleasure, regardless of direct usefulness or selfless emotion. But in a defensively organised society every person eradicates that artist inside, suppresses those urges as redundant and dangerous, as unwilling to yield to the moral and ideological discipline in force. And the artist is the one in whom these urges have prevailed, in whom the awareness of any usefulness whatsoever is weaker and gives way to pleasure and emotion, meaning giving way to unconstrained discharging of thoughts or urges – of what fills man's soul. The course of social life, providing people with diverse new phenomena and particularly in a complex and developing society, means that the content of thoughts or feelings that the artist must discharge in this manner is very often something at odds with the accepted norm, and even the artist of all people becomes the most susceptible to just such incitements, incompatible with the norm and with obligation as a compulsion. This means that between any defensively-organised society and its classes on the one hand, and art and the artist on the other, there must be a certain inherent contradiction. The artist is suspect for the whole, and feels suspected. But at the same time he feels in a way that, in his soul, he has one string more than the rest, that he, were he to want to, could with ease fulfil functions that are purely useful, just like others, while not all others, should they wish, would be capable of discharging the urges such as he can, or in the way that he does; therefore, sensing the whole's aversion, he also considers himself above the whole. To such claim, the whole responds with only pity and increased aversion; the antagonism becomes ever sharper, and in the eyes of artists assumes the form of some universal and essential antagonism between the artist individualist and the throng.

Yet this antagonism is by no means necessary and widespread. Indeed, mankind has lived for so long in a class system that we find it hard to imagine other relations. But it is precisely investigations into original art largely occurring in the era of a system not yet class-based, at the time of the primitive community, that demonstrate how then there is no such antagonism between the artist and the generality. There is none if only because artists are not some kind of distinct class of people, that the artist is always something else as well: both a maker and an otherwise useful clan member – and that anybody depending on the opportunities of their vital and social functions is also at times an artist. But the cause lies deeper still. This system emerged by itself, and with such benefit for all participants that it did not need to fight fiercely for its existence; neither do the people living in it sense that it is being bothered by new forces of some kind, later leading it to its doom, because those forces, simply encapsulated in the individual's appropriation of what is the exclusive fruit of their own personal measures, seem to be fully consistent with the entire existing and generally useful system. This is also why, if a certain monotony of actions, of habits, thoughts and human feelings is generated in this system, this occurs under compulsion, in general not with the aid of very violent prohibition,[3] but by itself, spontaneously. The same happens in the field of art as well. In this field, just as in any other, there is no conscious and violent aversion towards all variation, and neither is there opposition by the individual to variation encountered – in the customs and interests of the whole; in a word, there is no antagonism between the individual and society.

---

3   However, then as well certain powerful prohibitions exist, e.g. taboos, and more specifically sexual prohibitions [Kelles-Krauz's footnote].

Altogether it – antagonism – forms gradually, and is by no means of even strength in all eras and social forms. The Greek Republics know it only weakly, until the development there of monetary plutocracy, and that because slaves are considered outsiders if at all people, while among the Greeks themselves, although there is not total equality, the principle of all participating in civil life prevails – in a way as the weakened principle of the original community. Therefore there is no very strong and distinct ruling class, one that would have to give society a conservative-defensive character and iron out any variation, and thus also shackle art. Similar relations reoccur to a certain degree in the mediaeval city republics, where we also find beautiful examples of artistic and civil identity and awareness. But such a confined and despotic power, ruling on a grand scale and over a huge area, does appear in the Roman Empire. It is under its governments that one sees the strong development of the concept of the individual set apart from the whole due to thinking and feeling differently, persecuted for it, but precisely because of being persecuted and despised, so too above the surrounding generality that is unable to assess and understand this individual. Although in this era this concept is indeed only very weakly connected to artistic creativity, and this because the previous period surrendered art, and particularly the visual arts that left behind enduring mementos, into the hands of patrons, one must bear in mind on the other hand that both in the various forms of the day's pagan mysticism and the actions and ideas of Christianity, in the very dedication and even martyrdom, there is a great deal of that thoroughly aesthetic element, namely fulfilment, in the form of complete and moving emotion, deep urges of the spirit independent of any external dictates, goals or concerns for personal or even general benefit. But today, after the middle ages which are, after all, a repetition of the ancient world's history in slightly altered forms and with the addition of Christian ideas, a social-systemic power has also run rampant throughout the civilised world, its existence and duration depending on the strict and unchanging retention of the social-class principle, which had to defensively retrench and impose upon the whole of society certain dictates and interdictions, certain concepts of usefulness and obligation, to which the entire ideology and sensibility must be adjusted. And this power is capitalism. Only beneath its rule have all those elements of antagonism between the artist and the generality developed to the extreme, elements bequeathed to us by those earlier class-based systems. In the capitalistic system not everybody can be an artist, because the division of labour developed to extremity requires everybody to devote themselves solely to their trade and utilitarian work. This division of labour and the high requirements in regard to the technology of any art, handed down to us by several centuries of culture, mean that artists comprise some kind of separate stratum of people – just like manufacturers. But at the same time the artist in the capitalistic system is that person who did not want to, or who did not know how to, surrender to professional, ethical and political discipline; he is the suspect force of instability, and perhaps also disintegration; he is very often a person who, economically, is unable to make his own living, and he becomes a burden on others, upsetting the harmony of the general and obligatory wage-earning. In a class society, and particularly in capitalistic society, a good always has the attribute of an obligation, and an obligation – always the character of an external coercion. The artist in the meantime is the one who has retained his trait of wildness – meaning the era in which all people were, to a certain extent, artists; sometimes he is capable of great effort, but he cannot abide coercion. Art excludes obligation – until it becomes a pleasure as a reflex, or at least a painful emotion. Therefore capitalistic society has the longing to make the artist a pariah, and everything within it is arranged such as to surround artistic creativity with material and moral suffering, to almost fuse these into a single concept. Here the artist is opposing some kind of ruling social power with almost every reflex of his soul – and this very opposition already constitutes suffering. Yet at the same time the artist here, in this era, when at every step one encounters examples of innovators who at the beginning were persecuted and denounced, but who later were totally or partially victorious and were placed on pedestals, when the invention of print and altogether the intensification of relations between people forces the ruling class even more to apply all possible means of controlling and standardising minds, yet simultaneously enables the capable individual to influence and rouse huge crowds – the artist in these conditions, opposing society, not only suffers but feels more than ever his superiority over the generality of 'bread-eaters'. This pariah feels like a prophet. Art-suffering is simultaneously art-as-a-mission.

Needless to say, we have presented the most general tendency of the class society in regard to the arts (bearing in mind at all times that capitalistic society has, to date, been the mightiest of class societies), but it is of course only one tendency, alongside which others also function. After all, one cannot forget about the glaring fact of artists of all trades in total harmony with society and the ruling class, artists who not only are not pariahs, but who occupy the most honourable and best-paid positions, yet who are honoured with the rank of pariah. After all, we know that art may emerge on the occasion of any action in life; so why should not the ideas and feelings of the ruling class possess a certain ability of rising to the potency of selfless pleasure and emotion! Especially since this class used to be the fighting class, that it has its own past of suffering, of creating and of heroism, and that throughout past history one can find analogies – of the tone with its aspirations and harmonising interests. It is even a powerful temptation for persons gifted with artistic skills and talents, as in this manner one can easily become a prophet without being a pariah at all, and fulfil a mission without bearing a cross. The temptation is all the stronger since – as we know – every system leaves art, because of its distance from the fundamental functions, with relatively the greatest freedom in regard to the content and diversity of ideas, and that in this manner the urge for freedom, for breaking free of the norm that every artist feels, and the sublime feeling of independence related to this can achieve a certain level of fulfilment even in art generally and fundamentally not incompatible with the ruling system. Therefore, one can be a great artist of the word or of the brush, or even a powerful thinker, while at the same time – with the assistance of mainly historical resurrections – providing the system and the ruling class with the illusions essential for brightening up reality; one can in this manner brighten up this hard reality for the non-possessing classes as well. In this manner the stronger and larger artistic individualities can remain in harmony with the ruling system; as for the small and weaker, that relative freedom and variety that every system leaves for art, as well as the separation of art from the fundamental social matters, lends them an even easier way. All they have to do in their artistic creativeness is confine themselves to such forms and objects, to such a corner of the universe of phenomena, that where possible they do not touch at all, even from afar, those vital matters; that they do not offend them either with some dangerous idea or an excessively garish form. Sometimes the latter may even be admissible, as we shall see. Smaller artists can find many such niches where nobody will disturb them. The ruling generality will even gladly seek leisure and entertainment among them after the hardships and obligations of utilitarian life.

But let us return to those artists we spoke of above, and for whom we would have an enormous – though probably subjective – desire to call real artists, for whom art was a mission and could be suffering. Following a few centuries during which class inequalities sharpened unprecedentedly, and found extreme expression in centralistic absolutism based on a monetary economy, when the great mass of the nation was entirely brushed aside from all cultural life, while art – Baroque and Rococo, in all of its fields, from palace to opera – was solely a steward for enhancing the pleasures in the lives of the ruling strata, following these few centuries that the 16th, particularly the 17th, and even the 18th centuries were for Europe, when in parallel with the battle of the new class against the old system a great ideological movement also commenced in all battlefields, the fruit of which we are all ultimately still living with; it was then that those genuine artists, of whose type one is free to consider Schiller, created a new and revolutionary understanding of art as something higher and more laudable than ethics, since free entirely of any coercion, as something in which the contrast between the individual and society, between discretion and obligation, completely ceases to exist, because the individual as an artist, arbitrarily, for his own pleasure only, for satisfying his own urges, not only behaves but also feels and thinks nobly and well, such that he incorporates the highest usefulness into art, the highest ideal of society. Very often the whole is unable to understand such an artist or such art right away, but after all art sweeps them away and is the highest school of the most perfect human condition. This theory of art and such art were supposed to serve the revival of mankind. But following the Bourbon Restoration, which of course we understand here not only in the political sense, the theoreticians of the ruling system – defending itself in turn from any further transformation – also understood the extraordinarily momentous significance of such art and wished to take advantage of it. We said that art in a developed society, and particularly a class-based one, recedes from the fundamental social actions and in so doing loses in importance; we have seen that this happens mainly because these fundamental utilitarian actions are protected by an entire series of other means, such as the law, the state, organised religion and ideology in general; but when a particular system is threatened by such new forces that those means may seem insufficient, then art may once again emerge as the powerful means for mass suggestion that it was in primitive times. After all there is an artist dormant in every person, and after all there exists in everybody a natural aspiration to combine everyday life and everyday work with some kind of pleasure and some kind of emotion, and if only this miraculous transformation of the everyday obligation really does come to be, transformation of the ordinary utilitarian action and its connected dictates and beliefs into selfless pleasure and emotion, this sweet and radiant transformation of life into art, then that is precisely when, that is only when one can be sure that life such as it is and as it must be in the particular system, life thus defined and confined as the given ruling system wants to have it, has set its deepest roots in the people's souls and become the most resistant to all attempts at change and revolution. The theoreticians of the ruling system understood then that art may be the mightiest of educators in the system's service. And in keeping with all the rules and habits of this class system they did not wait until art would come to feel this way, but posed such strict requirements of it. Serve, be useful, do not eat bread for nothing! Art was granted a social office – just as Słowacki's Skierka was given the tough work with Grabiec.[4] It began to be understood solely as a tool for disseminating certain class ideas which, in the 19th century – and for reasons going beyond our investigations

---

4   An allusion to Słowacki's tragedy *Balladyna*.

here – frequently don national form. Art did not refuse the service demanded of it: but because this service, precisely because it was demanded and forced, goes against its nature, it only fulfils it within a distorted, indirect, imperfect form: in the form of tendentious art.

We are not asserting here by any means that tendency and art ruled one another out entirely, that a tendentious work could not be at all artistic. On the contrary, we believe that one could list plenty of works displaying a very prominent tendentiousness, a tendentiousness that was even fully deliberate and intended, yet which are works that possess undeniable artistic value. These works were created for a utilitarian purpose, with the goal of disseminating or consolidating a certain idea, yet due to the artist's skill or, to a certain degree, their own emotion, they are also a source of selfless pleasure and they evoke emotion. Of the multitude of examples that come to mind, I shall mention one that nobody will reject: *The Books of the Polish Nation and the Polish Pilgrimage* by Mickiewicz.[5] If by tendentious works of art we are to understand above all works of literature, they could be compared in the visual arts with works of (falsely) so-called applied art, meaning rather the arts and crafts movement. A beautifully carved chair also serves above all a utilitarian purpose, yet apart from that is undoubtedly a work of art. A bas-relief or statue, set apart from a utilitarian object (although there may be very many social elements contained within), is a pure and higher art. Only in such works does what constitutes the essence of art develop without constraint. Tendentiousness does not then immediately supplant the art in every work, but there is no doubt that it constitutes a grave danger for art. Being subject just like all ideas to systematisation, regulation, and the entailing hardening required by every ruling system, and all the more so a system that is highly class-based in character, such as today's, tendentiousness stands in the way of the further development and perfection of art, both in content and even in form. Ultimately only certain topics and a certain manner of treating them are permitted in this ministerial department of education, which art has been changed into. So because the deepest essence of artistry is, as we have seen, the aspiration for freedom and for novelty, so such a theory and practice of art, whether called moral or social or national, simply must have evoked a sharp reaction on the part of genuine artists. This reaction took on various forms. The most important for us is that artists declare that art has nothing in common with morality, nothing in common with society, nothing in common with the nation. It stands above all of these. The throng, the whole, usefulness and social interest – they all reach out their

---

5   See: Mickiewicz, Adam, 1833, *The Books and the Pilgrimage of the Polish Nation*, London: James Ridgway.

sticky tentacles to the artist from all angles, and strive in the most cunning of ways, including the most brutal, to make him their slave; but the artist breaks free of the polyp, shakes off the dusk of everything that is mundane, and rises into pure spheres known only unto him, ones the ordinary man is unable to reach. One poet does, indeed, and in a form that is even very elegant and so perfectly finished, call upon his confrères:

> Oh let us raise magnificent altars to beauty,
> Let love and gold cast their brilliance,
> Let the wine fill the crystal goblet;
> Let us adorn the head with roses, the face with joyous masks ...
> Let a statue bedeck each niche ...
> Let the song of bards sway us,
> Till all forbear any futile grief,
> And thought sinks into Olympian silence ...
> Yet onward – let there be no hungry among us!
>   W. GOMULICKI[6]

But on the other hand there is an emphatic protest on the part of the Parnassian Catulle Mendès:

> Pas de sanglots humains dans le chant des poètes.[7]

Art is not meant for society, it is not meant for anybody or for anything; altogether art is to be for itself only, art for art's sake!

When taking a closer look at this motto, this entirely natural reaction against the coercion of tendentiousness, we see that the reasons behind artistic creativity being simultaneously suffering and seemingly a mission, and behind

---

6   "O! wznośmy pięknu wspaniałe ołtarze,
    Miłość i złoto niech rzucają blaski,
    Wino niech szumi w kryształowej czarze;
    Skroń strójmy w róże, twarz w wesołe maski ...
    Niech posąg każdą przyozdabia niszę ...
    Niech nas pieśń wieszczów dopóty kołysze,
    Aż każdy smutków daremnych zaniecha,
    I myśl pogrąży w olimpijską ciszę ...
    Lecz wprzód – niech głodnych pośród nas nie będzie!
    (Gomulicki, Wiktor, *Głodnego nakarmić*, III, in: Gomulicki, Wiktor, 1978, *Poezje wybrane*, Warsaw: Ludowa Spółdzielnia Wydawnicza, pp. 16–17.)"

7   [From the French] Let there be no human tears in the song of the poets.

the artist feeling a social outcast yet at the same time an inspired prophet, have not stopped functioning at all. On the contrary, this motto results in exacerbation of the artist's antagonism with the whole of society, which now charges him with holding society's dearest ideals in disdain, or defiling them, but the artist – and I speak here of the most sincere and the most genuine of them, while of others I shall speak later – the artist feels, he is told by his deep and selfless urge for freedom, that even by breaking away from beneath the rule of these ideals he is not in reality trampling over them, but lending them some kind of super-utilitarian, as if super-human form, raising them to a power incomprehensible to others. Among such artists the concept of art for art's sake is by no means identical to the concept of art without ideas. They only instinctively seek some kind of ideological content, content that would not be today's and horizontal, that would be the property of the ruling system or any of today's parties and social tendencies surrounding us. They want to be taller than the present, generalising above all of time. They want art to present and to express something greater than everything that is born, that arises, and therefore that passes in society, and so in usefulness and in interests – something that is the greatest, meaning not passing away, something that is perpetual and absolute. This is how the well-known theory emerges, that as opposed to all those relative and variable social things surrounding us, art expresses that which always lasts in man despite all external changes, therefore something that is deepest, that can be found in the soul after discarding all the stratifications imposed by society. Clearly this theory also draws from philosophical sources. After all we know the theory of the invariability of human nature, appropriate for bourgeois rationalism. We know also various theories of the invariability of a certain creative element, or element governing the universe. With more rigorous investigation we could unearth the social origins of all of these theories – starting from the Eleatics – but that is not the job of the sociology of art, but that of the sociological history of philosophy. Then we would also see that in certain conditions and eras these theories play a revolutionary role, while in others they are the opposite, a tool of conservatism. Likewise in regard to this theory of art, which we shall return to in a moment. Let us just state in the meantime, that as a result of certain social conditions, art – in its search for freedom and independence – took precisely this theory, as a weapon, from the well-stocked arsenal of philosophy. And let us also add that this theory is frequently and easily linked to mysticism: that which lies dormant at the very bottom of the human soul, that which remains after shaking off all signs of social humanness, those elementary urges and intuitions that emerge in such moments of ecstasy or contemplation and constitute the deepest essence of art, these are the manifestations in man of the activity of some great, unknown and unfathomable superhuman, supernatural, changeless and irresistible force. In today's conditions of big-city life, of disintegration of the family and sexual anarchy, this theory may easily be defined more specifically, in such a manner saying that the eternal and greatest force dormant within us and manifesting itself in art is the urge for love. Here is not the place either for general investigation into the social origins of mysticism;[8] let us note only that the capitalistic system strongly favours its blossoming, because it features strongly the impossibility of clearly understanding the connection between distant, complex causes and social consequences, and the disconsolateness of people incapable of the bloody and almost bestial fight for existence, a revulsion towards the surrounding present day, a yearning for some kind of unknown calm and obedience.

In the theories of art discussed above, whether they are in the form of systematising rationalism or intuitive mysticism, we also see above all a certain type of protest against the existing system, and against its drive to grant art a servile character. In this meaning, in this role, the theories protect art from solidifying, from stagnation, and are a means of refreshing it. But after a certain length of their duration and in a certain category of theoreticians and artists, they also unveil their other side. In every class society, and particularly in that ruling today, the concepts of good and usefulness are opposed by another concept, one corresponding to new class currents that intend to remodel society. Moreover, they too not only autogenously emanate artistic creativity and sensitivity, but also – as we've pointed out above – spread throughout the new camp with the force of a certain moral compulsion, and they also reach for art to provide support with its suggestive and educational power. And sometimes, though less often, one hears voices from this camp demanding tendentious art. Artists also rebel against this demand, and apply their theory of the superiority of art over all things relative and social interests also to these new reformative social currents. And in relation to them art must retain its absolute freedom. In this case as well it has to be reiterated that art cannot serve any utilitarian goals, even if the most worthy and seminal for mankind, but that art is for art's sake. And in this point we are by no means denying artists their validity; a little later we shall pronounce precisely our thought on this matter, but for now we want to state that in this case the same theory has another meaning. In its previous form it turned against stagnation in art, and thereby against stagnation in society; now it is turning against social change – and this could also

---

8   For Greek mysticism (neo-Platonic), which exerted a powerful influence on Christian mysticism, we attempted to do this in a work entitled *Protest społeczny w starożytności* [*Social protest in Antiquity*], 'Głos' 1903 [Kelles-Krauz's footnote].

entail the danger of stagnation in art. Now, instead of hindering, this theory is beginning to make it easier for artists to remain in harmony with the ruling system, as it keeps them far from new social trends. A person with an artistic spirit, with a proclivity for freedom and novelty, leans by his or her very nature more towards them than anybody else. We shall also see later that in certain conditions he could identify with them while being an artist at the same time; but for that one has to be a strong artist. For now the weaker artist sees the danger of being caught by the wave and drawn away from art; without ceasing to be a person with other needs, he also senses the danger of opposing the ruling system in this particular way; and here the theory of art for art's sake comes to his rescue. He serves art alone, serves only disinterested beauty; his works will not contain that horizontal, everyday social content. If he is a brilliant thinker, then his works will have ideological content, but this content will bear precisely that character of the eternal absolute, and will be mystical or rationalistic. But with many other artists the slogan of art for art's sake is now expressed as a domination of form over substance. Any idea is always linked in some way or another with social interests, and if it does not necessarily have to it can very easily serve some kind of tendency; therefore, avoiding it is the easiest way to become independent of society, to be artistically free. In verse where attention has focused above all on exquisite rhyme and remarkable rhythm, in a painted or sculpted nude, still life or landscape – this freedom seems to be the most complete. The form really does become very independent here, while because it becomes the sole object of the artist's attention and efforts, this may lead to great perfection, while at the same time leaving room for all sorts of experiment, variety, newness or combination, for seeking something extraordinary, unprecedented, ultimately fanciful. In this manner art easily transforms into craft, in which – though not easy to master – many people can ultimately reach a significant level of perfection with the appropriate effort, simply through learning and experience. In addition rivalry develops between them, rivalry both for fame and quite simply for gain, and this pushes them yet further to strive to stand out with something unique, if only gaudy and fanciful. On the other hand, in a class and capitalistic society, but rich, developed and complex, gaudiness and fancifulness of form – as long as not involving a pointed challenge to the ruling system and in regard to content – no longer terrifies the ruling class, is not persecuted, and does not place obstacles in the way of the work's sale. After all, a rich ruling class frequently suffers from a surfeit of delights, while on the other hand every patron is characterised by vanity; both one and the other even demand that the most unusual of things be sought. For this reason this class sometimes even allows artists not only to opt for gaudiness and uniqueness in form, but also allows them to tickle their fancy with various eccentric ideas, even deliberately on display in the most blatant form exhibiting negations of morality and other 'sacred things' – as long as there is no sense of a deep and unshaken conviction held by the author … To which he, thinks the philistine, is an artist, that he were a madman and that I watch him. There's the guard making sure that he not damage…

Besides, indulging in the form and neglecting the idea in art was also, in a certain respect, a very healthy reaction against art being enlisted into forced service for the ruling ideas. Then tendentiousness became everything in a work of art, it determined the value assigned to it, which quite simply enabled non-entities to run rampant and hindered development in artistic technique. But then practising solely technique also hinders the development of art, and does not allow it to refresh. A certain degree of perfection is achieved, and this becomes a canon, a model, an academic ideal, but because form never exists anyway without a certain ideological content, this perfected form is only capable of expressing limited content and is hostile in advance to any attempts at introducing new content. The critical issue we have now reached, mainly regarding the permeation of new content in art, is as follows: scientific research has shown us that art emerges on the occasion of vital or social matters, that it emerges from them, from actions, feelings and social ideas, and that therefore every new social-ideological movement that is expressed in ethics, law and philosophy so too must give forth art. And this is because it must be accompanied by disinterested pleasure and emotion that bring to life a certain form that we call beautiful, as its centre, and it is this that these factors of pleasure and emotion must favour to the highest degree. Thus new social content simply forces itself into art through violence. On the other hand, though, social history has led to artists seemingly standing up to this with all their might, afraid of this – by infecting art with tendentiousness – compromising its freedom and independence, and also damaging the perfection of its form. As for us, we make no hesitation in asserting that since the social conditions once generated the concept of art-servant, the conscious pursuit for it to be the educator of people in a certain imposed direction, then it is extremely fortunate and good that a reaction formed against it, along with the entire artistic theory encapsulated in the motto of art for art's sake and in the cult of the form. Naturally, the absoluteness of this theory does not stand up to scientific theory in any point. The sociologist knows very well that artistic creativity never expresses any absolutely invariable forces, and all the more so transcendental, supposedly lying dormant deep within man, but always only such a man as created by the historical and surrounding social conditions; he knows also that art never is in reality amoral and asocial, but that even when it proclaims total indifference towards morality and society, or even their total negation, that whereas only in the first case it is not simply and exclusively a perfected technique of giving rise to pleasure (such as, for example, painting a still life), in reality it only expresses an obscure but strong desire for some other kind of morality and some other kind of society, from which coercion would be excluded. In the same way the establishing of an absolute contradiction between the freedom and independence of art as well as perfection of form on the one hand, and art being concerned with new social content, its fusing with new social currents on the other, is also wrong. This would be wrong altogether in regard to all new social currents; so it is all the more so entirely false when applied to the social currents of today. It is true that one can sometimes hear rather shrill demands coming from the womb of the new camp, that art serve it tendentiously, and that not always is that sense of golden artistic freedom properly appraised there – a sense that I consider one of the most beautiful flowers of history to have grown on the volcanic substrate of battles washed with the proud tears of lofty suffering. But it is also true that this concept of independence and non-conscientiousness is abused by the majority of artist-craftsmen today for shielding their very low egoism, cowardice or very distinct service for the mighty, that in many cases it is simply 'wool in the ears from human groaning'. Its noble meaning must be restored, and this precisely is also one of the great tasks for the new currents of history. Because in their very essence lies the battle with that external coercion, the 'transition from a land of necessity to a land of freedom' – as the dialectician declared, 'replacing that vexing government of people over people with the concordant administration of things' – as the economist said, and aiming for a 'morality without sanctions or obligation' – as says the modern philosopher. It is time therefore for ethics to again become art, and art ethics, as with Miller and Fichte. The demand for tendentiousness from art on the part of the new currents is only, I would say, the disease of their youth, the result of an insufficiently accurate appraisal of that actual but fleeting fact, that art is still either a tendency hostile to them, or is tendentiously indifferent towards them. However it is, it is a mistake, and a totally unnecessary mistake. There is no need in the least for a tendency from outside entered into the artist's soul, so that new social content, the ideal of the social good at all, would find artistic expression. On the contrary, this expression will be truly artistic and will act with the entire might appropriate to art only when during the creation of a work of art soaked with social content there is no thought at all in the artist's soul about some kind of social-didactic goal, when all vital-utilitarian basis has disappeared, and when we who sense these works of art do not sense in them any traces of some kind of purposefulness. Will anybody dare describe as tendentious Słowacki's work *Agamemnon's Tomb* or even *To the Author of Three Psalms*? They are not tendentious works, as neither was Zeus by Phidias, although they are full of social content, but that is because the content here is the body and blood of the artist, it is simply an urge that must discharge itself in precisely such artistic form.[9] And so too the new social idea must become the blood and body of some of the most beautiful and the most tender of human beings, it must out of duty become simply an urge, rise to the power of delight and emotion – because pain too can be delight – and then it will begin to give forth delectable flowers of art, dazzling with their colours, enchanting with their fragrance. I am not saying that this harvest has not yet begun here and there, but they are but smaller and sporadic flowers, they are still cornflowers and poppies scattered sparsely among the corn. The attitude thus understood among the new social currents in regard to art – and our scientific investigation demands we understand it thus – by no means threatens the perfection of form, and neither does it threaten at all those types of art in which social thoughts and feelings are only expressed very weakly and from very far afield, such as for example idyll, landscape, a study of only colours and shapes, or even still life. One thing about perfection of form, which is achieved mainly with very purposeful efforts, simply through work, is that it also really becomes art and is at its most potent in terms of action when the work reveals no trace of effort at all, when its creation in perfect form was quite simply a pleasure without coercion. Quite naturally, only the greatest of artists can achieve this degree, but it is untrue that any content at all could have hindered in the pursuit of the perfection of form. The new currents carry with them a pledge of comprehensive, unconstrained development of individuality, all of its preferences and inclinations, a promise of life from which – like an iridescent fountain from an abundant spring – pleasure and emotion are to gush forth. This life will want to be ornate and will adorn itself in the reproducing and combining of the colours, shapes and the sounds of nature. Except that this will happen not to the delight of patrons and the privileged, but for everybody and by everybody.

Thus the internal contradiction in the development of art to date shall be resolved; art, without ceasing to be social and socially defined, will become individual and free. By remaining pure pleasure and disinterested emotion, it will once again become important in life, and something dear to and loved by society.

Art will once again fuse with life.
Life will become art.

---

9 It is certainly sometimes difficult to place a strict border between a work that is tendentious and non-tendentious but filled also with the content concerned. As an example I give the already mentioned *Księgi pielgrzymstwa* [*Books of the Polish Nation and the Polish Pilgrimage*], and on the other hand – *Dziady* [*Forefathers' Eve*] [Kelles-Krauz's footnote].

CHAPTER 8

Psychiatry and the Science of Ideas[1]

In his work on 'the laws of the evolution of mankind' (*Die Entwicklungsgesetze der Menschheit*), published in Leipzig in 1888, which certainly suffers from a couple of formal shortcomings and may also be criticised in other aspects – but which nevertheless deserves to be better known than it is – the Romanian researcher Paul Weisengrün formulated a few laws of social development based on the promises of the 'economic materialism' of Marx, Engels and Morgan. If one were to exclude those that are rather an introduction to the fundamental issues, as well as those that too quickly lend shape to emerging currents, then one can cite the following:

One can distinguish three eras in the history of mankind according to the determining factors of evolution. In the first, species-related instincts and forms of reproduction are these factors; this is the era of primitive communism. Its disintegration pushes the factor of wealth-production into the foreground, a factor characterising history as strictly understood to this very day, the age of the dominion of individual production; genetic factors only have an influence here via economic forms. Finally the dawn of the third age is announced, to prevail when production begins to be regulated and anticipated by the common will of the people; familial and economic functions will then be performed with the help of intellectual measures, which will become the determining factor of evolution, giving man a greater sense of free will. To be precise, we have here two laws that we could call the law of determining factors, and the law of the consequences of these factors (*Gesetz der Triebfedern, Gesetz ihrer Nachfolge*).

History as rigorously understood is therefore defined by the ways of generating wealth; these are the base for the superstructure (*Überbau*) constituted by moral, legal, political, philosophical, religious, scientific, literary and aesthetic forms; the economic conditions of production shape the social substance to which every social form adapts. This is called the law of the economic base, which is the fundamental law of economic materialism. Finally: the social

---

1 Source: La psychiatrie et la science des idées, "Annales de l'Institut international de sociologie" 1895, pp. 253–303. The chapter below is a fragment of a longer essay. The piece is a polemic with one of the most important works of Max Nordau *Entartung* [Degenaration]. See: Nordau, Max, 1892, *Entartung*, Berlin: C. Duncker.

form lives for longer than social substance. This third law may be worded differently. To this day, an appropriate arrangement of social classes corresponds to each of the subsequent manners of production, with one of these classes prevailing. When a change in the manner of production, becoming essential, enables the transition of political power from one class to another, then the former of these classes will naturally strive to retain its dominion. As such the counterbalancing of all needs existing in society is essential, via the means and manners of satisfying them that are appropriate for a given form of production and a given class structure, and which correspond to the needs of the ruling class. The resulting relations between all fields of mental existence on the one hand, and the appropriate class area on the other, constitute the object of a separate part of sociology that happens to be consolidating, namely the psychology of classes, which could also be named historical sociology since it does not apply to the prehistorical era, in which there were not yet any classes. However, it is not necessary to delve deeply into the psychology of classes to acknowledge after what has been said here that wherever a positive conception of man's goals and obligations comes into play, we find – when boring deeper – one kind of class base or another. The dependence of moral systems and recommendations on the class basis is almost obvious to the impartial and delusion-free mind; it is more difficult to grasp and demonstrate in the case of phenomena further removed from the economic base, from the higher storeys of the edifice of social forms such as scientific and aesthetic theories. In order to understand this, let us note that the economic base can only influence the social form through direct modelling. The truth is that this is about a fundamental process involving direct mental responses to such or another phenomenon of satisfying needs; if a particular manner of satisfying them becomes established, then it creates a mental habit, expressed as moral or legal behaviour, or in the form of a political institution. This fundamental process occurs without a break, it establishes systems and then disperses them, just to then connect their atoms and create new wholes from them. But in the day when society has already come into possession of a traditional resource of various systems and is entering a new formation, class determinants are manifested differently, in a manner no less mighty though less discrete, a manner that could be defined as sorting. Every class then becomes blind regarding itself, creating the effect of it hiding from its own intellectual view all those elements of tradition that are radically incapable of harmonising with or counterbalancing the economic base. The rest involves transformation *ad usum Delphini*. And this is by no means about some *tabula rasa* of an antisocial human beast, but is precisely about the type of social perception that is the principle behind the modelling of social forms.

Since any scientific research is closely connected, to a lesser or greater degree, with the social existence of man, then all such research is to a lesser or greater degree exposed to the blindness of class egoism, to conservativeness. Because when the victorious class shapes society according to its needs, when it introduces a binding norm into all areas, the violation of which is treated as a crime because it threatens the existence of society in its current form, considered the ultimate and only possible form, then not only the law and public opinion codify this norm, not only religion and philosophy rush to sanction it, but so too numerous other sciences select their materials appropriately so as to support the desired deductions. Mr Nordau is right when he takes pity on the fate of philosophy, that alleged ruler of nations which, in reality, only follows needs and instincts and is supposed to find logically justified explanations for them; he is wrong, though, to believe that the role of psychiatry is totally different. Especially as he himself has played an extremely servile role here.

The shaping of society according to the perceptions of the ruling class, which I spoke of a moment ago, involves influencing human minds – the adaptive capabilities of which are not identical. As this influence proceeds, three separate categories emerge, differing purely quantitatively, and which when encountering the object of the battle become qualitative. The first category is characterised by a lower adaptive capability; for a long time the minds belonging to this category clutch tightly to the form of the social substance that has only just been overcome, tenaciously stoking hopes for a return, and for some time seeing salvation in the surviving legal institutions that have not yet been uprooted by the new spirit. The second category may legitimately be described as 'opportunistic', because its representatives, with moderate adaptive capabilities, settle quickly no matter what the social conditions; not holding distant recollections or far-reaching hopes, they live for the present. And finally the third category, the least conservative, comprising exceptionally mobile minds, those most desiring of novelty: this category transgresses social forms, like a train passing successive stations, barely stopping at them. As soon as certain judgments form in such minds and merge in them into systems, an outburst of new sensations scatters them and puts others in their place; as soon as the impressions obtained and the ideas formed satisfy such people, they are hungry once again. Two further groups should also be distinguished within this third category. The participants in the first, more preoccupied by the current social system (perhaps for purely external reasons), are incapable of abandoning their confines, and they satisfy their hunger for new impressions by drawing the boldest of consequences from the principles of the given system; there is a perfect and flexible German word for defining this action: *übertreiben*. This

I could give in French[2] as overstating or exaggerating; and when referring to life around them, they escalate matters in such an impetuous and unpredictable manner that they lead to true despair those who want nothing to do with such consequences. The second group breach the borders of the existing system, they sense the new social form, and they live for the dreams they connect to it. Depending on strength of will and the different environmental determinants, all these predispositions are manifested in action or remain within the sphere of contemplation.

One could ask: what determines the adaptive capability that differentiates minds if not their psychophysiological traits? Nothing else, of course; and Mr Nordau would be doing science a great favour were he to confine himself to investigating these psychophysiological conditions, as he did in the two chapters dedicated to mysticism and egotism, the presentation of which is what we were interested in. But he felt that he should lay down an hierarchy; and he did so arbitrarily, taking a point of view determined by class interests. We shall return to this in a moment.

Both groups in the third psychophysiological category describe, each in their own way, the brisk mind of each class, and its historical spur: the minds in the first group raise the existing norm right up to an abnormal absurd, while the minds of the second establish a new norm in place of the one that has had its day. However, we are observing here a phenomenon which, at first glance, seems to contradict the progressive character of the second group: it turns out that they treat the past with a large dose of affection, while these affections sometimes resemble the ideals of the most conservative minds that have just been overcome.

This phenomenon has been referred to so often whilst not understanding its meaning, that it would be worth stopping here for a while. Somebody once illustrated mankind's evolution as a spiral that constantly returns to the same points on the base circle, but is always relocated to a higher level. Such a spiral seems to describe well the true state of things, defined – I presume – by the constant and necessary law that one could call the destiny of revolutionary retrospection, and worded as follows: "Every motion aimed at changing the principles of the social system begins with a turn towards one of the eras of the more recent or more distant past".

The fact that this law is necessary is determined by the following circumstances: when a new social system removes and replaces the old, this happens

---

2 Nevertheless, the author proceeds to give the meaning of the term in Polish [translator's note].

because the old no longer satisfies needs that have become sufficiently noticeable and strong to bring about change. This change heads, of course, in a direction indicated by these needs, which because of their force have moved to the forefront of human life; and any 'superstructure' of legal, political and similar institutions that they fund shapes itself according to these needs. They are precisely what constitute the 'spirit of the laws'. And since the true basis of the transformation and new life manifests itself to people only via these laws and institutions, they begin to mould it, to develop, maintain and apply it to all manifestations of life. The inertia that causes acts of will to transgress predispositions in the psychological matter is explained in social matter by the application of the social form (moulded from needs) to the whole of social life; the consequences of this inertia are so more significant that people are unable to notice the uninterrupted changes taking place in the social substrate (economic and appropriate for the phase of historical development) and always react only to changes that, to some extent, are integral. Thus the unconstrained play of other categories of needs is hampered, and it is hampered yet further following every manifestation of dissatisfaction, since the ruling system, conservative in spirit, becomes increasingly exclusionary and intolerant. Minds injured in their needs turn away from the existing form, and seek something else. Let us recall the law of survival of the social form: here and there we still find the leftovers, the remains, of the former system; we know it from verbal and written tradition; and we discover that the category of needs dominating today was then subordinate to other needs, most of which – if not all – are analogical to the needs suppressed today. We can only seek salvation in what is known to us: thus we desire a return to that past. We desire it in the form in which it existed in the most conservative category of minds, the first in our classification; the minds of the third category in turn become too accustomed and adjust too much to the forms of the current system for them to give them up. One must take into account the problem of the oneness of the present and past; it solves itself by itself, since the entire process is a subconscious one. When barely visible transformations in the social substrate and the simultaneously increasing dissatisfaction join and lead to change in the existing system, the subjugation of this system creates a fusion with reconstitutions of the preceding system. The Hegelian and Marxist formula is verified: 'thesis, antithesis and synthesis' become reality. Yet the momentum snatches minds; and again the behaviour of institutions gives way to the satisfying of needs that are constantly changing and becoming the means for achieving the goal; a certain category of needs eliminates the new oppression and commands attention to be turned towards the recently rejected system, in which they were favoured; the pendulum swings again, and so it constantly repeats.

One can thus clearly see that the future system always takes the guise of a past one to some degree. In his brochure *18th Brumaire of Louis Bonaparte*, an example of a monograph of class psychology of exceptional value, Karl Marx asserts: "The tradition of all dead generations weighs like a nightmare on the brains of the living. And just as they seem to be occupied with revolutionizing themselves and things, creating something that did not exist before, precisely in such epochs of revolutionary crisis they anxiously conjure up the spirits of the past to their service, borrowing from them names, battle slogans, and costumes in order to present this new scene in world history in time-honoured disguise and borrowed language". These words display brilliant intuition of the law of retrospection. Its insightful application continues: "Thus Luther put on the mask of the Apostle Paul, the Revolution of 1789–1814 draped itself alternately in the guise of the Roman Republic and the Roman Empire, and the Revolution of 1848 knew nothing better to do than to parody, now 1789, now the revolutionary tradition of 1793–95".[3] Let us add that it was not the Revolution of 1789 that initiated the imitation of classic Antiquity: because this imitation constitutes a distinguishing feature of the emergence of the entire bourgeois class as a result of the inescapable reaction to the feudal system, which disregarded industrial and trading needs; it is the Renaissance that gives people the Revolution of the togas, the lictors and the curule seats. Then the needs ignored by the bourgeois society were directed towards the era preceding classic Antiquity, from which Engels deduced the Greek and Roman states, i.e. towards original communism. This is the theoretical contemporary renaissance, while Morgan deserves to be called the Erasmus of socialism. Therefore, if – as Marx says – the phantoms of Roman times watched over the cradle of the bourgeoisie, then the proletariat has anonymous heroes as its protectors, 'perennials', or in other words unidentified communities living one life and together perishing of hunger.

As we know, Marx and Engels accept the Hegelian principle of development through contradictions, a principle that can be interpreted as the law of revolutionary retrospection. A scholar relatively close to Marxism, though excessively universal for his ideas to be accepted in full (*allseitig* in the various meanings of that word), Friedrich Albert Lange, considered this idea deceptive. "The misleading appearance of an advance through antagonisms", he wrote in *The History of Materialism*, "rests upon this very fact, that the thoughts which dominate an era, or which appear as philosophical ideas, form only one portion of the intellectual life of a nation, and that very different influences,

---

3   Marx, Karl, 2008, *The Eighteenth Brumaire of Louis Bonaparte*, p. 15.

often the more powerful because so little apparent, are at the same time in activity, until they suddenly become in turn the dominant ones, while the others retire into the background".[4] And in another place he adds: "Without exactly resolving everything with Hegel into its opposite, it must be admitted that the operation of a great thought very frequently assumes an almost diametrically opposite tendency through a fresh combination with other elements of the age".[5] However, one can see that these comments are in keeping with my attempt at explaining the law of retrospection, and that Lange is wrong in thinking that he thereby proves the illusory character of the formula under investigation. On the contrary, by explaining it and continuing the procedure of setting it on its feet – in keeping with the famous intention of Marx or Engels (we cannot be sure whose): "we have put the dialectic that with Hegel stood on its head back on its feet again"[6] – he only makes it all the more evident. He could have even applied it for the chronology of philosophical systems that he ascertained in his first volume (empiricism, materialism, sensualism, idealism, scepticism or criticism), and which has already proven itself twice in history and is now beginning for the third time.

When taking into consideration development via contradictions, the global consequence of theses, antitheses and syntheses, we could arrange the different social systems into changeable and periodic series. By adding the epigenesis of needs to development, we would be introducing new series to this consequence, without departing from the common ground. For this purpose the needs and social systems would need to be classified, which I do not intend to tackle here. However, I shall draw attention to the fact that, essentially, without stopping at too many complex issues, two antagonistic principles may be distinguished that drive the wheel of the dialectic consequence: individualism and socialism; I understand these words as indicating the superiority of the individual's interests over the interests of society, and vice versa. When juxtaposing the social phases approaching or moving away from one of these principles, we can see that each of them relates to certain eras that swap preferences and in which each of them can find inspiration. Which confirms that elements of highly diverse historical provenance converge in the reforming aspirations of some contemporary era.

---

4 Lange, Friedrich, 1877, *The History of Materialism and Criticism of Its Present Importance*, vol. I, p. 57.
5 Lange, Friedrich, 1881, *The History of Materialism and Criticism of Its Present Importance*, vol. III, p. 272.
6 See: Engels, Friedrich, 1976, *Ludwig Feuerbach and the End of Classical German Philosophy*, Peking: Foreign Languages Press, p. 41.

This fact is not without significance. It leads to the defining of the proper role of this 'awakening of the dead' in the psychology of revolutionary movements. In the work mentioned above, Marx explains this as follows: "And in the austere classical traditions of the Roman Republic the bourgeois gladiators found the ideals and the art forms, the self-deceptions, that they needed to conceal from themselves the bourgeois-limited content of their struggles and to keep their passion on the high plane of great historic tragedy. Similarly, at another stage of development a century earlier, Cromwell and the English people had borrowed from the Old Testament the speech, emotions, and illusions for their bourgeois revolution. When the real goal had been achieved and the bourgeois transformation of English society had been accomplished, Locke supplanted Habakkuk".[7] And he adds: "Thus the awakening of the dead in those revolutions served the purpose of glorifying the new struggles ... of magnifying the given task in the imagination [...]".[8] And indeed, according to Spencer, the level of aesthetic delight defines this delight's remoteness from the fundamental processes of the species, from direct usefulness; according to Guyau this aesthetic level depends on the lesser or greater number of vital elements dissolved as if in the relishing of the beauty. The Polish sociologist Józef Karol Potocki joined these two levels, the first of which has leisure without effort as its basis, while conversely the second has the gravity of life – with the assistance of the psychological definition of leisure, which according to him is "every pleasant function of the organism in which the excellent adaptation of attention makes any effort superfluous, and even excludes consciousness, naturally together with the consciousness of the fundamental, utilitarian and non-aesthetic purposes of that function" (the article *Ginekologia i socjologia* [*Gynaecology and Sociology*] in "Głos Warszawy"[9]). Therefore, if we take into account the reference to remote historical eras convergent in terms of system with one's desired era, then it perfectly fulfils the two conditions set by Potocki for an idea to be able to become aesthetic delight. Because of their loftiness they have no direct connection with the current struggles or with the direct goal of the reform, involving the satisfying of certain needs hitherto neglected; but because of their scope, they are closely connected to these needs, even if only formally, and they thereby participate in the most important vital questions. Thus the role of those reminiscences of the past is to equip the turn to

7   Marx, Karl, 2008, *The Eighteenth Brumaire of Louis Bonaparte*, pp. 16–17.

8   Ibidem, p. 17.

9   Potocki, Józef Karol, 1894, *Ginekologia i socjologia*, Chapter IX, 'Głos' Warsaw edition, no. 12.

the future with an aesthetic element, to complete it with a dream; and it is recommended that the movement's artists be permeated with it.

I cannot agree with Marx when later he says: "The social revolution of the nineteenth century cannot draw its poetry from the past but only from the future".[10] This sentence is legitimate when falling from the lips of a sarcastic historian and addressing the people of 2 December.[11] Because after all the aesthetic elements of the past are perfectly justified and essential in every revolution, but nevertheless under one condition: that the past is sufficiently remote for it not to be intercepted by any of the current factions and for it not to have a direct connection with the fundamental and real processes of the revolution. This, though, is a separate issue, and so in the meantime I shall not tackle it.

I shall bring these remarks regarding the law of revolutionary retrospection and dialectic development through contradictions to a close with a certain comparison.

The phenomenon of motion going beyond the point of balance, or in other words vibrational motion, is fundamental and universal in nature. We could say that the social spirit vibrates during metempsychosis. It vibrates like a plucked string. If treated as a whole, the string performs simultaneously a few vibrational movements, while if examined in its parts, each of them performs quite complex motions, obedient to a few complex oscillations dependent on the shaping of the nodes. The nodes and the partial vibrations resulting from them correspond to the dialectic transformations and retrospectives in the womb of the great historical era; lengthening the string would enable the appearance of new nodes and new partial vibrations, just like development introduces new needs and new, partial to some degree or other, systemic series into the dialectic consequence. Ultimately the complex of partial and complete vibrations generates not only raw noise, but also pleasant sound; just as harmonious noises evoked by the recollections of a distant past give motion an aesthetic dimension, without which it would be incomplete.

Should I move on from this comparison, which, obviously, is only an ordinary comparison, to the hope that one day we will manage to create a precise formula for social vibrations? Although such allegory would be justified, I prefer to refrain – because Nordau is observing me carefully with a straightjacket at the ready. Did he not consider mysticism a contaminated chaotic association of thoughts and one incapable of attention – that mathematician

10   Marx, Karl, 2008, *The Eighteenth Brumaire of Louis Bonaparte*, p. 18.

11   Probably a reference to 2 December 1851, when the French president of the time, Louis-Napoleon Bonaparte, overthrew the Second Republic, and the same date of 1852 when he established himself as Emperor of the Second French Empire [translator's note].

imagining progress as integration, and the war of 1870 as an analytical equation? True indeed, that I would find myself among choice company in hospital: because du Bois-Reymond would definitely be taken there as well, since he recommends that all sciences turn to a single, definitive mathematical formula from which we would be able to deduce isolated moments of life in general, both the crossing of the Rubicon by Julius Caesar, and the exhaustion of the coal deposits in the world's mines. Verily, the great Helmholtz was fortunate to pass away before Nordau turned his attention to him: did he not go so far as to give this new science the special name of metamathematics?

However, let us abandon such far too easy polemic manoeuvres. The question that remains is: will the vibrating string ever achieve the point of rest, representing a complete and definitive synthesis, the harmonious satisfaction of all, absolutely all human needs? I myself do not believe it will; the very epigenesis of the needs would generate sufficient an obstacle here. However, in the entirety of social vibrations we have the right to observe a steady drive towards synthesising, and – as in mathematics – the asymptote of the curve may be acknowledged as describing these vibrations.

Despite his excessive positivism, Nordau has achieved an enormous leap into the realm of the unknown, which is appropriate to all believing positivists: for him the asymptote has been achieved, the spiral, shrinking, has soared, while we are witnesses to the moment when it becomes a straight line rising to the zenith. And here we have the ultimate social form; we are in it, stuck in it, and all that is left for us to do is but develop and protect these principles, so they may reach *ad astra* without obstacle!

But this, just like the objectiveness of this form, is not his illusion. Take a look rather at all social systems, right up to and including the bourgeois revolution: every one of them seemed to its representatives to satisfy, in a definitive and absolute matter, all the needs of mankind, and to ensure its happiness for always. Even more: it was precisely the bourgeois model that proclaimed this far and wide, with infinite certainty and, of course, sincerely. Its representatives understood perfectly the entire polemic value of the argument that 'it has already existed and did not satisfy mankind, who rejected it', as well as the entire force of the 'reactionary' label, and they began to abuse it. Because in forgetting that their revolutionary wishes had resonated with sympathy not only with the Greco-Roman world succeeding the primitive community, but also with the long period of unconstrained individualism of the human animal, *alalos*, not yet forming the society that preceded it, and that in fighting the mediaeval excess of restrictions against personality, they borrowed from Jean-Jacques Rousseau part of their ideals, including the ideal of the original era of a total absence of boundaries imposed on the individual, they related these offensive definitions to the mouthpieces of the new ideal, that – according to Morgan – would be the acknowledgment of the brotherhood of primitive communism, raised to a higher form.

For this job, psychiatry provides them with if not the most terrifying then at least the most dazzling weapon, for which it has paid – and let us not be afraid of stating this frankly – with the loss of its scientific character.

This is because it firmly took the point of view of the minds creating the second category; of those who are always pleased with the existing state of things; and by cunningly setting a stiff line at the transition point, it transformed the quantitative difference between health and mental illness into a qualitative difference. By adopting the criterion of the satisfied mass, it recognised those afraid of the new or those excessively enthusiastic as bearers of original deviation, and treated people of both the left and the right as deserving of the concern of sanctuary, only admitting as healthy those favouring the middleground. To justify before its scientific conscience this arbitrary transition from quantity to quality, it hurriedly adopted the idea of atavism, which it describes as "the organism halting at a standard of development below that achieved by the species as a whole".[12]

One should also add to this conception the belief in the current system's ultimacy and total incomprehension of the reformative element, which is the substance of idealisation of the distant future, and then one will be able to understand why psychiatrists find it so easy to flog – using the same insult 'regression!' – nymphomania, prostitution, women's struggles for self-reliance and opposition to the current model of the family, alike to an impulsive murderer or conspirator, and that in the country of the Carbonari!; and why they would demand shutting Ibsen's doctor Hockmann,[13] Huysman's character Jean des Esseintes,[14] grappling with public opinion (Huysman himself a society-hating eccentric), and the Zarathustra of Nietzsche, an opponent of any socialisation, all in the same cell.

This last fortuitous idea belongs to Mr Nordau,[15] who – putting it generally – is marked quite strongly and in a straight line by that kind of thinking (talking of which, could one not make of this a stigma of degeneration, similar to that of mystical thinking?), and equipped with an entire psychiatric arsenal, it

---

12   Nordau, Max, 1892, *Entartung*, vol. 2, p. 500.

13   Probably a reference to Dr Thomas Stockmann, protagonist of Henrik Ibsen's play *An Enemy of the People*.

14   Duke Jean des Esseintes, protagonist of the novel *À rebours* [*Against Nature*] by Joris-Karl Huysmans.

15   Nordau, Max, 1892, *Entartung*, vol. 2, p. 476.

lashes out to the left and the right. If somebody sets their own needs against the needs of the majority, which – let us note – every initiator of reform, every precursor of revolution must do, because he himself should sense a suppression of those needs in whose name he is supporting the dissenters, then a diagnosis is made immediately: such a person is heartless, has no compassion for their neighbours. Somebody else disperses the sober appraisals of the majority and proposes fresh ideas, therefore inescapably blurring to a certain degree the border between the known and the unknown: we know that such is the work of every precursor to intellectual revolution; however, he does not deserve our attention: he is but a poor mystic, thinking through the agency of illusions. Somebody finally draws their dissatisfaction from the legitimate pictures of current life: he has abnormal inclinations and a perverse taste. In criticising Ibsen's ideas regarding women and marriage, Nordau ridicules them: "The great reformer cannot grasp that mankind has already checked and rejected as something bad marriage by trial, as well as the preferences of maidens lacking rich experience in love and motherhood (Westermarck's authority is cited here). After all, he would be a degenerate if he did not see in the future the distant past".[16] Elsewhere he observes: "The belief that we are living on the eve of revelation, of liberation, of the imminent kingdom of the new era, is frequently observed among the mentally ill: it is a mystic delirium".[17]

The cited fragments enable a description of Nordau's class situation, although nowhere is it revealed directly, since both his field and medical pseudo-objectivism are an obstruction. He is a liberal conservative, and he corresponds to that moment of the bourgeois revolution in which it reveals – faced with the demoralising trends – a defensive tendency towards unification and consolidation, while on the other hand he emphasises yet more pointedly the principle of individualism in the form of self-help and the general obligation of intensive personal work, without which the entire system would come crashing down. He also proves a liberal conservative when we take into account his adoration of positivistic science and contempt for philosophical speculation, his attitude towards religion, his opinions regarding the family, Ibsen and Brandes, etc., and finally in the proposed remedies, which we shall shortly investigate. I confess that I was highly surprised not to find among those numerous madmen Paul Lafargue, with his 'right to laziness', or any socialistic theoretician; I explain this to myself by presuming that Nordau quite simply had not read them, as otherwise he certainly would not have failed to refer them to hospital, which I would urge him to do; unless his views were to change, which moreover I am

---

16   Ibidem, p. 216.
17   Ibidem, p. 481.

not afraid of, because – as Lange says – we should not expect people to notice the pupil in their own eye; therefore he will find in Marx's dialectic perfect ground for psychiatric exercise, and will deserve much more commendable laurels than those to decorate the forehead of the first 'objective' literary critic.

With Nordau the cult of protecting the majority is expressed to its fullest in his conviction that "the unnecessary taunting of the majority, serving only to satisfy an urge of little significance, is a sign of antisocial egotism".[18] Which, I believe, was uttered in the context of Oscar Wilde's eccentric trousers; could we, though, ask about the border between lesser and greater significance? Are such scruples in regard to excessively strict honesty not also a reprehensible attempt at standing apart from the majority?

Besides, the same Mr Nordau states that imitating people, and so listening too intently to their opinions, is a symptom of hysteria. This is not the sole contradiction, but it is a striking one: in regard to other questions Nordau unwittingly provides examples that for this spokesman of the middle ground madmen are both people of the right and people of the left, both those who fall behind and those who outpace him. Which is why in his second volume[19] he deprecates – as plucked from Parnas and egotistic – the preference for form manifested in art, and likewise diabolic amorality, and demonstrates the close connection between morality and society, quite rightly positing that that which is a manifestation of natural laws seems beautiful to us; while in his first volume[20] he considered outlandish the notion of Ruskin, that theoretician of the pre-Raphaelites, according to whom art is tied above all to the moral idea and pursues not the detail but the general law, the schema. We could therefore ask why Poe, Baudelaire or Rollinat are treated as degenerated necrophiles, while Valdès is presented as a truly philo-social artist, despite portraying a bishop in liturgical robes, his body being devoured by maggots, in a coffin. Does the perfect explanation meant to defend the latter,[21] namely that "the thought juxtaposing the insignificance of individual life with the greatness and eternity of nature is connected to a sublime element, whose presentation, as if constituting a function of the higher centres of the brain, is accompanied by a sense of delight", not lend itself perfectly for using in the case of the cursed aesthete-necrophiles?

Apart from the class stigma I spoke of a moment ago, Nordau is distinctly and fatally marked by occupational stigma. He has only dug through

18   Ibidem, p. 121.
19   Ibidem, p. 144.
20   Ibidem, p. 150.
21   Ibidem, p. 138.

psychophysiology and attaches next to no importance to the influence that society has on the mind's development, which results in the extraordinary narrow-mindedness of his aetiology. Although he indeed discerns that the character of deviation depends on the conditions of the environment, he practically always forgets this and only takes it into account in certain special cases, for example when concerning the impact of the artificial English civilisation or the effect of chancellor Bismarck's iron system on Nietzsche's mind. Yet in an entire mass of cases he has totally forgotten that the role of the 'degenerate' is at most similar to the influence of a concave or convex mirror deforming the image of reality. Thus he has not noticed that Tolstoy's aversion to his wife or Wagner's antagonism of the sexes derive from the awful manifestations of contemporary marriage, and so a purely social origin of an economic basis, and that the famous motto of Catulle Mendès, "Let there be no human tears in the song of our bards!", is largely a simple response to the commercial utilisation of ideals and contemporary suffering by various 'programmes', while today's excessive individualism is a reaction to the hard schemata of life imposed by society, despite the proclaimed 'laissez-faire' or the invasion of Panurge's sheep. He did not comprehend that Gautier's reduction of art to the occupation of an ordinary setter of verse reveals the invasion into this field of the capitalistic division of labour, while expansive industrialism subordinating to man all the forces of nature, reduced to artificial creations, bears fruit in the tastes of Baudelaire, dreaming of a white iron and marble landscape, Villiers de L'Isle-Adam, in love with the mechanical 'Eve of the future', and finally Huysmans, creating artificial nature. And after all he cites Gautier's opinion, according to which the cause of decadence is that artificial life has supplanted natural life in civilised societies! Neither has he understood the protagonist of Barrès, a typical manipulator of life and capitalist Viking, in the meaning given to this term by Hièn, or linked the definition of decadentism provided by Bourget – "a state of social atomisation, of individuals' independence in relation to society, of throngs of people incapable of performing everyday jobs" – with capitalism, its inherent competition and its excessively overgrown populace. Even if these psychiatric associations were overstated, we could say about Nordau that in focusing his attention he completely omitted the connections between the ideas, which – heaven forbid! – could also ultimately see him admitted to hospital.

Besides, his psychiatry totally refuses to cooperate when he has to explain where *verismo* came from in Italy, "beneath an eternally bright sky, among a beautiful, cheerful people using a melodious language",[22] and so a people not intended for systemic pessimism. Nordau truly seems not to know Sicily at all.

---

22   Ibidem, p. 412.

In the end – and once again the aphorism of the pupils may be recalled – he does not notice in the slightest that his fanatic attachment to distinguishing between the fine arts and his deprecation of any attempt at uniting them indicates perfect adaptation to contemporary systemic specialisation.

Two stigmas, of class and occupation, weigh down his work's final two chapters, containing a certain programme: the chapters on prognostication and therapeutics. Nordau deliberates on the future of human thought as an orthodox Darwinist, and proves very relaxed about its fate. In his opinion, those who cannot adapt must perish in the battle with the strongest, thereby freeing literature of their harmful influence. Mankind cannot currently adjust to the accelerated course of civilisation in a manner that is not fatiguing; in the future it will be the other way around; mankind will adjust this course to itself, and thus bring it to a halt, forgo reaching for new inventions, abandon the cities to return to the countryside, etc. Besides, one day poetry in general – a field so susceptible to degeneration – will utterly vanish or will be practised by women and children, the most emotional part of mankind; just as dance, once so significant, has lost its mighty role, just as legend and story have ceased to be depositories of tradition, just as speaking in verse is today almost an atavistic speech mannerism, and just like the novel, which draws the attention of ever fewer serious people.[23] Do you not find in such an alluring picture of the future the dream of a serious man of action, a man descended in a straight line – if I may use this terrible barbarism – from Plato, who wants to drive poets out of society so they would no longer disconcert the genteel spirit of our positive victories? Could dreams and ideals – mighty factors of social transition – really be longed for, or not frankly hated and despised by man, who considers the current social form the best and final form, seeing progress only in the application of his clear and unchanging principles in all areas and manifestations of human life?

As for the remedies that Mr Nordau hoped for, it seems almost superfluous to me to indicate their uselessness to people so poorly acquainted with the action of the driving forces behind the contemporary world. The individual struggle for a living, based on the class system with poverty at one extreme, and the boredom of delight at the other, does not eliminate neurosis but is – contrariwise – its source, especially as the irritated producers of newness have an ensured market among the hardworking bourgeoisie and have already become specialised in delivering the latter with 'redeeming entertainment', as Nordau termed all poetry. Before its disappearance, halting the fatiguing progress in technology and the growth of the great cities is impossible within the near future – for as long as the chaotic competition between producers and

---

23   Ibidem, p. 480.

the poverty of the buyers continues. In the end poetry never will be totally replaced by positive observation, since the investigation of a spaciously unconstrained universe must also be boundless in time, and so there will always remain some part insufficiently explained and susceptible to exploration by the imagination. Nordau does not confine himself to anticipating the remedies that time will bring, but proposes them himself. For example: one should proclaim publicly that this or that author is sick; society should be warned of the danger; yet the most effective means against mental contagion would be the creation of an association of professors, dignitaries and other influential figures, the aim being to point out and to boycott immoral and antisocial articles. I am so grateful! Even if Nordau were to stoop so low as to offer such a role to our Sociological Institute, I declare that I know not who in this company would be expected to impartially determine what deviation from the norm is harmful, and what useful, in regard to the goals of society as a whole?

We have familiarised ourselves with Mr Nordau's method: it is based on gradation and on establishing a criterion – all the more harmful, as concealed from the reader and probably also from the author himself – and likewise on applying it to some manifestation of intellectual life: that which oversteps the boundaries in one direction or another is deprived of its value and excommunicated. If similar method is used somewhere in science, then it would be the applied sciences, such as industrial chemistry, agronomy, or the exploitation of mines. It is also fully justified in the science of the application of ideas, in other words in propaganda and party polemics. Let psychiatry, wanting to maintain it, openly declare itself an enterprise for the selecting of ideas of one class or another: at least then honest people will know what category they are classed under, and the genuine, objective science of ideas will have less difficulty getting through to what constitutes real scientific value. This science investigates impartially – without idiosyncrasy and regardless of preferences – the relation between ideas and their correlative economic area (which, in the historical society, is expressed as the class area) and psychophysiological area. In our opinion, sociology derives from these two connected sources.

Nordau's work contains brilliant fragments on psychophysiology, to which I have drawn attention in my detailed account; however, due to the neglect of economic aspects and the disastrous influence of class stigma, it is unwittingly biased and therefore from a scientific point of view unsuccessful. I therefore allow myself the hope that even those who do not agree with my positive findings will share my objection regarding the incursion of arbitrary psychiatric method into the field of the science of ideas.

Translated from a Polish translation of the French original by Kajetan Maria Jaksender [translator's note]

CHAPTER 9

The Social Dialectic in Vico's Philosophy[1,2]

In his book about Vico,[3] Michelet explains why his *The New Science*, the first philosophy of history, came into the world in Italy. Well, it was because the Church there, defending itself against the attacks of Protestantism and wanting to prove, despite these assaults, its antiquity – though all in all, we should add, in order to retain its power over the entirety of its followers' intellectual lives – supported studies in history and linguistic studies while also scrupulously maintaining, even at the expense of the individual sciences, a scholastic universality, an association between all the sciences and religious philosophy. But this fact has a yet deeper significance: it is not solely the Roman Church but the entire established order that the author of *The New Science*, a predecessor of Haller and Hegel, seems to defend against the bold appearances of natural law and Cartesianism.

---

1 Source: Dialektyka społeczna w filozofii Vica, "Przegląd Filozoficzny" 1901, vol. 2, pp. 172–189.
2 In wanting to highlight through comparison the proper meaning for sociology of what I call the *law of revolutionary retrospection*, I have undertaken a number of studies into the various forms that, in the history of philosophy, have been adopted by the ideas of the golden age, the historical cycle, and the return of the past in the future; irrespective of the law of revolutionary retrospection, these studies provide an outline of the history of the cyclical concept of development of mankind, and thereby the same of the genesis of the so-called 'social dialectic' in Marxism. When one passes from classic Antiquity, from its mythology, its cynics, stoics, Platonists and followers of Plotinus, from the Middle Ages with their idea of original purity and their millenarianism – to modern philosophy, one encounters two mighty thinkers, G. Vico and J.J. Rousseau, who – each in a different spirit – tackle anew the thought of the return of the past in the future; from them it passes to German idealism and the French Utopians, and finally – we see it concentrated in our times in Marxism, dispersed in the systems of diverse social thinkers, from Spencer, Loria and Tarde to the historians of various schools, just as G. Ferrari and O. Lorenz.
    This article is dedicated to elucidating the idea of the return of the past in the future as seen by Vico. This brilliant thinker waited long for social science to show interest in him, but since the 60s, and particularly in recent years in Italy, much indeed has been written about him. As for myself, by no means am I writing a complete monograph about Vico, but only deliberate here in strict logical order what constitutes the premises or characterisation of his idea of *ricorso*. As far as I am aware, nobody has written about Vico from this special point of view [Kelles-Krauz's footnote].
3 J. Michelet, *Oeuvres choisies de Vico*, written in 1835, most recently published in Paris: Flammarion, 1894 [Kelles-Krauz's footnote].

Natural law emerges from a revival of Roman law in the Italian universities. Roman law, expressing the relations between isolated and independent individuals, returns at a time when associations – which during the Middle Ages shielded and bound the individual – are deteriorating with the growth in trade, under the influence of the demands of the increasing circulation and accumulation of money. The bourgeoisie, growing in power, are setting this law against the distinctions, exceptions and privileges of the Middle Ages: and this is why it is considered in keeping with the nature of man in general, in keeping with universal reason. Wherever the bourgeoisie blossoms, this natural law, this critical rationalism, becomes a compelling tool in their hands against everything that hampers their growth.[4] Grotius, Descartes and Pufendorf pave the way for Diderot and Rousseau. But in the period when Giambattista Vico (1668–1744) was alive, the economic, political, and intellectual flowering of the Italian bourgeoisie was held in check, the rule of religious and political dogma was ensured, and – even more so in Italy's south, Vico's homeland – there was no belligerent bourgeoisie. Therefore Vico assails Descartes' geometric method not only because of its sterility, its inability to create new ideas; he has particularly much to criticise about his individual criterion of truth. The sole criterion of truth, reiterates Vico echoing the theologians, is its creation: and so only the one Creator is the possessor of the entire truth, because to know and to act is for Him one and the same. As for René's (Descartes') 'clear and distinct concept', there is nothing to prove that it is not deceptive and subjective.[5] Man cannot aspire to achieve truth; but for the consolidation of the principles of his conduct, he may and he must be satisfied with the certainty indicated to him by the opinion of the whole, i.e. "judgment without consideration, acknowledged by the entire state, the entire nation, the whole of humankind".[6] Vico's opposition is even greater, if greater it is at all possible to be, to the theoreticians of natural law – Grotius, Selden and Pufendorf. Despite all of his adoration for Grotius, whom he extols as one of the most universal thinkers of modern times, he criticises them sharply, on several occasions, and at every opportunity.

---

4 Cf. Labriola's *Essais sur la conception matérialiste de l'histoire*, Paris 1897, Ch. VIII [Kelles-Krauz's footnote]. See: Labriola, Antonio, 1908, *Essays on the materialistic conception of history*, Chicago, IL: C.H. Kerr, pp. 179–201.

5 Vico, Giambattista, 1710, *De antiquissima Italorum sapientia*, Ch. II [Kelles-Krauz's footnote]. See: Vico, Giambattista, 1988, *On the Most Ancient Wisdom of the Italians*, Ithaca, NY: Cornell University Press, pp. 58–63.

6 *The New Science*, Michelet's French edition, p. 311, axioms 11, 12.

Grotius adopts the commonality of goods as the starting point for human history; in his opinion, this state is that most compatible with natural law. Only egoism and the corruption of customs led man to abandon this state of happiness; in everything that followed, starting from ownership, there is an element of evil, of licence, of contradiction with nature. Pufendorf, a student under Grotius, goes even further in his negation: in his opinion, law is based solely on the strength given to it by society, while in itself it is always arbitrary, artificial, and alien to reason. This is because reason is identified with nature: "Natural law", says Grotius, "is a rule surrendered to us by honest reason, a rule that allows us to adjudge whether a given fact is or is not in agreement with rational nature". And because this reason flowed forth from the state of nature in which a commonality of goods prevailed, so the entire activity of the proponents of natural law, with their individualistic criticism in fact always and necessarily leans towards a similar system, or at least towards a related moral ideal. Vico stands at the extreme directly opposite to these ideas. Even his general philosophical point of view holds him far removed from the thought that anything whatsoever exists that may be arbitrary and fundamentally evil. In one of his works, exceptionally interesting due to its form as it bears the complete stamp of scholasticism, written in 1710 and entitled *De antiquissima Italorum sapientia ex linguae latinae originibus eruenda*,[7] in which Vico demonstrates very adroitly that all his philosophical thoughts were precontained within the etymology of the Latin words, he expresses himself thus:[8] *Norunt id verum sapientes linguae latinae auctores, recta metaphysica, physica prava esse ... Prava sunt in natura et imperfecta, supra naturam recta pravorum regula ... Materia metaphysica, quia peculiares formae omnes sunt imperfectae, genere ipso, sive idea, continent optimam ... Forma physica nihil aliud nisi continens rei mutatio est ... Physica materia, quam libet formam peculiarem educat, educit optimam; quia qua via educit, ea ex omnibus una erat.*[9] So it is, in nature, in human reality, there are no perfect things; they are as they must be, because they cannot be

---

7   In English: *On the Most Ancient Wisdom of the Italians* [translator's note].

8   Chapter II, *De Generibus sive Ideis* and Chapter III, *De punctis metaphysicis*, pp. 62, 73, and 74, Ferrari edition, Milano 1835 [Kelles-Krauz's footnote]. See: Vico, Giambattista, 1988, *On the Most Ancient Wisdom of the Italians*, pp. 58–66.

9   "The wise creators of the Latin language knew indeed that supernatural things are simple, while natural ones are warped ... In nature – things warped and imperfect; above nature – a simple thing, the rule of warped things. Because all individual forms are imperfect, therefore the supernatural possesses the best form, as only a type by itself, i.e. an idea ... Physical shape is nothing other than the constant transformation of things.... Whatever shape is adopted by the natural world, this shape is the best, because the path leading to this form was the only one (possible) of them all. [Footnote: Kazimierz Kelles-Krauz.]

other than they are, and therefore the best possible. Perfection, the measure and precept of worldly things, exists, but it exists beyond and above nature. And further: "Fate, which is to say the will of God, may in general be only good, although to our understanding, constrained by egoism, it may seem bad".[10]

Can one not presume that one is hearing Hegel? Such is often the impression when reading the works of this Neapolitan philosopher, and particularly when he contemplates social phenomena from the same point of view. And thus for example Vico stands against the notion that any existing institution could be artificial. In his work *De iuris universi principio et fine uno* (1720), containing the first outline of his philosophy of history, he contends the theorem of Epicurus, Machiavelli, Hobbes, Spinoza and Bayle, that laws were the invention of the mighty aimed at managing the ignorant. "Certainly", he says, "usefulness provides the opportunity for the emergence of law, but honesty always constitutes its raison d'être".[11] Power establishes the law, that is true; but then power is based on reason. Later, in his *Scienza nuova*, Vico negates that even non-Christian religions were solely the product of deception: they resulted from the inherent, non-imposed gullibility of the first people.[12] The same may be said of monarchy: the first, domestic, did not emerge from a compulsion inflicted on people previously free, but from the very nature of things, from the process of creation of the family; the second, the people's, is "the form of government best adapted to human nature when reason is fully developed":[13] and so always, according to the words of Pomponius, *rebus ipsis dictantibus regna condita.*[14] Vico responds to Plato's dream of a future republic governed by the best with the laconic title itself of one of the chapters in his work: *On the Eternal Natural Commonwealth, in Each Kind Best, Ordained by Divine Providence.*[15] He expounds that in every historical period, those who were the best compared to their contemporaries ruled, and they ruled for as long as they were the best, and that "the world is always governed by those who are naturally fittest". This acknowledgement of the fulfilled fact, this type of social Darwinism, if

---

10   See Chapter VIII [Kelles-Krauz's footnote]. See: Vico, Giambattista, 1988, *On the Most Ancient Wisdom of the Italians*, pp. 105–108.

11   See Michelet's translation, p. 183 (J. Michelet, *Oeuvres choisies de Vico*) [Kelles-Krauz's footnote].

12   Book II, Chapter II, § 1 [Kelles-Krauz's footnote]. See: Vico, Giambattista, 1948, *The New Science of Giambattista Vico*, Ithaca, NY: Cornell University Press, p. 100.

13   Vico, Giambattista, 1948, *The New Science of Giambattista Vico*, p. 341.

14   [From the Latin] Kingdoms are founded at the dictation of things themselves [Kelles-Krauz's footnote].

15   Book IV, Chapter V [Kelles-Krauz's footnote]. See: Vico, Giambattista, 1948, *The New Science of Giambattista Vico*, pp. 377–384.

on the one hand it provides a glimpse of the counterrevolutionary philosophy of the early 19th century, on the other it is ultimately nothing other than the philosophical application of the leading thought of divine judgments....

In these conditions, what right and capacity for judging what exists, for protecting against fait accompli on the principle of supposed natural law may individual reason have? Above all it is unable by itself to understand what is necessary for society as a whole: "Man is mainly attached to his own personal interest; therefore, Providence is needed to keep him in the social order and to lead him by its justice through the successive forms of socialisation: family, borough, nation, and mankind".[16] Precisely legislation, knowing man as he is, exploits his weaknesses to make social virtues out of them.[17] Further, in the name of what higher principle would the individual's reason, and their personal sense of natural law – which by their very essence are changeable and historical – command them to have self-esteem? A mistake made by all theoreticians of natural law involves precisely the notion that "when the natural law of human nations ensued ... and upon which the philosophers and moral theologians based their understanding of the natural law of fully unfolded eternal reason, the phrase was fitly reinterpreted to mean that the natural law of nations was ordained by the true God".[18] One of the main meanings of *The New Science* involves just that, that it is the history of human views, the history – as Vico says directly – of human nature.[19]

Vico shows us (in book IV) the consequence of the three natures, three kinds of custom, types of law, natural and those of governments, that they correspond to: languages, laws, various authorities and reasons, and demonstrates with facts that "[s]o far was the natural law of the developed human reason of Grotius, Selden and Pufendorf (whom we always encounter together in his writings) from being current by nature through all times in all nations!".[20] If in the meantime, in the cited apostrophe against Epicurus, Machiavelli and their imitators, Vico protests against their opinion that in his opinion derogates the law, that "it changes appropriately to the place and time", then there is no contradiction here in the least: if he promises to prove that "law is essentially eternal truth, unchanging either in time or in space", then this is in a totally different meaning: because the "real God is the foundation of real law,

---

16   Vico, Giambattista, 1948, *The New Science of Giambattista Vico*, p. 211.

17   Book I, Chapter II, axiom 7 [Kelles-Krauz's footnote]. See: Vico, Giambattista, 1948, *The New Science of Giambattista Vico*, pp. 5–6.

18   Vico, Giambattista, 1948, *The New Science of Giambattista Vico*, p. 212.

19   Ibidem, p. 100.

20   Ibidem, p. 323.

just as He is the basis of true religion", and God implements this sole law in the wake of various forms. And because the thought of God is implemented in mankind, then what the commonality or majority of humankind sense as right should serve as a principle in social life, and "let him who would transgress these [bounds of human reason] beware lest he transgress all humanity".[21] This is precisely about the individual's conviction that there exists something above their own reason; and as such it is ultimately about the proving of law on the basis of metaphysics "denying us the misfortunate ease of investigating whether the law is right".[22]

As for human nature, then although Vico does not want to place it above everything else as the Epicureans do, he is far from the thought of repressing it in the manner of the stoics. They are both, he says, reclusive doctrines. In society man should be guided, but not by depriving him of his nature: this is what constitutes the raison d'état of the *foederum generis humani* (relationships of the human race) – the institutions of marriage, or tombs, etc. "Governments [...] must have suited the nature of the men governed" (ax. 69), and even "things do not settle or endure out of their natural order", proclaims axiom 8 – and it might seem that this axiom is based on the adoption of a certain point to which things should always tend, in other words to some kind of reformative or even revolutionary criterion, if not for the fact that it simply expresses – one hundred years before Haller – the thought that man's natural state is life within society. Vico also maintains that his principles of law arose on the basis of "real knowledge of human nature – but this human nature has its beginnings in the true God" (p. 184); the assertion that it is God who makes history through a nation constitutes the fundamental principle of his social philosophy.

The author of *The New Science* harshly berates Pufendorf for his hypothesis – one probably worthy of Hobbes himself – that man, at the beginning of his existence, was thrown into the world without the help and care of God; Grotius in turn is reproached for saying that his system would remain intact, even if the concept of God were to be removed from it.[23] In fact, in his definition of natural law Grotius says that if honest reason indicates to us that a particular deed is moral or immoral, then this means that God, the creator of nature, commands or prohibits it of us. He speaks just like all determinist-theists, defenders of the ethical independence of the individual from social gravitas, from

---

21 Ibidem, p. 94.

22 *De iuris universi,* etc., in: Michelet, Jules, 1894, *Oeuvres choisies de Vico,* p. 183 [Kelles-Krauz's footnote].

23 *In acta Lipsiensia,* in: Michelet, Jules, 1894, *Oeuvres choisies de Vico,* p. 203 [Kelles-Krauz's footnote].

the eastern doctors of the church (Origen) to the founders of Protestantism; he says the same as will say his successor Descartes, who proves the reality of the external world's existence with the argument that God cannot deceive us. Vico, the faithful Catholic, the supporter of St Augustine's doctrine; Vico the pupil of Jesuits, the pupil of that determined Scotist Ricci, and thus the heir to the entire authoritarian theory of deistic indeterminism must take a totally different position. In his opinion God is manifested beyond doubt in the ideas and deeds of people, but only people as a whole – "in the objective spirit" as Hegel would say; humankind does indeed possess an inherent sense of justice,[24] but this is manifested not in the individual, but in the entire human race; Grotius and others thus err by not wanting to acknowledge external justice, i.e. dominion.[25]

Under this umbrella of Providence, that giver of the peoples' natural law,[26] Vico frequently expresses thoughts quite akin to the views of the creators of natural law, from which later – following the loss of this safety valve – revolutionary conclusions were extrapolated. He himself understands very well that "monarchs would surely fall were they to forbid the worship of God".[27] But by feeling protected in this way, he deduces ownership – just like the naturalists he fights – from the occupation of land,[28] and even at the threshold of the first society he sets down a certain kind of social contract, consciously concluded between the mighty and against the subjects – because he explains the transition from patriarchy to aristocracy in the following way: when the strongest of the original giants formed families, the rest came to live under their care and power; but in time these servants (*famuli*) rebelled against the patriarchs, by which they forced the latter to join together in a political body for the purpose of defence. Thus, on the one hand, the family fathers were forced, for the restoration of obedience among their household members, to grant them land (hence *clientes, clientelae*); on the other hand they subordinated sovereign domestic authority to the dominion of the state they belonged to. "Otherwise", says Vico, "it becomes impossible to understand in what way civil government resulted from domestic authority".[29] However, by no means does the fact that

---

24   "My book is based on the principle of justice innate to human kind": G. Vico, in a letter to the prelate Esperti, in Michelet, Jules, 1894, *Oeuvres choisies de Vico*, p. 176 [Kelles-Krauz's footnote].

25   Vico, Giambattista, 1948, *The New Science of Giambattista Vico*, p. 111.

26   Ibidem, p. 209.

27   Michelet, Jules, 1894, *Oeuvres choisies de Vico*, p. 459.

28   Vico, Giambattista, 1948, *The New Science of Giambattista Vico*, p. 206.

29   Ibidem, p. 161.

the social contract – if we are to acknowledge this concept – thus has its beginnings in violence and deception, mean that anybody had the right to demand its revision, since it all finds fulfilment in tune with the divine plans.

One can also observe with Vico, despite his enormous erudition, an almost Cartesian contempt (also resembling that of Rousseau) for men of learning, for the accumulated yet contradictory testimonies of philosophical and philological gravitas. "So, for purposes of this inquiry", he says, "we must reckon as if there were no books in the world".[30] Yet when the rationalists turned from books to appeal to the judgments of their own reason, they transferred from the womb of the civilisation oppressing them to the fictitious state of nature, while Vico conversely, wanting to create *The New Science*, desired to "burrow into the bottomless and extensive library of mankind's universal acumen, so as to browse through the earliest demotic authors who preceded writers by more than a thousand years",[31] or to word it differently – to descend to the true state of nature, to the prehistoric state of people.

The sense of history developed with such extraordinary subtlety and strength constitutes a separate trait shown by Vico in the flood of rationalism. Although he also acknowledges eternal and unchanging truths, these truths are above nature.[32]

This historical sense is identified with sober realism, which is summarised in that sentence addressed against Bodin: "The law of reason is the moralists' natural law. The law of advantage and strength is the natural law of the peoples. And the peoples complied to it, as lawyers say: *usu exigente humanisque necessitatibus expostulantibus*".[33] This structure of Vico's mind allows him to express thoughts, to make discoveries that make him the predecessor of many of the most outstanding sociologists of more modern times. The most famous of these thoughts, the one that most earned him the admiration of the democrat Michelet, is reducing the greatness of Homer and the greats in general to the activity of human masses, as if dissolving their personalities in the masses. Apart from this we find that, for his day, he has many a thought of brilliance. With his division of history into three ages, and by his very description of these ages, he precedes Comte; with his granting poetry a place earlier

---

30   Ibidem, p. 85.
31   In acta Lipsiensia, in: Michelet, Jules, 1894, *Oeuvres choisies de Vico*, p. 206.
32   De nosi temporis studiorum ratione, in: Michelet, Jules, 1894, *Oeuvres choisies de Vico*, p. 152.
33   From the Latin: "On the command of practice, on the demand of human needs" [Kelles-Krauz's footnote].

in history than prose – [he precedes] historians of civilisation of the measure of Tylor; his mythological and historical critique is quite simply amazing in its ideas.[34] With him we encounter reasoning similar to Świętochowski's argumentations about 'the poet as original man'; the germs of Bachofen's[35] theory, such thoughts on the beginnings and the position of religion – albeit pagan religion – as were later expounded by Feuerbach;[36] the entire Roman history is explained by *The New Science* not otherwise than through the struggle of the classes on an economic foundation.

All of this of course was no obstacle to Vico dedicating his *The New Science* to Cardinal Corsini, or to the latter – as elected Pope – accepting it with much praise. In order for such ideas to lose the favour of the guardians of the established order, as well as for Vico to obtain the recognition of this order's scientific opponents, what was needed was above all a reconciliation of the historical and realistic point of view with 'human rights', which was only the work of the 19th century and economic materialism. In the 18th century the totality of these ideas was held in check only by the momentum of the revolutionary bourgeoisie (which was already *in potentia* revolutionary in 1728, when Vico's book was published), and as such it comes as no surprise that not only did the "verbose Neapolitan advocates, following much drink and in a state approaching sleep"[37] not understand him particularly well, but also the philosophers gathered around the Science Journal[38] of Leipzig and the entire 18th century suspected him of solely wanting to defend Catholicism and condemned him to oblivion.

• • •

---

34 Ajax and Horatius Cocles, themselves conquering thousands, forty Normans scattering an entire army of Saracens – 'themselves' meaning at the head of all their sons, slaves, and household members beneath the father's name (book II, Chapter V). The bull abducting Europa, the Minotaur, and the winged horse Perseus – these are the symbols of the privateers (Chapter VI), etc. [Kelles-Krauz's footnote].

35 Juno was the wife and sister of Jupiter, because the first marriages, sanctified by auspice, were between brothers and sisters [Kelles-Krauz's footnote].

36 Axiom 54; "This by the eternal property that when men fail to see reason in human affairs, and much more if they see it opposed, they take refuge in the inscrutable counsels hidden in the abyss of divine providence". (Vico, Giambattista, 1948, *The New Science of Giambattista Vico*, p. 313). See also: Marx, Loria, etc. [Kelles-Krauz's footnote].

37 Vico, Giambattista, *Autobiography of Vico*, in: Michelet, Jules, 1894, *Oeuvres choisies de Vico*, pp. 105, 136.

38 This is a literal translation of the name given in Polish by the author [translator's note].

Knowing two traits of Vico's mind, his historical and critical sense, and his belief in a divine plan, it is easy to understand that he must reject the notion of
a golden age that is the centre of gravity of the historical cycle in concepts
of antiquity. In fact, as an example Vico directly accuses Plato – one of the
masters he venerates the most highly – of having committed a serious error in
accrediting primitive people with so many virtues. But Vico, in this case as well
outpacing the method of critique of his day, is not satisfied with only stating
the mistake; he also explains it. Thus in his opinion the beginning of human
history presents itself as follows:[39] Following the deluge (his system begins
after the deluge, thanks to which the golden age of the Christian paradise is
beyond the reach of his critique) giants came into the world, and possessed
an entirely beastly nature. They lived like beasts, in a total commonality of
women and goods, without social bonds or laws, among murder and poverty.
But they heard the roar of thunder and fear overcame them. Fear pushed them
to hide in caves and evoked a certain sense of shame when satisfying their passions. As a consequence, some of them abducted one woman each, becoming
their husband and lord. Thereby marriage – the first law, the first *foedus generis
humani*, extracting man from his beastly state – came into being. Thus God,
with the help of thunder, caused the human beasts to take the first step on
the road to civilisation. Vico himself compares this change to the achievement
attributed by the pagans to Saturn: essentially, we see here the traces of the
influence exerted on him by one of his favourite classics, Virgil.

Then began the age of the patriarch, the age in which the father of the family
was simultaneously its king, its wise man and its priest. These families, initially
comprising only kin, since each formed from a single couple, settled in the
hills. The beginning of the great human ideas dates back to this period. Thanks
to the theocratic government of the patriarch, one could say that the people
are in direct relations with the deity, and poetry, religion and sacrifice appear.
In Vico's terminology, this is the age of divinity or the poetic age. Those family
fathers ensuring the safety of those beneath their dominion had an evident
superiority over the godless giants who still retained a commonality of goods
and the resultant disputes.[40] So too the giants soon came to beg the fathers for
their care, offering them in exchange their obedience. The fathers governed
in the name of divine will, and constituted an oracle; they were at the same
time the social, intellectual and religious leaders of their families. This is the
reason why the poets extolled this age, one in which 'the gods reigned on
Earth'; this is precisely what led Plato astray, and aroused his longing for the

---

39   Mainly book II, Chapters IV and V, *The New Science* [Kelles-Krauz's footnote].
40   Vico, Giambattista, 1948, *The New Science of Giambattista Vico*, p. 161.

times when "the philosophers were kings, the kings – philosophers".[41] At the same time, though, this was an age of boundless authority of the father over his children, an age of cruel sacrifice: with Plato himself we encounter just such a family father from the golden age in the person of Polyphemus. "We may conclude from all this how empty has been the conceit of the learned concerning the innocence of the golden age observed in the first gentile nations. In fact it was a fanaticism of superstition which kept the first men of the gentiles, savage, proud and most cruel as they were, in some sort of restraint by main terror of a divinity they had imagined".[42]

Such presents itself the golden age, the state of nature, the original happiness, the commonality of goods – in the light of the 'new philosophical critique', while among other things *The New Science* has the significance, the 'appearance',[43] of such critique. Although indeed there is nothing here from which the golden material of the retrospective ideal may be woven. Besides, one should not look for the ideal, for the ideal society, in history, in a certain specified era of the past: there exists an "ideal law, eternal, which holds power in common society contained within the divine thought, and in the likeness of which the societies of all times and all countries are established".[44] Only such a conception enables the reconciling of man as he currently is with man as he should be:[45] and for having suggested this thought to him, Vico does not cease to glorify the godlike Plato. Eternal ideal history: three words that encapsulate the concept of Vico's *recorsi*, the recurring cycles. Having finally reached the main section of our subject, we shall make a closer investigation.

• • •

Vico himself writes that an important task of his was to "lay out an ideal, eternal history, the phases of which would serve as a model for the course of universal

---

41   Ibidem.

42   Ibidem, p. 159.

43   With his profundity and acumen, Vico himself defines the multifaceted scientific momentousness of the historiosophic method that he discovered, listing seven 'aspects' (*aspetti*) what his *Scienza nuova* has, according to the direction to be applied and highlighted in a given case: 1. Civil (social) theology; 2. Philosophy of authority, i.e. ownership; 3. History of human ideas (of human nature). 4. New philosophical critique (of great people, etc.); 5. An ideal eternal history; 6. A new chronology (explaining the beginnings of humankind); 7. A new system of the natural law of the peoples [Kelles-Krauz's footnote].

44   *Autobiography*, in: Michelet, Jules, 1894, *Oeuvres choisies de Vico*, p. 59 [Kelles-Krauz's footnote].

45   Michelet, Jules, 1894, *Oeuvres choisies de Vico*, p. 77.

history of all times ... complying with certain everlasting traits as manifested by the social system in the emergence, settling and falling of nations".[46] To find "divine providence and common to all nations, namely the common sense of the human race, determined by the necessary harmony of human things, in which all the beauty of the civil world consists ... once these orders were established by divine providence, the course of the affairs of the nations had to be, must now be and will have to be such as our Science demonstrates, even if infinite worlds were produced from time to time through eternity, which is certainly not the case".[47]

Naturally Vico himself was unable to understand the entire momentousness of this undertaking. He only wanted to create a 'civil theology of divine Providence', nonexistent until his time since only natural theology had been addressed,[48] and with its assistance force rebellious social thought to obey. But his striking figure stands at a historical turning point, at which 'civil theology' transforms into a social science based on the correctness of facts, the conformity of will, and subordination of individuals' resistance to social laws – a social science which, today, is the strongest foundation of aspirations for social reform.

We emphasise above the term conformity ... in the changeability of places and time. These are two areas over which Vico unfolds the dominion of his ideal history and conducts his investigations. In the first he is the harbinger of modern ethnology, since he articulates one of its main principles: the principle of the shared nature of the peoples (words used for the title to one of the chapters in *The New Science*[49]), the principle of the autogenous, and unimitated, similarity of social evolution in all nations;[50] and some idea of his perspicacity is given by the fact that he discovers the identity of the social state of Japan at

---

46   *Autobiography*, in: Michelet, Jules, 1894, *Oeuvres choisies de Vico*, p. 78 [Kelles-Krauz's footnote].

47   Vico, Giambattista, 1948, *The New Science of Giambattista Vico*, pp. 92–93.

48   Ibidem, p. 90.

49   Vico, Giambattista, *Principi di Scienza nuova d'intorno alla commune natura delie nazioni* [Kelles-Krauz's footnote].

50   Compare book I Chapter I. The chronology of the nations in the following order: Jews, Chaldeans, Phoenicians, Greeks and Romans. Each of these nations developed entirely independently of others. Hegel later puts the nations in a sequence, in order to demonstrate with them the dialecticism of his Idea: Vico does not need to distort the facts. See also his *De constantia iurisprudentis*, in which he fights the presumption that laws of the Ten Tables in Rome were an imitation of the laws of Solon, and proves that they were entirely self-generated [Kelles-Krauz's footnote].

the moment of the arrival there by European missionaries with their feudalism (in general with *mens heroica*, with that 'heroic spirit' appropriate, for example, to the Romans in the era of the Punic Wars[51]).

The second area is the proper field of *ricorso*. Thus the history of nations has, above all, a certain defined course (*corso*) (see the title of book IV). How does this historical schema look? We already know its first two stages: the pre-social state, and the 'godly' age. At the moment when the people who had remained till that moment in the beastly state escaped from the care and authority of the family fathers, and when the latter – having led through their exploitation to rebellion – finally united for the purpose of defence and ceded land to the rebels, thereby concluding a double contract – a contract between the fathers themselves, and a contract of the fatherly state with the state of the clients – established the first non-familial society, then with this moment we step into the heroic age, characterised by the natural law of strength, by customs irascible and sensitive in regard to honour, by wars, privateering and republican-aristocratic government: an age embodied perfectly in the person of Achilles. The period of the kings' rule in Rome also corresponds to this age. The term *patria (res)* derives from the joining of the 'fathers'. This organisation, spawned on the ground of class struggle, lives among constant class struggle. The plebeians shortly start to demand rights identical to those of the 'fathers': the right of marriage (*connubia patrum*), rights written in order to make them independent of the caprices of the knighthood, etc., and in order to acquire these rights they strive to demonstrate knightly deeds in wars, thereby wanting to prove themselves equal to the patricians, serving their homeland entirely naturally, "in order to preserve their comfortable existence".[52] Finally, despite the hateful resistance of the patricians, the plebeians obtain their first concession through the establishing of the institution of census, thereby marking the transition to democracy, meaning to the human age. (In the Middle Ages, 'man' still signifies a serf). At that time human nature really is human, equalitarian, comprehensive, moderate, favourable and sensible; language itself, in the age of gods comprising only gestures (the *acta legitima* of the Romans are one of the relics of this language), in the heroic age – signs and short words that have to this day remained the language of military commands, adapts to this nature and by becoming segmented, becomes at the same time accessible and understandable to all. "In virtue of this sovereignty over languages and letters, the free peoples must also be masters of their laws, for they impose on the laws the

---

51   Vico, Giambattista, 1948, *The New Science of Giambattista Vico*, p. 74.

52   Ibidem, p. 78.

senses in which they constrain the powerful to observe them".[53] One can see here how consistent, versatile and deep Vico's historical 'monism' is!

Besides, monarchy belongs to the 'human' age on the same principle as democracy. This age possesses a "human government in which the equality of rational nature, constituting a proper attribute of mankind, is reflected in civic and political equality. All citizens in this era are born equal, whether because they have popular government, or the government of monarchy places all subjects on a level of identical rights, itself only holding a purely civic superiority over the citizens in its commanding of the armed forces" (p. 556). Monarchy is only the final and essential consequence of democracy – at the moment when the latter becomes corrupt and is torn apart by factional disputes.

The beastly state of 'nature'; the divine, theocratic age; the heroic-aristocratic age; the age of people – democratic and monarchical; such is the course of history. In certain circumstances it is faithfully repeated: and this is the *ricorso* (Michelet translates this as *retour*, or return; see book V; we would say merry-go-round).

An example of such a return exists. Following the collapse of the Roman world, the populace found itself in a beastly state – with wars of everybody against everybody, in a state analogical to that the giants were in after the deluge. This was followed in turn by the formation of families and shelters, by a period of 'long-lasting barbarianism', in other words feudalism, the institutions of which – as Vico demonstrates with amusing philological comparisons characterised by erudition – recreate the institutions of the Roman patriciate; and ultimately democracy and monarchy.[54]

Such is Vico's entire idea of the revival of the past in the future. Ultimately it is nothing other than the stoic idea of cycles limited to history, though with the admittedly very important difference that the God of the stoics, the 'spirit of the world', lives together with the world, just like the later Hegelian absolute, while Vico's God – absolute and pre-existing – perpetually recreates his unshaken thought.

Perpetually? To infinity? Such is the first question that comes to mind when we want to delve deeper into Vico's mind. And we have to answer it in the negative. Because there exists the "eternal natural royal law by which the nations

53 Ibidem, p. 308.

54 Vico attempted yet another partial application of his *ricorso* idea: according to Michelet (p. 136), in his posthumous panegyric on Countess Althan, he made a noteworthy comparison of the war for the succession of the Spanish throne with the Second Punic War [Kelles-Krauz's footnote].

come to rest under monarchies".[55] Monarchy flowing from democracy, 'popular' monarchy, may crown and bring a felicitous conclusion to the mundane
wandering of a nation; this may endure without end, and in itself it bears no
germ of disintegration. That fatal return only threatens society for as long as
there exists a democratic republic, always tending to degenerate into anarchy.

If society, says Vico, is not saved from democratic anarchy by the formation
of monarchy or the arrival of healthier peoples who conquer it, then it must
out of necessity return to the state of original barbarianism through everybody
fighting everybody else for riches. Yet when this merciless battle ultimately reduces people to but a few, then the given quantity of items essential for life
is again sufficient, and once again they become open to more noble feelings
and commence anew the eternal course of history. Mankind is reborn from its
flames like the phoenix.[56]

This is also why the fifth book of *The New Science* bears the following title:
'The recourse of human institutions which the Nations take when they rise
again' (in the original: *Del ricorso delle cose umane nel risurgere che fanno le
nazioni*).

The strictly conservative nature of the cycle idea with Vico is thereby outlined even more clearly: the necessity for all the miseries of history to begin
anew, for a collapse into a beastly condition, is the punishment of Sisyphus
suspended by God like Damocles' sword above any excessively tempestuous
democracy, putting off for too long the execution of His eternal plan to seek 'repose' in monarchy. The same abasement could also be the sole consequence of
attacks by rebels who, enticed by the charm of the golden age would attempt
to overthrow popular monarchy.[57]

It is out of necessity that this spirit of the entire system excludes any supposition that ancient social systems might be reborn in a higher form.[58] In fact
his idea boils down simply to the conditional periodicalness of human history.
It is also tied to the comparison of human life to the existence of a single man:
Vico tells us of the attributes of the 'childish world', of the similarity between

---

55   Vico, Giambattista, 1948, *The New Science of Giambattista Vico*, p. 340.

56   Ibidem, p. 382.

57   Of interest to note is that Le Bon, in his *Psychological Laws of the Evolution of Peoples*, imi-
      tating Vico's conception of recourses and using it in the same counterrevolutionary spirit,
      threatens Europe with a new invasion of barbarians in the event of victory for socialism ...
      [Kelles-Krauz's footnote].

58   It would not be inappropriate here to point out, if one were to want to imitate Vico's
      philological method, that *ricorso* in Italian also means 'menstruation' [Kelles-Krauz's
      footnote].

a poet, a child and primitive man,[59] in such a manner that it brings to mind at the same time the modern biological law of 'embryogenic concentration' and certain theories of literary degeneration.

Cycles considered as a whole may only reoccur with complete sameness. Yet if Vico does not consider a return to the beastly condition following the fall of the Roman Empire as entirely similar to the condition of the giants after the deluge, then this may be explained in that the ancient world did not fall into this state simply as a result of its own disintegration, but that this decomposition was halted by the arrival of healthier nations.

If one can seek in Vico the idea of the past being reborn in a higher form, this is not as a consequence of cycles, but as a consequence of ages within the womb of one and the same cycle. This thought is accompanied by ideas that later as well are occasionally connected to it: the ideas of a law that only later, among the Marxists, was called the law of survival of the social form following the disappearance of the appropriate content, the transition of institutions into their opposites, of thesis – antithesis – synthesis. All these ideas are to be found with Vico only in their germ, and they do not play much of a role in his system (with the exception of the 'law of survival'); however, they do testify to the keenness of his historical flair, and deserve to be considered, if only due to the issue of Vico's possible impact on Hegel and Comte, or at least the kinship of these intellects.

Chapter VI of book IV of *The New Science*, titled: *On the manner in which each social form mixes with the preceding*,[60] is based on the following axiom: "when men change they retain for some time the impression of their previous customs".[61] Which for example is why the fathers, after having passed from the beastly state into the familial state, retained their inherent cruelty for some time; which is also why their communities after this were initially a mixture of aristocracy and the domestic monarchy of the family fathers; otherwise it would be impossible to understand in what way civil society emerged from familial society. Later still democracy retained the custodial power of the aristocrats and popular states were ruled by aristocratic bodies (for example the Roman senate). One could compare this historical theory of Vico's with his psychological theory, summarised in the following words

---

59   Axiom 37. See: Vico, Giambattista, 1948, *The New Science of Giambattista Vico*, p. 20.

60   The actual title is: 'Other proofs taken from [mixed commonwealths, that is from] the tempering of the state of a succeeding commonwealth by the government of the preceding one' (Book IV, Section XIII).

61   Vico, Giambattista, 1948, *The New Science of Giambattista Vico*, p. 338.

(*De antiquissima Italorum sapientia*[62]): "*Quod nos vulgo imaginari, Latini mem-orare dicunt. Homini enim fingere nihil praeter natur am datur*".[63] There even exists an example of such memory-imagination, of such retrospective imitation in discovering – between two different cycles: speaking about the rebirth of Roman law in the Italian universities, Vico ascribes this to the fact that this law, having emerged in the democratic 'human age' of antiquity, also corresponded to the needs of the new 'people's' age just beginning, making it clear at the same time that the law that he calls the natural law of civilised nations could have contributed to an acceleration in the progress of modern 'democracy'.[64] However, all these thoughts are neither connected into one with themselves or with the following thoughts also deserving attention: "But finally the family fathers, having become great by the religion and virtue of their ancestors and through the labors of their clients, began to abuse the laws of protection and to govern the clients harshly ... they had thus departed from the natural order, which is that of justice".[65] In this manner this one and the same institution turned in the course of time from being just to unjust. The plebeians, wanting to attain equality, rivalled with the patricians in their abidance of the laws, customs and patricianly religion. Thus the tool for the oppression of the plebeians became the tool of their liberation. The survival of the social form serves here as the basis for transition from the existing form to its opposite.

And so, finally, the 'thesis – antithesis – synthesis' and the dialectic revival of the past in a higher form: the first customs (of the divine age) were characterised by piety and religiosity, which had overcome the original animality; the second – (of the heroic age) – impetuousness and irascibility, and for this reason they may be considered to some extent a relapse of the original animality; the third – 'human', 'based on duties', constitute a kind of return to patriarchal piety in a higher form. "People begin from unity in domestic monarchy, pass through governments of the minority, the majority and the whole, and once again come to unity (of a higher kind) in a civil monarchy".[66]

In defiance of his entire system, Vico seems even to bequeath to his successors a certain kind of longing for the golden age, and the wish that at least one of this age's real virtues might be reborn in a higher form. This longing applies to the versatility of the people of that day, a trait thanks to which the wise men

---

62   Ferrari edition, p. 81 [Kelles-Krauz's footnote].
63   "There where we use the term 'to imagine', the Latins said 'to remember'. Because man can only think up what is in nature" [Kelles-Krauz's footnote].
64   Vico, Giambattista, 1948, *The New Science of Giambattista Vico*, p. 120.
65   Ibidem, p. 378.
66   Ibidem, p. 161.

of the 'golden' age, the family fathers, were equally as great as the philosophers, the lawmakers, the chiefs, the orators and the poets,[67] since the father of a family simultaneously fulfilled all duties that then corresponded to these appellations of today. This wish, which coming from Vico does not surprise us, and which he expressed in his speech: *De nostri temporis studiorum ratione*, was for the modern university to provide its students with everything that once a single person, for example Aristotle or Plato, gave their pupils, so that the encyclopaedia of sciences be reborn (*disciplina vere rotunda, De iuris univ. etc*).[68]

However, this is an exception that is not fundamental at all. The fundamental attribute of Vico's idea of the historical cycle is that lost happiness does not return to people waiting in a state of longing, but only unshakable destiny – which they cannot avoid in any way – is fulfilled. No rebellion is of any use: all that remains is to surrender to higher will. Yet in the sequence of theologians stretching from Plato to Hegel, Vico is the one who inseminated the Absolute Idea with the nourishing juice of historical realism.

---

67   Ibidem, p. 265.
68   In: Michelet, Jules, 1894, *Oeuvres choisies de Vico*, p. 187.

Bibliography

Major Works Cited

Abramowski, Edward, 1897, Les bases psychologiques de la sociologie (Principe du phénomène social), Paris: V. Giard, E. Brière.

Abramowski, Edward, 1898, Le matérialisme historique et le principe du phénomène social, Paris: V. Giard.

Anderson, Benedict, 1983, Imagined Communities: Reflections on the Origin and Spread of Nationalism. London, UK: Verso.

Barth, Paul, 1890, Die Geschichtsphilosophie Hegels und der Hegelianer, Leipzig: O.R. Reisland.

Beaussire, Émile, 1865, Antécédents de l'hégélianisme en France, Paris: Germer Baillière.

Bellamy, Edward, 1888, Looking Backward: 2000–1887. Boston, MA: Ticknor & Co.

Beltov, 1956, The Development of the Monist View of History, Moscow: Foreign Languages Publishing House.

Benjamin, Walter, 1968, Illuminations. New York: Schocken Books.

Bieńkowski, Wiesław, 1973, Kazimierz Kelles-Krauz: życie i działalność, Warsaw, Poland: Państwowe Wydawnictwo Naukowe.

Borzym, Stanisław, Floryńska, Halina, Skarga, Barbara and Walicki, Andrzej, 2000 (eds), Zarys dziejów filozofii polskiej 1815–1918, Warsaw, Poland: PWN.

Castells, Manuel, 2012, Networks of Outrage and Hope, Malden, MA: Polity Press.

Champion, Edme, 1887, Esprit de la révolution française, Paris: C. Reinwald.

Comte, Auguste, 1903, A Discourse on the Positive Spirit. London, UK: W. Reeves.

Croce, Benedetto, 1898, Essai d'interprétation et de critique de quelques concepts du marxisme, Paris: Giard et Brière.

Durkheim, Émile, 1951, Suicide. A Study in Sociology. New York: The Free Press.

Durkheim, Émile, 1982, The Rules of Sociological Method. New York: The Free Press.

Engels, Friedrich, 1902, The Origin of the Family, Private Property, and the State, Chicago, IL: C.H. Kerr.

Engels, Friedrich, 1976, Ludwig Feuerbach and the End of Classical German Philosophy, Peking: Foreign Languages Press.

Fester, Richard, 1890, Rousseau und die deutsche Geschichtsphilosophie, Stuttgart: Göschen'sche Verlag,

Flint, Robert, 1874, The Philosophy of History in France and Germany, Edinburgh and London: William Blackwood and Sons.

Foucault, Michel, 1990, The History of Sexuality. New York: Vintage Books.

Franck, Adolphe, 1893, Réformateurs et publicistes de l'Europe au XVIII siècle, Paris: Calmann Lévy.

Gomulicki, Wiktor, 1978, Poezje wybrane, Warsaw: Ludowa Spółdzielnia Wydawnicza.

Haller, Karl von, 1822, Restauration der Staatswissenschaft, Winterthur: Die Steinerische Buchhandlung.

Hartmann, Eduard von, 1884, Philosophy of the Unconscious, London: Trübner.

Hobbes, Thomas, 1996, Leviathan. Oxford, UK: Oxford University Press.

Kovalevsky, Maxim, 1890, Tableau des origines et de l'évolution de la famille et de la propriété, Stockholm: Samson et Wallin.

Kareev, Nikolai, 1896, Starye i novye etiudy ob ekonomicheskom materializme, Petersburg: Tipografiia M.M. Stasiulevicha.

Kołakowski, Leszek, 1978, Main Currents of Marxism: The Founders, the Golden Age, the Breakdown, New York: W.W. Norton & Company.

Krause, Karl, 1851, Das Urbild der Menschheit, Dresden: Arnoldischen Buchhandlung.

Kuhn, Thomas, 1962, The Structure of Scientific Revolutions.

Labriola, Antonio, 1897, Essais sur la conception matérialiste de l'histoire, Paris: V. Giard, E. Brière.

Labriola, Antonio, 1908, Essays on the Materialistic Conception of History, Chicago, IL: C.H. Kerr.

Labriola, Antonio, 1912, Socialism and Philosophy, Chicago, IL: C.H. Kerr.

Lafargue, Paul, 1895, La propriété, origine et évolution: thèse communiste, Paris: Ch. Delagrave.

Lange, Friedrich, 1877, The History of Materialism and Criticism of Its Present Importance, vol. I, Boston, MA: James R. Osgood and Company.

Lange, Friedrich, 1881, The History of Materialism and Criticism of Its Present Importance, vol. III, London: Trübner & Co.

Lévy-Bruhl, Lucien, 1890, L'Allemagne depuis Leibniz, Paris: Hachette.

Lévy-Bruhl, Lucien, 1903, The Philosophy of Auguste Comte, New York: G.P. Putnam's Sons.

Lévy-Bruhl, Lucien, 1926, How Natives Think. New York: Alfred A. Knopf.

Limanowski, Bronisław, 1875, Socyologija Augusta Comte'a, Lviv: Drukarnia J. Dobrzańskiego i K. Gromana.

Loria, Achille, 1893, Les bases économiques de la constitution sociale, Paris: Felix Alcan.

Lukács, György, 1967, History and Class Consciousness. Studies in Marxist Dialectics. Cambridge, MA: MIT Press.

Mannheim, Karl, 1997, Ideology and Utopia. New York: Routledge.

Marx, Karl, 1894, Capital. A Critique of Political Economics, vol. III: The Process of Capitalistic Production as a Whole, New York: International Publishers.

Marx, Karl, 1906, Capital. A Critique of Political Economics, vol. I The Process of Production of Capital, Chicago, IL: C.H. Kerr & Company.

Marx, Karl, 1955, The Poverty of Philosophy. Answer to the Philosophy of Poverty by M. Proudhon, Moscow: Progress Publishers.

Marx, Karl, 2008, The Eighteenth Brumaire of Louis Bonaparte. New York: International Publishers.

Marks, Karl, Engels, Friedrich and Lenin, Vladimir, 1972, On Historical Materialism. A Collection, Moscow: Progress Publishers.

Masaryk, Tomáš Garrigue, 1898, Die wissenschaftliche und philosophische Krise innerhalb des gegenwärtigen Marxismus, Vienna: Verlag Die Zeit.

Mehring, Franz, 1938, The Lessing Legend. The Origins of German Middle Class Culture, New York: Critics Group Press.

Michelet, Jules, 1894, Oeuvres choisies de Vico, Paris: Flammarion.

Mickiewicz, Adam, 1833, The Books and the Pilgrimage of the Polish Nation, London: James Ridgway.

Mickiewicz, Adam, 2016, Forefathers' Eve, London, UK: Glagoslav Publications.

Morgan, Lewis H, 1877, Ancient Society or Researches in the Lines of Human Progress from Savagery through Barbarism to Civilization. London, UK: MacMillan & Company.

Nałkowski, Wacław, 1904, Jednostka i ogół: szkice i krytyki psycho-społeczne, Krakow, Poland: Czatowicz.

Nordau, Max, 1892, Entartung, Berlin: C. Duncker.

Plekhanov, Georgi, 1976, Selected Philosophical Works, vol. II, Moscow: Progress Publishers.

Pöhlmann, Robert von, 1893, Geschichte des antiken Kommunismus und Sozialismus, Munich: C.H. Beckiche Berlagsbuchhandlung.

Plato, 1931, The Republic. London, UK: Oxford University Press.

Rousseau, Jean-Jacques, 1761, A Discourse upon the Origin and Foundation of the Inequality among Mankind, London: R. and J. Dodsley.

Rousseau, Jean-Jacques, 1920, The Social Contract & Discourses. London, UK: J.M. Dent & Sons.

Rousseau, Jean-Jacques, 2005, On the Origin of Inequality, New York: Cosimo Classics.

Simmel, Georg, 2005, Rembrandt. An Essay in the Philosophy of Art. New York: Routledge.

Simmel, Georg, 2016, The View of Life, Chicago, IL: University of Chicago Press.

Snyder, Timothy, 1997, Nationalism, Marxism, and Modern Central Europe: A Biography of Kazimierz Kelles-Krauz, 1872–1905. Cambridge, MA: Harvard University Press.

Sztompka, Piotr (ed). Masters of Polish Sociology, Wrocław, Kraków, Poland: Zakład Narodowy im. Ossolińskich.

Tarde, Gabriel, 1895, La logique sociale, Paris: Félix Alcan.

Tarde, Gabriel, 1903, The Laws of Imitation, New York: Henry Holt and Company.

Tarde, Gabriel, 1989, L'opinion et la foule, Paris, France: Les Presses universitaires de France.

Thomas, William. I., 1928, The Child in America: Behavior Problems and Programs. New York: Alfred A. Knopf.

Vico, Giambattista, 1948, The New Science of Giambattista Vico, Ithaca, NY: Cornell University Press.

Vico, Giambattista, 1988, On the Most Ancient Wisdom of the Italians, Ithaca, NY: Cornell University Press.

Wallace, Alfred Russel, 1899, The Wonderful Century, New York: Dodd, Mead and Company.

Weber, Max, 2011, Methodology of Social Sciences. Brunswick, NJ: Transaction Publishers.

Żarnowska, Anna. 1962. Kazimierz Kelles-Krauz (1872–1905), in: Kelles-Krauz, Kazimierz. Pisma wybrane, Warsaw, Poland: Książka i Wiedza.

Selected Works Written by Kazimierz Kelles-Krauz

Hochfeld, Julian (ed.), 1992, *Kazimierz Kelles-Krauz. Pisma wybrane*, vol. 1 and 2, Warsaw, Poland: Książka i Wiedza.

[Kelles-Krauz, Kazimierz] 1901a *J.J. Bachofen*, 'Prawda' 21 (43), 22 (44), in: *Pisma wybrane*, vol. 1.

[Kelles-Krauz, Kazimierz] Esse, Elehard, 1901, *Comtisme et marxisme*, 'Revue Socialiste', no. 197, in: *Pisma wybrane*, vol. 1.

[Kelles-Krauz, Kazimierz] *Czy jesteśmy patriotami we właściwym znaczeniu tego słowa?*, in: *Pisma wybrane*, vol. 2.

[Kelles-Krauz, Kazimierz] 1901b, *Czym jest materializm ekonomiczny*, 'Prawda' 37–39, in: *Pisma wybrane*, vol. 1.

[Kelles-Krauz, Kazimierz] 1905a, *Demokracja w nowoczesnym ustroju państwowym*, 'Głos' 1, 3, 4, 8, 11, 12–14, 17, 18, 21, in: *Pisma wybrane*, vol. 2.

[Kelles-Krauz, Kazimierz] 1901c, *Dialektyka społeczna w filozofii Vica*, 'Przegląd Filozoficzny' 2, in: *Pisma wybrane*, vol. 1.

[Kelles-Krauz, Kazimierz] 1900a, *Ekonomiczne podstawy pierwotnych form rodziny*, 'Krytyka' 8, in: *Pisma wybrane*, vol. 1.

[Kelles-Krauz, Kazimierz] 1905b *Kilka głównych zasad rozwoju sztuki*, 'Poradnik dla samouków' pt. 5, vol. 2, in: *Pisma wybrane*, vol. 1.

[Kelles-Krauz, Kazimierz] Esse, Elehard, 1897, *Międzynarodowa polityka proletariatu (w kwestii wschodniej)*, 'Przedświt', 10, in: *Pisma wybrane*, vol. 1.

[Kelles-Krauz, Kazimierz] Luśnia, Michał, 1905, *Niepodległość Polski a materialistyczne pojmowanie dziejów*, 'Krytyka' 4–5, in: *Pisma wybrane*, vol. 2.

[Kelles-Krauz, Kazimierz] Luśnia, Michał, 1899, *Niepodległość Polski w programie socjalistycznym*, 'Krytyka' 4, in: *Pisma wybrane*, vol. 2.

[Kelles-Krauz, Kazimierz] 1900b, *O tak zwanym kryzysie marksizmu*, 'Przegląd filozoficzny' 2–3, in: *Pisma wybrane*, vol. 1.

[Kelles-Krauz, Kazimierz] Luśnia, Michał, 1900, *Ostatnie nieporozumienie*, 'Przedświt' 7, in: *Pisma wybrane*, vol. 2.

[Kelles-Krauz, Kazimierz] Luśnia, Michał, 1903, *Porachunek z rewizjonistami*, „Przedświt" 10, 11–12, in: *Pisma wybrane*, vol. 2.

[Kelles-Krauz, Kazimierz] 1906, *Portrety zmarłych socjologów*, Warsaw, Poland: Księgarnia Naukowa, in: *Pisma wybrane*, vol. 1.

[Kelles-Krauz, Kazimierz] 1903a, *Program narodowościowy Socjalnej Demokracji Austriackiej a program* PPS, 'Przedświt' 7, 8, in: *Pisma wybrane*, vol. 1.

[Kelles-Krauz, Kazimierz] Luśnia, Michał, 1904a, *Rewizja programu agrarnego?*, 'Przedświt' 9, 10, in: *Pisma wybrane*, vol. 1.

[Kelles-Krauz, Kazimierz] 1903b, *Ruch społeczny w starożytności*, 'Głos' 21, 22, 24, 26, in: *Pisma wybrane*, vol. 1.

[Kelles-Krauz, Kazimierz] 1901d, *Rzut oka na rozwój socjologii w XIX stuleciu. Wiek XIX*, 'Prawda', in: *Pisma wybrane*, vol. 1.

[Kelles-Krauz, Kazimierz] Michał Luśnia, 1891, *Sartor sarritus albo czy się Ostoja ostoi?*, 'Przedświt' 11, in: *Pisma wybrane*, vol. 2.

[Kelles-Krauz, Kazimierz] Esse, Elehard, 1899, *Socialistes polonaise et russes*, 'L'Humanité Nouvelle', in: *Pisma wybrane*, vol. 2.

[Kelles-Krauz, Kazimierz] Luśnia, Michał, 1902, *Widoki rewolucji*, 'Przedświt' 8, 9, in: *Pisma wybrane*, vol. 2.

[Kelles-Krauz, Kazimierz] Luśnia, Michał, 1904b, *W kwestii narodowości żydowskiej*, 'Krytyka' 1, 2, in: *Pisma wybrane*, vol. 2.

[Kelles-Krauz, Kazimierz] 1903c–1904, *Wiek złoty, stan natury i rozwój w sprzecznościach*, 'Przegląd Filozoficzny' 3, 4 (1903), 1 (1904), in: *Pisma wybrane*, vol. 1.

Directory of Persons Referenced

Abramowski, Edward (1868–1918), Polish philosopher and socialist.

Abu Bakr (573–634), companion to Muhammad and the first Caliph.

Andler, Charles (1866–1933), French Germanic scholar and philosopher.

d'Argenson, French aristocratic dynasty.

Arkwright, Richard (1732–1792), English inventor.

Arminius (approx. 17 BC–21 AD), chieftain of the Germanic Cherusci tribe.

Babeuf, François Noël, pseudonym used by Gracchus (1760–1797), radical French politician of the French Revolution period.

Bachofen, Johann Jakob (1815–1887), Swiss lawyer and anthropologist.

Ballanche, Pierre-Simon (1776–1847), French writer and philosopher.

Barrès, Maurice (1862–1923), French novelist and nationalist.

Barth, Paul (1858–1922), German philosopher.

Bauer, Bruno (1809–1882), German philosopher and historian.

Bax, Ernest Belfort (1854–1926), British philosopher and socialist.

Beltov, pseudonym used by Georgi Plekhanov (1856–1918), Russian revolutionary and Marxist theoretician.

Bernheim, Hippolyte (1840–1919), French physician and neurologist.

Blanc, Louis (1811–1882), French socialist and historian.

Blanc, Ludwig Gottfried (1781–1866), German philologist.

Bloch, Iwan (1872–1922), German dermatologist and sexologist.

de Bonald, Louis Garbiel Ambroise (1754–1840), French philosopher and politician, proponent of royalism.

Bonnet, Charles (1720–1793), Swiss philosopher and naturalist.

Bourget, Paul (1852–1935), French writer.

Brandes, Georg (1842–1927), Danish literary critic and philosopher.

Brunetière, Ferdinand (1849–1906), French writer and critic.

Büchner, Ludwig (1824–1899), German philosopher, representative of scientific materialism.

Buckle, Henry Thomas (1821–1862), British historian of culture.

Bugiel, Włodzimierz (1872–1937), Polish doctor and man of letters.

Cabet, Étienne (1788–1856), French socialist and philosopher, a proponent of utopian socialism.

Cunow, Heinrich (1862–1936), German theoretician of Marxism, member of the Social Democratic Party of Germany.

Deschamps, Léger Marie (1716–1774), French Benedictine and philosopher, proponent of Utopian socialism.

Dicaearchus of Messana (345–258 BC), Greek geographer, apprentice of Aristotle.

Drumont, Édouard (1844–1917), French writer and nationalist.

du Bois-Reymond, Emil (1818–1896), German doctor, researcher of the nervous system.

Dühring, Eugen (1833–1921), German philosopher and socialist, critic of Marxism.

Ferri, Enrico (1856–1929), Italian criminologist and socialist.

Fireman, Peter (1864–1963), Russian economist and chemist.

Flint, Robert (1838–1910), Scottish philosopher and theologian.

Fouillée, Alfred (1838–1912), French philosopher.

Fournière, Joseph-Eugène (1857–1914), French socialist.

Gautier, Théophile (1811–1872), French writer and playwright.

Giddings, Franklin Henry (1855–1931), American sociologist and economist.

von Görres, Joseph (1776–1848), German journalist and writer.

De Greef, Guillaume (1842–1924), Belgian philosopher and sociologist.

Grotius, Hugo (1583–1645), Dutch jurist, one of the creators of international law.

Guizot, François (1787–1874), French historian and politician.

Guyau, Jean-Marie (1854–1888), French philosopher and poet.

Guyot, Yves (1843–1928), French economist and politician.

von Haller, Karl Ludwig (1768–1854), Swiss lawyer.

Hermann, Konrad (1819–1897), German philosopher.

d'Holbach, Baron Paul (1723–1789), French philosopher of the Enlightenment.

Hotman, François (1524–1590), French lawyer and writer.

Hugh (Hugon) of Saint Victor (1096–1141), a mediaeval philosopher, theologian, mystic, founder of the Parisian Platonic-Augustine 'St Victor's School'.

Iselin, Isaak (1728–1782), Swiss philosopher of law.

Jaurès, Jean (1859–1914), French socialist leader.

von Jhering, Rudolf (1818–1892), German lawyer.

Kareev, Nikolai (1850–1931), Russian historian.

Kautsky, Karl (1854–1938), Czech-Austrian Marxist theoretician.

Kidd, Benjamin (1858–1916), British sociologist.

Kołłątaj, Hugo (1750–1812), Polish Roman Catholic priest and political activist.

Kovalevsky, Maksim (1851–1916), Russian sociologist, representative of evolutionism in the social sciences.

Krause, Karl Christian Friedrich (1781–1832), German philosopher.

Krzywicki, Ludwik (1859–1941), Polish Marxist and sociologist.

Kudrin, pseudonym used by Nikolai Rusanov (1859–1939), a Russian socialist.

Labriola, Antonio (1843–1904), Italian philosopher and theoretician of Marxism.

Lacombe, Paul (1834–1919), French historian.

Lafargue, Paul (1842–1911), French Marxist philosopher.

Lange, Friedrich Albert (1828–1875), German philosopher and sociologist.

de Lapouge, George Vacher (1854–1936), French anthropologist and theoretician of racism.

Lasalle, Ferdinand (1825–1864), German lawyer and socialist.

de Laveleye, Émile Louis Victor (1822–1892), Belgian economist.

Lazarus, Moritz (1824–1903), German philosopher and psychologist.

Lessing, Gotthold Ephraim (1729–1781), German writer and philosopher.

Letourneau, Charles Jean Marie (1831–1902), French anthropologist.

Lévy-Bruhl, Lucien (1857–1939), French philosopher and sociologist.

Lexis, Wilhelm (1837–1914), German sociologist and economist.

von Lilienfeld, Paul (1829–1903), Russian politician, proponent of organicistic sociology.

Lippert, Julius (1839–1909), Austrian historian.

Littré, Émile (1801–1881), French philosopher and lexicographer.

Longuet, Hubert (1518–1581), French lawyer and writer.

Loria, Achille (1857–1943), Italian political economist.

de Mably, Gabriel Bonnot (1709–1785), French philosopher and politician.

Maine, Henry Sumner (1822–1888), British lawyer and sociologist.

de Maistre, Joseph (1753–1821), Savoyard political philosopher and diplomat, a proponent of conservatism.

Marsilius of Padua (1275–1343), Italian philosopher.

Masaryk, Tomáš Garrigue (1850–1937), Austrian-Czech politician, philosopher and sociologist, first president of Czechoslovakia.

Maurer, James Hudson (1864–1944), American union activist.

Mehring, Franz (1846–1919), German politician and historian.

Meléndez Valdés, Juan (1754–1817), Spanish poet.

Mendès, Catulle (1841–1909), French poet and playwright.

Merlino, Francesco Saverio (1856–1930), Italian lawyer and anarchist.

Mikhaylovsky, Nikolay (1842–1904), Russian sociologist and literary critic.

Mirtov, pseudonym used by Pyotr Lavrov (1823–1900), Russian philosopher and sociologist.

Morelly, Étienne-Gabriel (1717–1778), French philosopher, proponent of Utopian socialism.

Morgan, Lewis Henry (1818–1881), American anthropologist.

Möser, Justus (1720–1794), German jurist and social theorist.

Nordau, Max (1849–1923), Hungarian-Jewish physician and philosopher.

Novikov, Jakov (1849–1912), Russian sociologist.

Oresme, Nicole (1320–1382), French philosopher.

Ortes, Giammaria (1713–1790), Venetian priest and economist.

Pope, Alexander (1688–1744), English poet.

Posada, Adolfo (1860–1944), Spanish sociologist, a representative of so-called regenerationism.

Potocki, Józef Karol (1854–1898), Polish political activist and poet.

Pouchet, Felix-Archimède (1800–1872), French naturalist, proponent of the theory of spontaneous generation.

von Pufendorf, Samuel (1632–1694), German historian and theoretician of law.

Ricci, Matteo (1552–1610), Italian Jesuit.

Rogers, Thorold (1823–1890), British economist and historian.

Rollinat, Maurice (1846–1903), French poet.

Roscelin of Compiègne (approx 1050–1120), mediaeval philosopher and theologian, considered the founder of nominalism.

Ruskin, John (1819–1900), English art critic and writer.

von Savigny, Friedrich Carl (1779–1861), German lawyer.

Schäffle, Albert (1831–1903), German sociologist.

Schenk, Samuel Leopold (1840–1902), Austrian embryologist.

Schmidt, Konrad (1863–1932), German economist.

Seignobos, Charles (1854–1942), French historian.

Selden, John (1584–1654), English theoretician of law.

Słowacki, Juliusz (1809–1949), Polish Romantic poet.

de Staël-Holstein, Anne-Louise Germaine (1766–1817), French writer and columnist.

Stammler, Rudolf (1856–1938), German philosopher of law.

Staszic, Stanisław (1755–1826), Polish Roman Catholic priest and writer.

Steinthal, Heymann (1823–1899), German philosopher and philologist.

Stuve, Peter (1870–1944), Russian economist and politician.

Świętochowski, Aleksander (1849–1938), Polish writer and educator.

Thibaut, Anton Friedrich Justus (1772–1840), German lawyer.

Tugan-Baranovsky, Mikhail (1865–1919), Ukrainian economist and politician.

Turgot, Anne Robert (1727–1781), French economist and politician, general controller of finance during the reign of Louis XVI.

Tylor, Edward Burnett (1832–1917), British anthropologist, a representative of cultural evolutionism.

Wallace, Alfred Russel (1823–1913), British naturalist.

Ward, Lester Frank (1841–1913), American botanist and sociologist.

Weber, Alfred (1868–1958), German sociologist and culture theoretician.

Weisengrün, Paul (1868–1923), German philosopher.

Weishaupt, Adam (1748–1830), German philosopher.

Weitling, Wilhelm (1808–1871), German socialist, a proponent of utopian socialism.

Westermarck, Edvard (1862–1939), Finnish philosopher and sociologist, who conducted studies into sexuality.

William of Champeaux (approx. 1070–1121), mediaeval philosopher and theologian.

Wolf, Julius (1862–1937), German economist.

Wundt, Wilhelm (1832–1920), German physician and psychologist.

Name Index

Subject Index

www.ingramcontent.com/pod-product-compliance
Lightning Source LLC
Chambersburg PA
CBHW070916030426
42336CB00014BA/2434